The Moral Leader

Challenges, Insights, and Tools

Sandra J. Sucher

 Routledge
Taylor & Francis Group

LONDON AND NEW YORK

First published 2008
by Routledge
2 Park Square, Milton Park, Abingdon, OX14 4RN

Simultaneously published in the USA and Canada by Routledge
711 Third Ave, New York, NY 10017

Routledge is an imprint of the Taylor & Francis Group, an informa business

© 2008 Sandra J. Sucher

Typeset in Minion and Bell Gothic by
Florence Production Ltd, Stoodleigh, Devon

British Library Cataloguing in Publication Data
A catalogue record for this book is available from the British Library

Library of Congress Cataloging in Publication Data
Sucher, Sandra J.
  The moral leader: challenges, insights, and tools/Sandra J. Sucher
      p. cm.
   Includes bibliographical references and index.
   1. Leadership – Moral and ethical aspects.   2. Business ethics.   I. Title.
   HD57.7.S835 2007
   174'.4 – dc22   2007006494

ISBN10: 0–415–40063–5 (hbk)
ISBN10: 0–415–40064–3 (pbk)
ISBN10: 0–203–94064–4 (ebk)

ISBN13: 978–0–415–40063–3 (hbk)
ISBN13: 978–0–415–40064–0 (pbk)
ISBN13: 978–0–203–94064–8 (ebk)

To students of "The Moral Leader" course,
past, present, and future

Contents

CONTENTS

Acknowledgments

"The Moral Leader," a literature-based course on leadership, has a storied past of its own, and I am grateful to all who have contributed to it. Brought to Harvard Business School in the 1980s by Robert Coles, psychiatrist and educator, the business school was just one of Coles' stops, which included the Harvard schools of medicine, law, architecture, politics, divinity, education, and design.[1] In each of these settings, Coles demonstrated the value of using literature to explore moral decision-making and leadership. His views on moral leadership are recorded in many of his books; those interested in the origins of "The Moral Leader" course will particularly enjoy *The Call of Stories: Teaching and the Moral Imagination*, Coles' description of how he came to a literature-based approach and how it influenced him and those fortunate enough to have been his students. *Lives of Moral Leadership: Men and Women Who Have Made a Difference*,[2] also by Coles, presents profiles of individuals he considers to be moral leaders; it, too, sheds light on how moral leadership can be defined and, more important, how it is lived.

Following Coles were a small cadre of HBS instructors, all committed to learning through literature, who contributed to the course. Scotty McLennan, presently Dean of Religious Life at Stanford University, developed his own version, as did Mary Gentile, now a thoughtful and creative advisor on business ethics and ethics education who openheartedly involved herself in this project since I first outlined it to her, providing advice that helped shape my views on how to make "The Moral Leader" accessible to students and instructors alike.

My immediate predecessor in the course is Joe Badaracco, who has generously served as a mentor, sharing his complete teaching files, allowing me to watch an entire semester of the course being taught, and encouraging me in the development of my own course and the texts that describe it. Joe has reflected on literature he finds valuable to leaders in *Questions of Character: Illuminating the Heart of Leadership through Literature*.[3] He extracts realistic, imaginative, practical, and by no means obvious lessons from the stories he writes about, perfectly illustrating what it looks like to study literature for the useful and powerful lessons it can provide to leaders of all stripes.

"The Moral Leader" project is based on my own version of the course; it includes this textbook, an instructor's guide for those interested in teaching the course or in adapting parts of it to their own courses: *Teaching "The Moral Leader": A Literature-Based Leadership Course* (Routledge, 2007), and a website (www. Routledge.com/textbooks/9780415400640). These were developed with Barbara Feinberg, my long-time collaborator, who has strengthened every aspect, from the design and lesson plans of the course, to the structure and contents of all the materials that document it. This textbook has benefited especially from Barbara's intellectual reach: her knowledge of topics from moral philosophy to history to the arts of war gave invaluable direction to the gathering of background information on each of the texts we study, no mean feat when you consider a literature that encompasses thousands of years and multiple continents and cultures.

Joshua Bellin, research associate of infinite curiosity and flexibility, picked up on Barbara's suggestions and brought them to life; Josh's ability to unearth relevant and surprising facts about the contexts of the various characters and their situations is only surpassed by the range and clarity of his writing.

Bianca Buccitelli inherited the last phase of the project – the process of bringing the instructor manual and this student textbook to print. A calming and steady influence, Bianca is a gifted administrator and research associate.

Colleagues at Harvard Business School aided the development of this project, beginning with those who first approached me with the possibility of teaching "The Moral Leader," and including colleagues who provided feedback on various drafts of the texts. My thanks to the following for these and other kindnesses: Lynda Applegate, Regina Bento, Srikant Datar, Willis Emmons, Charlie Fine (on loan from MIT), David Garvin, Jan Hammond, Bob Hayes, Matthew Kumar, Deishin Lee, Lynn Paine, Tom Piper, Roy Shapiro, Peter Tufano, and Noel Watson. This project was supported by the Harvard Business School's Directors of Research; I am grateful to them.

Francesca Heslop, my editor at Routledge, is responsible for publishing all of "The Moral Leader" materials, and for encouraging me in the development of this student textbook; I thank her and Simon Whitmore for their vision, persistence, and good advice.

Thanks to my family for love and support: Richard, Libby and Andrew; Susan and Stuart; Mark and Jane; and to my parents: Gerald Sucher (1920–2005) and Jean Sucher (1922–2006).

NOTES

1   Robert Coles, *The Call of Stories: Teaching and the Moral Imagination*, Boston, MA: Houghton Mifflin Company, 1989, pp. xvii–xviii.
2   Robert Coles, *Lives of Moral Leadership: Men and Women Who Have Made a Difference*, New York: Random House, 2000.
3   Joseph Badaracco, *Questions of Character: Illuminating the Heart of Leadership through Literature*, Boston, Mass.: Harvard Business School Press, 2006.

Introduction

Chapter 1

Overview of "The Moral Leader"

"THE MORAL LEADER" COURSE

Welcome to "The Moral Leader," a course that has intrigued and enriched thousands of students since it was first offered in the 1980s as an elective at the Harvard Business School. In class, students debate morally challenging situations that arise from reading and thinking through powerful novels, plays, short stories, and historical accounts; these are international in scope, illuminating timeless tests of moral decision-making and leadership. The aim of this literature-based course is to develop your ability to identify, describe, and analyze moral problems, and to think clearly about how to act in consequence.

The readings for the course, previewed in this book, are arranged in a flow of thirteen sessions, divided into three modules – Moral Challenge, Moral Reasoning, and Moral Leadership – that move us through an exploration of the topic of moral leadership. The flow highlights a succession of questions that constitute the thrust of the course: *What is the nature of a moral challenge? How do people "reason morally"? What do these look like when they are undertaken by leaders – individuals who must make decisions under conditions of responsibility for others? How is moral leadership different from any other kind?*

While philosophical in form, these are intensely practical questions, born of our desire to make good, morally satisfying decisions when we are in leadership roles. Our ability to grapple with them, alone and with others, is a step on the road to moral action.

The reading list for the course draws on fictional and historical accounts set in the US, Great Britain, Nigeria, Japan, Thailand, Greece, Antarctica, and Italy. You will read about challenges people faced more than two thousand years ago and as recently as September 11, 2001, in times of war, and of peace, and in unsettling periods in between. The varied settings, times, and situations reinforce the universality of moral challenge and the requirement for leaders to develop their abilities to describe and analyze moral problems, to think them through, and to act.

As you will discover, the literary and historical material will allow us to examine moral action through the lens of others' moral challenges and subsequent choices.

Table 1.1 *The "Moral Leader" readings*

Reading	Setting	Format
Module I: Moral Challenge		
Endurance: Shackleton's Incredible Voyage Alfred Lansing	Antarctica, 1914	Historical account
Antigone Sophocles	Ancient Greece	Play
Blessed Assurance Allan Gurganus	1940s America	Novella
Things Fall Apart Chinua Achebe	Early twentieth-century Nigeria	Novel
Module II: Moral Reasoning		
Trifles Susan Glaspell	Rural America, early twentieth century	Play
Principles of Biomedical Ethics Tom L. Beauchamp, James F. Childress		Text excerpts
The Sweet Hereafter Russell Banks	Contemporary America	Novel
The Remains of the Day Kazuo Ishiguro	Britain between world wars	Novel
A Man for All Seasons Robert Bolt	Sixteenth-century England	Play and movie
Module III: Moral Leadership		
The Prince Niccolò Machiavelli	Sixteenth-century Italy	Treatise
The Secret Sharer Joseph Conrad	1890s off the coast of Siam	Short story
Truman and the Bomb *Just and Unjust Wars* Michael Walzer	World War II, beyond	Text excerpts
Personal History Katharine Graham	1970s America, recalled	Autobiography
A Good Life Ben Bradlee		Autobiography
American Ground: Unbuilding the World Trade Center William Langewiesche	Post-September 11th USA	Eyewitness account

Unlike a case-based discussion, we see beyond a "what would you do" situation to realize the consequences of decisions that protagonists actually make; this perspective on cause and effect, on action and impact, takes us from speculation of what *might* happen to a consideration of what *did* happen and why.

The classes thus provide a laboratory for understanding how morally charged situations develop and are shaped through choices, and the results they produce. The opportunity to see a situation all the way through this process is essential to understanding how to anticipate the effects of moral leadership. It also provides us, in the classroom, with the opportunity to refine, validate, or revise our own thinking about moral assessment and our determination of action as potential leaders.

AN APPROACH TO UNDERSTANDING MORAL LEADERSHIP

What is it about "The Moral Leader" course that is so compelling? Why have so many students participated in it year after year? And why has it attracted a series of dedicated instructors who have at once personalized the curriculum but kept its basic approach intact? Many answers to these questions come from your fellow students, those who have taken the course at the Harvard Business School and are eager to share their views with you,[1] and are combined with my own reflections.

Prior to becoming a faculty member at HBS, I spent twenty-five years as a senior executive, doing the hard work of improving corporate and organizational performance and witnessing first-hand the complexities of leadership, particularly when moral issues are at stake. In redesigning the course, which I've now taught nine times, I've brought that corporate experience into the equation in order to have you focus intently on the practical aspects that come from "The Moral Leader" approach to learning.

So in the next sections you will hear from your fellow students and from me. We are all encouraging you on!

Why study moral leadership?

The student responses are in italics.

- *In some way I will characterize "The Moral Leader" as a Renaissance class – one that is made to expand your perception of the world and of yourself in a broad but very tangible direction. It covers issues (1) that are inevitable for us to face in some shape or form, (2) whose outcomes could be very important in our lives, causing great amounts of either joy or grief, and (3) for which normally we do not tend to think ahead of time, making us fairly unprepared when we encounter them.*
- *Thus, if you want to learn about the issues of power which tend to compromise multiple moral issues, or whether preconceived strong moral rigidity is the right format in which to address delicate moral issues, or what morality really is, this is a course for you.*

5

Looking back on my years of corporate life, I know that many things happen that cannot be anticipated. But the need to make decisions in situations in which ethical or moral questions arise is as certain as the sun rising and setting, baked into the conflicts of serving constituencies with different interests and into the endless temptations of a measurement-based life.

In my experience, organizations offer few (if any) venues in which such concepts can be discovered, challenged, and refined. Yet you may worry – and rightly so – that you will face situations with moral and ethical stakes and that you will be unprepared for such moments, left to rely on gut feel and instinct.

"The Moral Leader" approach can help you in your struggle to define your own notions of morality, moral action, and moral leadership. The course provides a place where you can think out loud (and on paper) about the challenges of leading while contending with moral problems, and you will have some stunning examples to learn from (both positive and negative).

Practicing moral decision-making

*   *Morality is not something that can be switched on like a light when you assume a leadership role. Taking the time mentally to flex your morality muscle in the relative security of a classroom gives you a sense of your individual stance on moral issues before you are leading others and making moral judgments that impact more than just yourself. Ultimately, how we will each react in a morally challenging situation is something we shan't be able to predict until the moment comes, but this class is a step towards taking every possible preparation to ensure that when faced with a challenge we will have some experience to draw upon – even if it is through the lessons of our protagonists.*

One advantage of "The Moral Leader" approach is the way its readings and debates replicate the kind of involvement in the life of others that is the stuff of organizational existence: The fast friendships, long-standing enmities, close connections, unavoidable rivalries, and dependence on others that characterize a lifetime spent in organizations. No one succeeds (for long) in organizations who is not good at "reading" others, but learning how to read another person is very hard to teach. Literature is good at this – it's what it is for.

Learning through literature

*   *The study of literary and historical leaders does indeed question, confront and challenge preconceived notions about moral reasoning, moral challenge and moral leadership. You'll be surprised at how much impact the study of such characters will have on your own thought processes.*
*   *This course does not take you through moral challenges in the business context. Although the Ken Lay/Enron analogies will strike you throughout the course, you will not actually be studying corporate fraud and malfeasance.*

I have come to believe that the course is intense, powerful, and practical precisely because it does *not* focus solely on problems situated in contemporary organizations. Instead, the readings take us far and wide, back thousands of years, and deep into other cultures. Effective leadership requires intimacy and breadth, the ability to connect oneself to oneself and to connect to others. This is a lifelong search with boundaries that stretch well beyond any particular organization or assignment, well beyond, in fact, the professional careers that any of us pursue. A course like "The Moral Leader" allows us to develop self-awareness and a hunger to understand the broader world we live in. The curiosity and self-knowledge we gain is a powerful combination, one I believe will serve you well in *all* the roles you will play.

Engaging in moral debate

- *Be prepared to be uncomfortable in discussing certain issues like race, religion, culture (yours and others'), but also be willing to contribute to the discussion, even where you know your view will be vastly different from others (as long as you're respectful). It's hard to be a mere participant in this class and learn at the same time – you have to be willing to test your thoughts and ideas, have them challenged quite forcefully and either defend yourself or concede a change of mind.*

Another advantage of "The Moral Leader" is having the chance to experience your real (perhaps better or even best) self in the presence of others, experiencing what it feels like to say what you are thinking, to struggle to put your thoughts into words, to take risks on ideas that are half-formed, or cynical, or exploratory. These, too, are necessary skills for individuals who work in organizations – the ability to locate yourself through thoughts and words, and to take risks to say things that others may not want to hear, or might disagree with profoundly. A topic like moral leadership invites such a search for authenticity, and you will find yourself working hard, very hard, to describe your ideas and to react, real-time, to the ideas of others.

Confronting differences

- *My primary suggestion would be to come into the class discussion with a completely open mind since sticking to your initial thinking can limit your learning. I have found that in prior discussions I have come in with one conclusion on the reading and have left with a completely different one. It's easy in a class like this to have preconceived notions, so you must work hard to let new ideas in.*

"The Moral Leader" will expose you to the many ways in which even smart, well-intentioned, articulate individuals can differ from each other. Organizational life and leadership require the ability to search for common ground on a wide variety of topics. Yet each of us pursues this search in the (sometimes conscious, sometimes unconscious) belief that our ideas can't really be that different from others', that the assumptions and reasoning processes of others are more or less like our own.

In "The Moral Leader," you will see how differently your classmates think about notions that to you seem obvious and self-evident. In addition, you will be exposed to characters and situations that force you well outside of yourself – that require you to enter into worlds that are vastly different from your own. Both of these facets of the course will prepare you, better than you might have been, to navigate the differences in worldview and opinion that await you in your professional (and personal) life.

USING THIS TEXT

This textbook has been created to enhance your participation in "The Moral Leader."

The following chapter, a "Guide to Literature-based Learning," describes approaches that have proved effective in reading and analyzing the materials and in preparing for class sessions. It also features additional advice from students on their own techniques for study and class participation.

The three main topics of the course – Moral Challenge, Moral Reasoning, Moral Leadership – are then examined. Each begins with a module map – a one-page capsule view of major module themes and readings. There is also a module preview, a brief look at some of the ways the topics have been considered by, for example, philosophers, social and natural scientists, and researchers on leadership.

Each class session is focused on a specific literary text or historical account and has its own dedicated chapter, designed to aid your preparation and to enrich your analysis. The chapters include:

- a selected quote (or series of quotes) from the text that takes you into the heart of the story, situation, or characters we will focus on;
- an overview of themes and questions posed by the text;
- assignment questions;
- historical background, illuminating the context of the reading and the situation;
- author biographies.

A few of the readings are included in an appendix to this textbook, but most are assigned as individual texts. The textbook closes with an annotated bibliography of additional readings on moral leadership.

NOTES

1 Students participating in "The Moral Leader" in Fall 2006 responded to an email survey that invited them to share their perspectives on the course with future students. With candor, thoughtfulness, and generosity, they responded to two questions: (1) In introducing "The Moral Leader" to other students, what would you have wanted to know about the course before you began it? (2) In thinking about how to prepare for class and how to participate productively in it, what thoughts, advice, and suggestions would you share with future students of "The Moral Leader"? The excerpts included are verbatim.

Preparation

Chapter 2

Guide to Literature-based Learning

READING THE MATERIAL[1]

> The point is that in the activity of literary imagining we are led to imagine and describe with greater precision, focusing our attention on each word, feeling each event more keenly – whereas much of actual life goes by without that heightened awareness, and is thus, in a certain sense, not fully lived . . . So literature is an extension of life not only horizontally, bringing the reader into contact with events or locations or persons or problems he or she has not otherwise met, but also, so to speak, vertically, giving the reader experience that is deeper, sharper, and more precise than much of what takes place in life.[2]

This topic may be unexpected and puzzling because it provides suggestions on how to read. But, in fact, you have already in your educational career honed your skills at various types of reading, ranging from literary analysis, which may focus on the careful hunt for symbol, theme, and use of language; to the type of reading skills associated with executives, i.e., the ability to skim, pick out important points, do some (but not exhaustive) analysis, and come to a point of view – grounded in data and analysis – that you can defend.

In "The Moral Leader," the materials we read include fiction, history, biography, autobiography, and plays, in several instances complemented by extracts from philosophical and ethical writings. These works require yet another approach to reading, analysis, and judgment-formation. While different, however, it is no less rigorous and disciplined than other approaches.

The following reading framework will help you engage in the material of the course and prepare yourself for class discussion. This framework operates at two levels.

LEVEL ONE: READING FOR REACTION

The first level is what we'll call *reading for reaction* – often visceral reaction – to the story and the characters and the decisions they make, or, for the philosophical writings, to the nature of the arguments that are being laid out. Part of the pleasure of this course is the uniformly high quality of writing we are treated to, and this writing can grab our attention, and our emotions, in very powerful ways. It is critical for us to know what grabs us – what strikes us as compelling, or angering, or dismaying, or inspiring – since these emotions give us pointers for what we want to focus on as we look at the texts in more detail. The philosopher Martha Nussbaum, author of the quote above, observed that emotions are themselves modes of vision, or recognition.[3] So, as you are reading and reacting, you are monitoring your reactions – so that you can eventually understand *why* you respond the way you do.

But "The Moral Leader" is not a "great books" course. We are here to learn from these works, not only to react to them. There are assignment questions for each class that ask you to engage in particular analyses, interpretations, and judgments, as well as in personal connections. These questions imply that you do more than just read for reaction. The questions benefit from the next level, where we do the work necessary to learning.

LEVEL TWO: READING FOR DEPTH AND LEARNING

The second level is *reading for depth and learning*. At this level you are examining the material carefully from three perspectives: description, analysis, and judgment.

Description

While description sounds easy enough, in "The Moral Leader" it means getting into the mind of a character or the heart of an argument – people (and ideas) that are, or may be, very different from you and your own ways of thinking. The questions you ask of yourself are: Do I really understand this person or this point of view? Could I articulate what makes this person tick? Could I expound on this idea?

This particular skill, the ability to understand other people and other ideas, is probably one of the most important capabilities you can acquire in making you effective in organizations. As you may well know from your own experience, nearly all of the meaningful work you do will involve your ability to engage other people and their ideas, so focusing on careful description – the ability to get inside other people and their ideas – is critical.

Because the material in "The Moral Leader" is varied, not every character you meet or every idea you encounter will be immediately "likeable." Indeed, you discovered this when you reacted to the material. But the process of description asks you to enter fully into the general context and specific situations of characters, and to appreciate the complexities of the ideas presented. In contrast to reaction, where you yourself were (viscerally) responding, in description you are essentially taking yourself and your reactions out of the equation.

Analysis

The analysis perspective asks you to make sense of what you read, looking at the characters, actions, context, and ideas in a more conceptual way. Whereas the description perspective asks you to imagine yourself as someone else or to understand other viewpoints, the abstracting process of analysis helps you to examine what's going on and how arguments unfold. Analysis begins your search for the reasons why certain situations develop the way they do, why people behave in certain ways and not others, what makes arguments different from one another.

Much of the work we do when we analyze is *pattern recognition*, looking for noteworthy or surprising trends in available data, or for specific, identifiable types of situations, actions, or modes of reasoning. In "The Moral Leader" we aim to expand the number and kinds of patterns that you recognize and can draw on for analysis.

For example, you will start to develop an understanding of fundamental types of moral problems. Being able to characterize a situation as belonging to a class of moral problem (for example, problems of conflicting rights) is a first step in wrestling the problem to the ground, a way of making it more tractable. You will also be exposed to different moral theories, or perspectives, from which to engage in moral analysis, judgment, and decision-making. Over time, you will begin to recognize strands of these moral perspectives in the justifications that characters offer for their actions – another pattern to look for that helps you understand how they are thinking and deciding.

These approaches will augment the analytical skills and instincts you bring to the material and will increase your ability to analyze the texts we study. The assignment questions for each class will build on these general skills, and will focus them on particularly important issues to examine and to understand.

Judgment

The third perspective is judgment, the hardest of all to come to *after* description and analysis. That is, we are all tempted to "judge" right off the bat. This course emphasizes, however, that judgment is what we do last. After allowing yourself to react to what you've read, then delving into a deeper understanding of what you've read – only at this point are you truly ready to make a judgment. "Judgment" is your best-considered evaluation of characters and their actions, of ideas and their implications – on the basis of having done the work of reaction, then of description and analysis.

Good judgment – judgment that others will consider and feel compelled to respond to – requires careful preparation. The most persuasive judgments are those that come packaged with reasons – well laid out arguments, supported by data of various kinds, that explain how you arrived at this position and not some other. As you flesh out your arguments, you will find that you challenge your own thinking, clarifying, refining, and helping you understand the nature of the judgments you make.

Summary of reading framework

You'll find this course much more rewarding if you become aware of reading at both of these levels: reading for reaction as well as reading for depth and learning. Discipline in reading this way assists in class discussion because you will be clear on the perspective you are speaking from.

- Is your comment a description – an attempt to help us really (i.e., objectively) understand a character and her situation and context, or an idea?
- Do you have a way of interpreting events or actions or characters or arguments that helps us see the material in a clearer and richer light – in short, are you analyzing?
- Are you judging – speaking from the vantage point of your own prior description and analysis, and your values, experience, and considered beliefs?

READING THE MATERIAL: STUDENT TIPS AND SUGGESTIONS

The student responses are in italics.

When to read

- *Don't leave the reading of the book till the last minute. I have noticed a marked difference in my class performance when I've read the book a day or two in advance of the class time as opposed to finishing it a few minutes before class. (This might just be a function of your subconscious working on analyzing the issues in the book – without really setting aside time to answer specific questions.) I would highly recommend getting the reading done a day in advance of class to give yourself a chance to think over the moral issues in the reading and come to form your own opinion on them. Last-minute reading allows little time for thought development.*

Background readings

- *The background information [to each reading] is key. Sometimes I have read it before the book, and sometimes I have read it after. I am not sure which approach I like more; nevertheless, I always find that the context is instrumental in aiding my understanding of the story.*

Take notes

- *Read the questions that will be discussed in class before reading the book, so you can flag passages as you read them, rather than hunting through the book later to find the parts that best relate to the questions.*
- *Write down notes for yourself/mark parts of the text/fold pages (i.e. whatever it takes) where something strikes you. This is more of a gut feel about things – so, if anything strikes you as worthy of more thought/discussion, note it!*
- *Mark passages while you are reading that somehow represent moral challenge, reasoning, leadership, etc. It is very powerful to be able to cite specific lines from the reading during the discussion that can support and clarify your points.*

Build connections

- *Putting yourself in the character's shoes when reading a novel/play for class is key. You will find that a lot of the decisions the character makes that you are critical of as a reader you are quite sympathetic to when putting yourself in that same situation. This leads to a much deeper understanding of the underlying motivation for actions and reactions that we are bound to witness in our future life and career.*
- *Try to relate the story, character or dilemma to something in your life to make it more tangible.*
- *Try, as you're reading, to connect the week's text to other texts in the course that you've read – it's really fun when you see how your thought process develops across weeks, and it's also useful to apply the learnings from one week to other weeks.*

PARTICIPATING IN CLASS

"The Moral Leader" is a rigorous discussion-based course, a forum for learning that allows you to participate in a process of personal and collective exploration. By participating actively, you will find that the course offers an excellent venue to develop your own skills in discussion, listening, persuasion, and debate.

This would be true of any seminar-style course, but is particularly relevant to "The Moral Leader." The course crosses boundaries that are not normally crossed, allowing questions raised by the texts about moral decision-making, race, class, cultural practices, and religious beliefs to be pursued, both as ends in themselves and as rehearsal for the kinds of discussions that will be necessary for you and other twenty-first-century leaders to facilitate.

Good listening and discussion skills are essential – a life-long pursuit for any leader – but sometimes we wonder what criteria to use to determine how well we are communicating our thoughts and ideas, and how well we are engaging with the thoughts and ideas of others. Table 2.1 illustrates some of the fundamental elements of effective communication in a course like "The Moral Leader".

Table 2.1 Discussion skills for "The Moral Leader"

Discussion skill	Behaviors
Analysis	Careful reading; able to reference text easily and correctly
	Identifies patterns or themes
Debate	Good defense of point of view with back-up data from text
	On-point rebuttal; direct, clear response to another's comment or question
	Able to escalate or deepen argument
Listening	Respectful and attentive to speakers; closely follows discussion
	Able to summarize others' views and arguments accurately
Teamwork	Builds on others' contributions
	Helps others understand text, frameworks, or concepts
	Helps others clarify their views or change them
Exploration	Open to revising personal views
	Adds new layer or poses larger question
	Proposes novel argument or interpretation
	Proposes new direction for discussion
Use of personal experience	Illuminating example: Helps others see new angle or understand topic in more depth
Continuity	Maintains flow of discussion
	Creates links across texts or class sessions
	Good summary: Draws strands of discussion together

PARTICIPATING IN CLASS: STUDENT TIPS AND SUGGESTIONS

The student responses are in italics.

Be yourself

- *Speak your mind in class. This isn't a typical business course where you should structure your thoughts along frameworks – the discussion is geared towards introspection and deep examination of an issue, so share your thoughts openly.*
- *Feel free to challenge interpretations openly and to bring personal as well as current affairs and business analogies into your comments. It helps you and the class bring a direct association to the character/situation under discussion.*

Be sensitive

- *In terms of participation, speak sensitively since some of the issues discussed in the course might be delicate or personal. I feel it's important to ensure your classmates feel comfortable to participate openly as the greatest learning comes from listening to others' ideas.*

Stay flexible

- *As for actual discussion – come in with an open perspective and really engage in the conversation at hand – it will take turns that you never could anticipate, and as a participant you have to be nimble and open enough actively to listen and contribute to the discussion.*
- *When it comes to participating productively, my trick is to ask myself explicitly if I agree with everything said in the class. That is, as each person speaks, I ask myself whether I agree with the comment. This allows me an opportunity to speak at any moment in the class, it keeps me very engaged in the discussion and, most importantly, it has truly helped me in defining my own views on being a moral leader.*

Reflect *after* class

- *I find the introspective aspects of the course to be the most valuable, and would encourage trading time spent analyzing other characters for more time spent on self-reflection (developing your own framework, considering times when you've been at your moral best and worst, what you'll change, etc.).*
- *The thing that makes this class most powerful to me is the next step (past understanding characters) of contrasting their behavior with how you might behave. I think my real insights come when I think about what I would do and what I would like myself to do.*

NOTES

1   Harvard Business School Case 9–605-027, Revised August 23, 2006. Copyright © 2006 by the President and Fellows of Harvard College.
2   Martha Nussbaum, *Love's Knowledge: Essays on Philosophy and Literature*, New York: Oxford University Press, 1990, pp. 47–48.
3   Ibid., p. 79.

Moral Challenge

Moral Challenge Module Map

Central theme	Text and setting	Storyline	Preparation
Survival: The challenge of right versus wrong	*Endurance,* by Alfred Lansing Antarctic, 1914	How Ernest Shackleton saved the members of an Antarctic exploration expedition	Historical account: 280 pages
The challenge of right versus right	*Antigone,* by Sophocles Ancient Greece	A clash of competing "rights" in which neither side yields	Play: 60 pages
The challenge of a moral dilemma	*Blessed Assurance,* by Allan Gurganus 1940s America	A young, white insurance collection agent is torn between helping his black clients and his need for employment	Novella: 60 pages
The challenge of new principles	*Things Fall Apart,* by Chinua Achebe Early twentieth-century Nigeria	An Ibo clan confronts the arrival of Christian missionaries and British colonial authorities	Novel: 210 pages

Chapter 3

Moral Challenge Preview

I will refer to the case of a pupil of mine, who sought me out in the following circumstances. His father was quarrelling with his mother and was also inclined to be a "collaborator" [with the Nazi forces in France]; his elder brother had been killed in the German offensive of 1940 and this young man, with a sentiment somewhat primitive but generous, burned to avenge him. His mother was living alone with him, deeply afflicted by the semi-treason of his father and by the death of her eldest son, and her one consolation was in this young man. But he, at this moment, had the choice between going to England to join the Free French Forces or of staying near his mother and helping her to live. He fully realized that this woman lived only for him and that his disappearance – or perhaps his death – would plunge her into despair. He also realized that, concretely and in fact, every action he performed on his mother's behalf would be sure of effect in the sense of aiding her to live, whereas anything he did in order to go and fight would be an ambiguous action which might vanish like water into sand and serve no purpose. For instance, to set out for England he would have to wait indefinitely in a Spanish camp on the way through Spain; or, on arriving in England or in Algiers, he might be put into an office to fill up forms. Consequently, he found himself confronted by two very different modes of action; the one concrete, immediate, but directed towards only one individual; and the other an action addressed to an end infinitely greater, a national collectivity, but for that very reason ambiguous – and it might be frustrated on the way. At the same time, he was hesitating between two kinds of morality; on the one side the morality of sympathy, of personal devotion and, on the other side, a morality of wider scope but of more debatable validity. He had to choose between those two.

Jean-Paul Sartre, "Existentialism is a Humanism,"
lecture given in 1946

THE NATURE OF A MORAL CHALLENGE

What are moral challenges? What form do they take, and how do we identify them?

The subject of moral challenge – the kind of wrenching decision Sartre's student had to make – is a practical foundation for beginning our study of moral leadership. Later in the course we will ask how we might usefully *reason* about moral challenges, (which we will address in Module II: Moral Reasoning), and how we might act upon them and use these aptitudes to demonstrate *moral* leadership (which we will cover in Module III: Moral Leadership). Before then, we need to understand our own *moral awareness* – the personal framework people use to recognize morally charged situations, and the types of such situations – *moral challenges* – that any of us might face.

This module comprises four readings that will help clarify and reveal the complexities of four different types of moral challenge. In it, we will consider ethical problems from a variety of perspectives and in a range of situations, from the mundane – the challenges of an insurance collection agent – to the cataclysmic – an entire Antarctic expedition stranded in icy waters.

The module comes at the beginning of the course because it forces us to start at the beginning: To consider why and how moral issues are perceived by people in particular situations. When is a challenge a *moral* challenge? What makes us believe that a *moral* issue – as opposed to, for example, a legal issue – is at stake? As we begin our progress through these readings, many of us believe we have an intuitive sense of what we mean by "moral"; we know we are in the terrain of right and wrong, and of judging whether a particular decision or action is morally sound. But we might wonder: Where do these moral views come from?

THE VIEW FROM PHILOSOPHY

Of course, philosophers have broached the topic of moral philosophy – also called ethics. They have broadly addressed the question of the origins of our moral sentiments in two different ways: Either morality exists independently of humanity or it is a human invention. The Greek philosopher Plato championed the first approach, claiming that, like mathematical principles humans must accept, live by, and cannot change, morality exists as an abstract "spirit-like" entity. Most religious theologians reached similar conclusions, arguing (in various ways and to various degrees) that morality is determined by a god or gods, and therefore exists independently of humanity.

The second approach, which argues against morality as a spirit-like object, or against morality as being of divine origin, has roots as old as the first approach, having been championed, for example, in the Greek philosophical tradition of Skepticism. Today, that approach is expressed through notions of individual relativism – the belief that individuals create and live by their own moral standards;

and of cultural relativism, which suggests that moral prescriptions come from within societies, and thus different societies may have strikingly different moral codes. Common to both of these ideas is the assumption that morality is, to one degree or another, a human invention.[1]

A NOTE ON TERMINOLOGY

As we read, study, and debate, we will use the words "ethics" and "morality" interchangeably. There is no consensus definition of these terms, and even philosophers use them differently, as is suggested by the following entry from *The Oxford Companion to Philosophy*:

> **ethics and morality:** "Morality" and "ethics" are terms often used as synonyms: an ethical issue just is a moral issue. Increasingly, however, the term "ethics" is being used to apply to specialized areas of morality, such as medicine, business, the environment, and so on. Where professions are involved, a governing body will typically draw up a code of ethics for its members. "Ethics" in this sense can be thought of as a subset of morality, being that aspect of morality concerned with moral obligations pertaining to the practice of a profession. On the other hand, some philosophers, from Socrates to Bernard Williams, use "ethics" in a broad sense to refer to reflective answers to the question "How should I live?" If we accept this broad sense of "ethics," then morality becomes a subset of ethics, being that aspect of ethics concerned with obligation.[2]

THE VIEW FROM SOCIAL SCIENCE

Aside from philosophy, empirical research has also attempted to answer the fundamental question of the origins of morality and of our moral awareness. For example, Emile Durkheim, commonly regarded as a founding father of modern sociology around the turn of the twentieth century, argued for a sociological–cultural approach. He posited that morality is the deeply ingrained respect for collective society and the social order held by each individual; rules, maxims, and laws therefore have no moral authority on their own unless they are sanctioned by society as ideals that transcend individual needs or desires.

Extended to the field of anthropology, this approach has been used to explain the wide diversity in moral assumptions, often called "codes," among different societies and cultures[3] – one of which, the Ibo of nineteenth-century Nigeria, we will meet in the last reading of this module, *Things Fall Apart* by the Nigerian author Chinua Achebe.

Sigmund Freud, the founder of psychoanalysis and another turn-of-the-century theorist, came to a different conclusion. Freud's underlying assumption was that an individual's subconscious desires and motivations manifest themselves in actual behavior. He approached the issue of morality from a biological perspective, claiming that people – irrespective of society and culture – are "not gentle creatures who want to be loved and who at the most can defend themselves if they are attacked; they are, on the contrary, creatures among whose instinctual endowments is to be reckoned a powerful share of aggressiveness."[4]

Although he agreed with Durkheim that morality comes from society, Freud also believed that morality exists because of the universal necessity of regulating and controlling human behavior. Morality is therefore instilled in children through their development of a conscience (roughly what he termed the "superego"), which internalizes society's mores through emotional mechanisms such as guilt in order to minimize aggressive tendencies.

Contrasting to Freudian notions of internal regulation spurred by societal demands, behavioral theories, such as those propounded by the psychologist B. F. Skinner, asserted that, through external rewards, punishments, and imitation, children learn and internalize society's moral codes.[5]

THE VIEW FROM DEVELOPMENTAL PSYCHOLOGY

Throughout the remainder of the twentieth century, the field of developmental psychology used these foundations to flesh out more intricate and nuanced theories of moral awareness.

Jean Piaget, a Swiss psychologist, typified this approach by noting that "socialization in no way constitutes the result of a unidirectional cause such as the pressure of the adult community upon the child . . . Rather . . . it involves the intervention of a multiplicity of interactions of different types and sometimes with opposed effects."[6] This approach thus acknowledges that morality within society can be challenging and often conflict-ridden. In this module, Sophocles' play *Antigone* will allow us to explore the clash of two firm, but different, moral imperatives. Similarly, *Things Fall Apart* will illustrate how competing moral views are approached by those living in dynamic and changing societies and cultures.

One of the best known and most influential theories of developmental psychology has been Lawrence Kohlberg's description of stages of moral judgment. Positing that moral awareness develops in children *and* in adults, Kohlberg and his colleagues began a systematic inquiry into this moral development terrain. His work, and that of many researchers subsequently, suggested a developmental progression that ranged from an externalized sense of right and wrong enforced by obedience and punishment – most often (but not solely or necessarily) found in children – to an internalized appreciation of moral principles with which an individual constantly interacts.[7] This research suggests that by facing, discussing, analyzing, and acting on a succession of moral challenges, individuals can develop increasing moral awareness and judgment over the course of their lives.[8]

In this module, we will have an opportunity to witness an example of this turbulent process of moral development ourselves, in Allan Gurganus' novella *Blessed Assurance.*

TYPES OF MORAL CHALLENGE

While philosophers, social scientists, and empirical research help us understand moral awareness and its development, identifying and analyzing the *kinds of moral challenges* people face is equally important, and has also been a focus of examination.

Plato, for example, in questioning the universality of certain moral principles, asked: "To speak the truth and to pay your debts ... even to this are there not exceptions? Suppose that a friend when in his right mind has deposited arms with me and he asks for them when he is not in his right mind, ought I to give them back to him?"[9] For Plato, the answer was clear-cut: Protecting others from harm is a more compelling moral imperative than speaking the truth or paying debts.

Two thousand years later, Jean-Paul Sartre, the twentieth-century French writer and philosopher, found the student's dilemma noted above – whether to fight the Nazi occupation or to stay and console his mother – a more difficult scenario with no right answer. Moral arguments could be mounted on each side.

In their research, developmental psychologists have typically used such confounding ethical dilemmas as a basis for interviews with subjects; for example, Kohlberg's "Heinz Dilemma" questions whether a husband, after exhausting all other options, would be justified in stealing an unaffordable but life-saving medication from a pharmacist for his critically ill wife, who otherwise would certainly die.[10]

The complexity of options in such situations makes it all the more important to look carefully and critically at how we think about the right thing to do, especially if we are to come to terms with what we believe is right. Literature, and fiction in particular, can illuminate these timeless human issues, placing characters in situations that we can then ponder, analyze, and debate.

RIGHT VERSUS WRONG CHALLENGES, RIGHT VERSUS RIGHT CHALLENGES, AND TYPOLOGIES OF MORAL CHALLENGE

If moral challenges pose varying degrees of difficulty, and require a diverse array of considerations, then it is little wonder that philosophers have attempted to create a typology or scheme for categorizing types of moral challenges. One distinction they make is between a *right versus wrong* situation and a *right versus right* situation.

Right versus wrong challenges are described as those with clear, or mostly unambiguous, ethical imperatives, which point to a right answer, however difficult (or simple) that answer may be. As the first reading of this course, Ernest Shackleton's fight for his crew's survival will shed light on this type of challenge.

No matter how perilous Shackleton's situation in the frigid Antarctic seas was, however, leading ethicists have argued that true ethical dilemmas only exist in *right versus right* scenarios, which are "genuine dilemmas precisely because each side is firmly rooted in one of our basic, core values."[11]

Right-versus-right dilemmas have been further classified into different types of challenges. Rushworth Kidder, an ethicist, identifies four basic "dilemma paradigms" in which competing values exist on both sides of a moral challenge. These four paradigms – general categories into which he believes all moral challenges can be classified – are, first, telling the truth versus maintaining loyalty; second, considering the needs of the individual versus considering the needs of the community; third, accounting for short-term versus long-term considerations; and, fourth, weighing the ideal of justice against the competing imperative of mercy.[12] As useful as his paradigms are, however, very little in the study of ethics is simple or universally accepted; diverse typologies, paradigms, and ways of considering moral challenges compete and coexist.

OVERVIEW OF READINGS IN THIS MODULE

The readings in this module have been selected to reveal and illuminate the complexity of four different types of moral challenge.

- **The challenge of right versus wrong.** *Endurance,* the story of Ernest Shackleton's leadership of twenty-seven men stranded when their ship sinks in the Weddell Sea off the coast of Antarctica, will allow us to examine a *right-versus-wrong* dilemma, which, in this case, is the challenge of survival.
- **The challenge of right versus right.** *Antigone* will suggest the complexity and potential tragedy of a *right-versus-right* scenario, represented in the play by two competing "rights," or moral positions, one taken by Antigone, and the other by Creon, king of Thebes.
- **The challenge of a moral dilemma.** In *Blessed Assurance,* we will follow the decisions and actions of Jerry, a young white agent who collects funeral insurance premiums from poor African-Americans in the American South. This novella will provide insight into the actual process of responding to a *moral dilemma* – a type of right-versus-right conflict in which competing positions cannot be reconciled.
- **The challenge of new principles.** *Things Fall Apart,* a story of the conflict between the Umuofia, an Ibo clan of Nigeria, and Christian missionaries and British colonial authorities, will illuminate the challenges posed by *new moral principles* to both individuals and societies as a whole.

NOTES

1 For a short and comprehensive summary of these debates, see J. Feiser, "Ethics," *The Internet Encyclopedia of Philosophy*, 2006, online: http://www.iep.utm.edu/e/ethics.htm (accessed December 7, 2006).

2 *The Oxford Companion to Philosophy,* New York: Oxford University Press, 2005, p. 271. See also Thomas Mautner, *A Dictionary of Philosophy,* Cambridge, MA: Blackwell, 1996, for definitions of ethics, p. 137, moral, p. 276, moral philosophy, p. 277, morality, pp. 278–279, and *The Cambridge Dictionary of Philosophy*, Cambridge: Cambridge University Press, 1999, for definitions of ethics and related concepts, pp. 284–289, and morality, p. 586.

3 Elliot Turiel, *The Culture of Morality*, New York: Cambridge University Press, 2002, pp. 36–40.

4 Sigmund Freud, *Civilization and Its Discontents*, translated and edited by James Strachey, New York: Norton, 1961, p. 58.

5 Ibid., p. 95.

6 Quoted in ibid., p. 97.

7 Kohlberg's six stages are: (1) behavior based on punishments and rewards, (2) the idea that "good" behavior is in one's own self-interest, (3) the "good boy/girl" attitude, in which an individual tries to gain the approval of others through appropriate behavior, (4) a recognition of the merits of abiding by the law and acting on obligations of duty, (5) recognition of the "Social Contract," that is, the mutuality of social relations and the corresponding concern with the welfare of others, and (6) a conscience based on universal principles. See R. Barger, "A Summary of Lawrence Kohlberg's Stages of Moral Development," University of Notre Dame, 2000, online: http://www.nd.edu/~rbarger/kohlberg.html (accessed December 8, 2006). Researchers in the field of evolutionary biology similarly assert that the ability to reason morally is "hard-wired" in us. See, for example, Marc D. Hauser, *Moral Minds: How Nature Designed Our Universal Sense of Right and Wrong*, New York: Ecco, 2006.

8 Ibid.

9 http://classics.mit.edu/Plato/republic.2.i.html (accessed December 13, 2006).

10 Lawrence Kohlberg, Dwight Boyd, and Charles Levine, "The Return of Stage 6: Its Principle and Moral Point of View," in Thomas Wren (ed.), *The Moral Domain*, Cambridge, MA: MIT, 1990, p. 154.

11 Rushworth Kidder, *How Good People Make Tough Choices: Resolving the Dilemmas of Ethical Living*, New York: Fireside, 1995, p. 18.

12 Ibid., pp. 18–22.

Chapter 4

Endurance: Shackleton's Incredible Voyage

Survival: The challenge of right versus wrong

SHACKLETON'S AVERSION to tempting fate was well known. This attitude had earned for him the nickname "Old Cautious" or "Cautious Jack." But nobody ever called him that to his face. He was addressed simply as "Boss" – by officers, scientists, and seamen alike. It was really more a title than a nickname. It had a pleasant ring of familiarity about it, but at the same time "Boss" had the connotation of absolute authority. It was therefore particularly apt, and exactly fitted Shackleton's outlook and behavior. He wanted to appear familiar with the men. He even worked at it, insisting on having the exact same treatment, food, and clothing. He went out of his way to demonstrate his willingness to do the menial chores, such as taking his turn as "Peggy" to get the mealtime pot of hoosh from the galley to his tent. And he occasionally became furious when he discovered that the cook had given him preferential treatment because he was the "Boss."

But it was inescapable. He was the Boss. There was always a barrier, an aloofness, which kept him apart. It was not a calculated thing; he was simply emotionally incapable of forgetting – even for an instant – his position and the responsibility it entailed. The others might rest, or find escape by the device of living for the moment. But for Shackleton there was little rest and no escape. The responsibility was entirely his, and a man could not be in his presence without feeling this.[1]

ENDURANCE: THEMES AND QUESTIONS

What is moral leadership?

All of us who serve as leaders, or who aspire to leadership roles, try to determine what good and effective leadership consists in. **But is good leadership, even excellent leadership, the same as *moral* leadership?**

There is no better place to begin to answer this question than with the story of Ernest Shackleton. On December 14, 1914, the *Endurance,* a 144-foot-long three-masted barkentine, a ship built for the ice and heavy seas of the South Pole, left South Georgia, the southernmost outpost of civilization, a desolate island and whaling station. Its destination was the continent of Antarctica, the goal of its leader and crew, the "last great polar expedition" – crossing Antarctica on foot. On August 30, 1916, Shackleton, the expedition's British leader, collected the 27-member crew for their return trip to South Georgia.

In between was a 21-month ordeal that began with the sinking of the *Endurance* in the Weddell Sea off the coast of Antarctica, followed by 497 days on ice floes and in small boats, then a numbing 4-month wait for stranded crew members on Elephant Island to see if Shackleton's (and 5 other crew members') 17-day dash in an open 22-foot boat over 850 miles of some of the worst seas on the planet had been successful in reaching South Georgia to acquire a ship large and sturdy enough to save them. Not a single member of the crew had been lost.

Endurance: Shackleton's Incredible Voyage can serve as a laboratory for us, a place to begin to learn about leadership. The historical account was written from diaries and interviews with members of the expedition. In this intimate portrait of leadership we observe a leader and those led in close quarters and over long stretches of time.

Even if we hope we never face a challenge like Shackleton's, we wonder how we might fare as the leader of a group in such extreme straits. We'll be interested in how Ernest Shackleton maintains the morale, stamina, and hope of the crew of volunteers, seamen and civilians alike, people who need to believe in their leader but who are experienced enough not to be easily fooled by false promises or unrealistic assessments of the challenges they face.

Survival: a challenge of right versus wrong

Through Shackleton, we can begin to develop our own views on **the burden of leadership: what moral decision-making looks like under conditions of responsibility for others.** And let there be no mistake about it: There were plenty of decisions to be made in the days and months that passed between the sinking of the *Endurance* and the crew's final rescue. When to leave and when to stay; what to preserve and what to leave behind; how to pass the time when no progress could be made – Shackleton faced an unending stream of decisions, providing us with a vivid picture of the lived reality of leadership and the concerns, worries, and responsibilities that come with it.

But since our goal is to understand how moral leadership differs from leadership of any other kind we'll want to dig deeper, and ask: **What responsibilities do leaders face when their own lives are at stake, and when the lives of those who are in their keeping are at risk? What is permitted? What is required? What is prohibited?**

Shackleton's decisions can be examined in light of these questions, questions that plumb the challenge of survival, questions of right versus wrong that Shackleton faced, not once, but thousands of times over the course of the 21 months. Should he try to save the whole crew, even those who were too sick to help and who might slow them down, perhaps fatally, when they needed to respond to changing conditions of sea and weather? How about the shirkers – those who refused to cooperate and do their fair share of work? Should he keep the crew together, or allow the stronger and more capable and able-bodied men to try to find a means of rescue for the rest? These were some of the viable options that Shackleton faced.

The role of context in moral decision-making

We'll also be able to examine **the role of context in moral decision-making**. From the moment the *Endurance* is trapped in the pack ice of the Weddell Sea, it is evident that Shackleton's decisions, even if tactically flawless and morally sound, will still be tested in a situation over which he has little, if any, control. The heavy seas and winds and implacable currents of the Weddell Sea will play a large role in the outcome of the expedition, forcing us to consider this special requirement of leadership – **the need to act in an uncontrollable world.**

What does morality consist in?

The satisfying outcome of Shackleton's story – all of the crew saved – will also allow us to begin to explore **what we mean when we use the term "moral."** We will have the opportunity to examine Shackleton's actions and his motives – the story of how he came to the expedition, and what personal goals he had for it. This allows us to begin to consider **the factors that we believe should be taken into account in moral judgment.** Does Shackleton demonstrate moral leadership because he saves the crew? Is that all that is required? Are there other tests that we should use to assess him, other criteria that he must meet before we call him a moral leader? Our work in answering these questions will lay the groundwork for subsequent inquiry into moral challenge, moral reasoning, and moral leadership, and what they mean to each of us.

ASSIGNMENT

READING: *Endurance: Shackleton's Incredible Voyage,* by Alfred Lansing.

1   Was Shackleton a moral leader? How do you know?

ENDURANCE: BACKGROUND

We are routinely treated to media coverage of events around the globe, making us familiar with tsunamis and drought and with the challenges of individuals and nations thousands of miles away. We debate topics such as climate change, global warming, and other environmental threats that can only come from a perspective that is truly worldwide, one that stretches, in fact, beyond our planet. So it may be hard to imagine what it was like to live at a time when parts of the world were virtually unknown, and when nations and individuals competed for the honor, and related political and commercial influence, that came with exploration. The following background materials will help bring you back to the time of Ernest Shackleton. They sketch the broad context of geographical exploration among European nations, and then the more particular story of British exploration, and the history of the explorers of Antarctica, including Ernest Shackleton.

European competition and geographical exploration

Historians commonly refer to the last decades of the nineteenth century as the beginning of the "New Imperialism," when vast tracts of land worldwide – from Africa, to India, to Southeast Asia, to China – were brought under European control. Geographical and scientific exploration was inherently bound with the momentum of European imperialism. For instance, just as Britain was gaining control over parts of Africa, British explorers were simultaneously seeking the sources of great African rivers such as the Niger and the Nile. These intrepid explorers were often seen as heroes and sources of pride to their country; their exploits were widely circulated in writing, and captured the popular imagination. Through exploration – "discovery" – territories (even those previously inhabited) could be "claimed."

Britain's Royal Navy, arguably the strongest in the world until World War II (1939–1945) and the linchpin of its Empire (the world's most extensive), played a direct role not only in geographic exploration, but in scientific exploration as well. Charles Darwin, the naturalist and originator of the theory of evolution, for instance, sailed aboard a Royal Navy ship, the famed HMS *Beagle*. Similarly, Britain's Royal Geographic Society, which was instrumental in spearheading, formalizing, and disseminating geographical and scientific exploration in the nineteenth century – including Polar exploration – viewed itself as an agent of both science and Empire. Its original prospectus of 1830 claimed that the advantages of exploration were not just "of the first importance to mankind in general," but "paramount to the welfare of a maritime nation like Great Britain with its numerous and extensive foreign possessions."[2]

As industrialization spread across Europe, newly unified nation-states such as Italy and Germany, along with older, more established powers such as France, sought to compete with Britain (and with each other) for power, trade, and prestige. Nearing the turn of the century, this competition became especially fierce between Britain and Germany, and was manifested most spectacularly in a naval arms race.[3]

Control of the water had attained paramount importance, and this control was not purely about armaments; it was also about charting, mapping, and exploring the seas.

Great Britain and Polar exploration

The exploration of the Arctic seas and the Antarctic continent, although having little to do with any distinctly military posturing, was seen as a source of prestige, and, as such, explorers into the region were treated as national heroes. Antarctic exploration was pursued partially because of the challenge of conquering the last frontier that existed – in the words of Ernest Shackleton, "You can't think what it's like to walk on places where no man had been before."[4] It was also, in a sense, seen as an international sport. Britain's greatest adversaries in reaching the South Pole, for example, were not Germany, Italy, or France, but rather Norway (see timeline chart on p. 34), a country that hardly participated in the European power struggle and indeed remained neutral in World War I (1914–1918), and America, which was to be Britain's eventual ally in that conflict. These were not rivalries in any bitter sense, and indeed British explorers such as Captain Robert Scott often consulted more experienced Norwegian polar explorers for advice.[5]

For Britain, the pride associated with exploration at the turn of the century was especially alluring. Captain Scott's expedition to Antarctica aboard the *Discovery* in 1901, on which Shackleton served, departed Britain "with the unanimous backing of their countrymen," an important development at a time when Britain's role in the next century was deemed uncertain.[6] Queen Victoria had died earlier in the year, and meanwhile the British Army was suffering continuing setbacks in the Boer War in South Africa against the ethnically Dutch Boer militias. As one newspaper trumpeted, "Even in the throes of an exhausting struggle, we can yet spare the energy and the men to add to the triumphs we have already won in the peaceful but heroic field of exploration."[7] When Shackleton returned from his command of the *Nimrod* Antarctic expedition in 1909, he came back a hero, with one newspaper commentating that "It is pleasant to think that in spite of the moanings we hear from time to time on the decay of British manliness, our people are still as swift as ever to idolize the Man of Action."[8]

Antarctic exploration until *Endurance*

Eighteenth and nineteenth centuries

One of the most celebrated explorers of all time, Captain James Cook, sailed on several landmark journeys through the southern hemisphere in the last half of the eighteenth century. His reports of large seal populations on the islands surrounding Antarctica triggered an onslaught of British and American sealers into the area; the Industrial Revolution in England had suddenly made seal and whale oil indispensable (mineral oil was unknown at the time), and meanwhile seal skins were coming into fashion for women's coats. During the first decades of the

ERNEST SHACKLETON: BIOGRAPHY

Ernest Shackleton was born outside Dublin in 1874 to an Anglo-Irish family, and moved with his family to London as a child. In 1890 he joined Britain's merchant navy (not an organized fleet, but a term that included all privately and publicly owned merchant ships flying the British flag), and by 1898 he had achieved qualifications to be the master (captain) of a merchant ship. After being introduced to Sir Clement Markham, he was offered a position on Captain Scott's 1901 expedition on the *Discovery*. Shackleton returned to England in 1903 in ill health, having suffered on the journey from scurvy.

Shackleton immediately began seeking a means of returning to Antarctica, and resigned from the merchant navy in order to raise funds. He failed in the short term to do so, and attempted a series of jobs ranging from journalism to politics. Eventually, he came to work for a Scottish industrialist, William Beardmore, who agreed to support Shackleton's 1907–1909 voyage on the *Nimrod*. The expedition came within 97 miles of the South Pole before being forced to turn back, partially because Shackleton continued Scott's folly of using ponies instead of dogs (despite the advice of more experienced Norwegian explorers). None-the-less, the expedition achieved success in locating the South Magnetic Pole and returned to Britain to wide acclaim. He published a book on the Antarctic, and embarked on a series of lecture tours, including to Norway, where his successes also met an enthusiastic response.

When his celebrity waned with the "Race to the Pole" between Scott and Amundsen, Shackleton embarked on various business ventures, which came to little. Shackleton's announcement of another journey in 1913, to cross a large swath of unmapped Antarctica, was originally greeted with skepticism, especially since the pole had already been reached. None-the-less, he bought a Norwegian ship, which he renamed the *Endurance*, and assembled a crew. When war was declared in Europe in 1914, Shackleton offered his ship and his men to the Royal Navy, but was given permission to proceed to the Antarctic.

Following the *Endurance* adventure, Shackleton was commissioned into the Army as a major, and gave a lecture tour after the war. However, he soon became ill and began drinking heavily. In 1921 he took the opportunity to go south once again on the *Quest*. In 1922 he died of a heart attack on that voyage, while on the island of South Georgia, where he was buried.

nineteenth century, this booming trade was responsible for much of the continuing exploration in the Antarctic region.[9]

Throughout the century, scientific exploration also continued apace, originally centered around a search for the South Magnetic Pole[10] led by the British Royal Navy and by Captain James Ross in particular. Learned societies proliferated

Table 4.1 Antarctic expeditions at the turn of the twentieth century

Expedition and vessel	Leader and financing	Comments	Results
1901–1904 The British National Antarctic Expedition, aboard the *Discovery*	Captain Robert Falcon Scott, with the backing of Sir Clements Markham and the British government	Limited use of skis, limited knowledge of how to handle dogs. Lack of nutrition caused scurvy. Ernest Shackleton, a member of the expedition, was severely weakened.	Biological experiments conducted and important geographical discoveries made. Distance from pole reached: 463 miles
1907–1909 The British Antarctic Expedition, aboard the *Nimrod*	Sir Ernest Shackleton, privately financed	Used ponies instead of dogs, which proved to be a mistake on the icy terrain. Illness plagued the expedition, and Shackleton was forced to leave members behind before returning for their rescue.	Numerous geographical and biological discoveries made. South Magnetic Pole discovered. Distance from pole reached: 97 miles
1910–1912 Norwegian expedition on the *Fram*	Roald Amundsen (of Norway), privately financed	Adept use of skis and dogs allowing for efficient travel, use of seal meat to forestall scurvy, well planned, and fortunate with weather	First to reach South Pole. Returned safely
1910–1912 Expedition aboard the *Terra Nova*	Captain Scott, privately financed	Continued use of ponies, little use of skis, unlucky with weather	Scott and polar expedition party reached pole soon after Amundsen, but perished on the return journey

Source: Adapted from Eleanor Honnywell, *The Challenge of Antarctica*, London: Anthony Nelson, 1984.

Note: Scurvy was a common ailment suffered by sailors, and could at times prove fatal. Only in 1912 was it discovered that scurvy is caused by a deficiency in vitamin C.

throughout the century, and helped support and spur this research. The International Geographic Society passed a resolution in 1895 declaring that "the exploration of the Antarctic Regions is the greatest piece of geographical exploration still to be undertaken."[11]

Financing voyages

While the Royal Navy had funded voyages of science and exploration in the past, the naval arms race with Germany prevented it from directly funding an expedition to the Antarctic at the turn of the century. Rather, Sir Clement Markham, president of the Royal Geographical Society and determined to beat the Norwegians and the Americans to the South Pole, raised money for the first major Antarctic voyage; he was eventually given a grant by the British government. Markham chose the captain, Robert Scott, an officer in the Royal Navy, for the 1901 voyage on the *Discovery*.[12] Scott's crew included Shackleton.

Subsequent voyages were privately financed. Shackleton, for his first Antarctic voyage as a commander in 1907 on the *Nimrod*, actively engaged in fundraising, and expected great financial returns in publishing contracts and lecture tours. He even negotiated a £10,000 deal with a publishing company for advance rights to his account if he succeeded in reaching the Pole.[13] Scott, not as enthusiastically, also had to raise funds for his doomed expedition aboard the *Terra Nova* in 1910, in which he raced the Norwegian Roald Amundsen to the South Pole (Table 4.1).

BACKGROUND BIBLIOGRAPHY AND FURTHER READING

Driver, Felix. *Geography Militant: Cultures of Exploration and Empire*, Oxford: Blackwell, 2001.
Theorizes about the connections between exploration and empire, and provides concrete examples. See specifically Chapter 2 on the Royal Geographic Society.

Honnywell, Eleanor. *The Challenge of Antarctica,* London: Anthony Nelson, 1984.
Details the history of Antarctic exploration, including in-depth discussions of the major expeditions at the turn of the twentieth century.

Mortimer, Gavin. *Shackleton and the Antarctic Explorers*, Dubai: Carlton Books, 1999.
Provides an in-depth account of Scott's, Shackleton's, and Amundsen's voyages, and also gives detailed biographical information on each of these explorers.

"Royal Naval History: Maintaining Naval Supremacy 1815–1914," Royal Navy, online: http://www.royal-navy.mod.uk/static/pages/3540.html (accessed December 11, 2005).
Provides the history of the Royal Navy throughout the nineteenth century, including voyages of exploration and the naval arms race with Germany.

Shackleton, Ernest. *Shackleton: The Polar Journeys*, Cork: Collins Press, 2002.
A compilation of Shackleton's writings on both the *Nimrod* and *Endurance* expeditions.

ALFRED LANSING: BIOGRAPHY

Alfred Lansing was born in Chicago in 1921. During World War II (1939–45), when he was nineteen, he began a six-year tour of duty with the US Navy. While in the Navy, he was promoted to the rank of ensign and received a Purple Heart, a medal awarded by the President to members of the armed forces who are wounded (or killed) in battle. After leaving the Navy in 1946, he attended college, graduating from Northwestern University in Chicago in 1950.[14]

Lansing became a professional writer, journalist, and editor, explaining that "I have a great many opinions about writing, but I'm afraid that all of them are unprintable; furthermore, it's been my experience that most writers don't talk about their craft – they just do it."[15] He began his career as a bureau manager for the United Press, a global news agency. He later served as a staff writer for *Collier's*, an illustrated news and literary magazine that employed highly regarded writers such as Ernest Hemingway and Winston Churchill; he also worked as the Outdoor Editor for *Collier's*, having a specific personal interest in Japanese gardening. His professional career also included working as an associate editor for *Reader's Digest*, a popular and best-selling general-interest magazine, as well as becoming an editor for Time Books.[16]

Lansing is best-known for his freelance work, especially for his thoroughly researched work *Endurance: Shackleton's Incredible Voyage*, first published in 1959. The book has since been regarded as a classic; the 2002 paperback edition was its twenty-seventh printing.[17] A few years after its first publication, Lansing also published an abridged edition under the title *Shackleton's Valiant Voyage*.

"Throughout the book," a laudatory book review exclaimed, "the extremely thorough research undertaken by the author is evident. Lansing conducted extensive interviews with the survivors of the expedition, as well as gaining access to many of the diaries kept by the men during their ordeal."[18] As part of his research, he became a member of the Scott Polar Research Institute in Cambridge, England, in 1957.[19]

For his work on *Endurance*, Lansing was awarded a Secondary Education Board Book Award, as well as a Christopher Little Award. The latter prize, which he received in 1960, is given to books dealing with important subjects concerning the public good that are based on "sound and spiritual principles" and that are presented with solid literary craftsmanship with the goal of reaching a wide audience.[20]

Lansing died in 1975, his last job being editor of the Bethel, Connecticut, *Home News*, a weekly newspaper.[21]

AUTHOR BIBLIOGRAPHY

"10 Authors Cited: Christopher Literary Prizes Given by Movement," *The New York Times*, March 21, 1960, p. 19.

"Alfred Lansing, 1921–1975," *Contemporary Authors Online*, Thompson Gale, 2006, online: http://galenet.galegroup.com.ezp1.harvard.edu/servlet/ BioRC (accessed December 7, 2006).

Obituary for Alfred Lansing, *The New York Times*, September 4, 1975, p. 38.

Smith, Holly. "Against All Odds," *The Geographical,* 1999, vol. 71, no. 10, p. 67.

NOTES

1   Alfred Lansing, *Endurance: Shackleton's Incredible Voyage*, New York: Carroll & Graff, 1999, pp. 85–86.
2   Quoted in Felix Driver, *Geography Militant: Cultures of Exploration and Empire*, Oxford: Blackwell, 2001, p. 40.
3   "Royal Naval History: Maintaining Naval Supremacy 1815–1914," Royal Navy, online: http://www.royal-navy.mod.uk/server/show/nav.3854 (accessed December 7, 2006).
4   Quoted in Gavin Mortimer, *Shackleton and the Antarctic Explorers*, Dubai: Carlton Books, 1999, p. 8.
5   Ibid., p. 16.
6   Ibid., p. 18.
7   Quoted in Ibid., p. 18.
8   Ibid., pp. 50–51.
9   Eleanor Honnywell, *The Challenge of Antarctica*, London: Anthony Nelson, 1984, pp. 18–21.
10 The magnetic poles, whose locations shift over time, are the center of the Earth's magnetic activity and differ from the actual geographic poles through which the Earth's axis runs.
11 Ibid., pp. 22–26.
12 Mortimer, op. cit., p. 12.
13 Ibid., p. 34.
14 "Alfred Lansing, 1921–1975," *Contemporary Authors Online*, Thompson Gale, 2006, online: http://galenet.galegroup.com.ezp1.harvard.edu/servlet/BioRC (accessed December 7, 2006)
15 Ibid.
16 Obituary for Alfred Lansing, *The New York Times*, September 4, 1975, p. 38.
17 Lansing, op. cit.
18 Holly Smith, "Against All Odds," *The Geographical,* 1999, vol. 71, no. 10, p. 67.
19 *Contemporary Authors Online*, op. cit.
20 "10 Authors Cited: Christopher Literary Prizes Given by Movement," *The New York Times*, March 21, 1960, p. 19.
21 Lansing obituary, *The New York Times*, op. cit.

Chapter 5

Antigone

The challenge of right versus right

ANTIGONE: There is no shame in honouring my brother.
CREON: Was not his enemy, who died with him, your brother?
ANTIGONE: Yes, both were brothers, both of the same parents.
CREON: You honour one, and so insult the other.
ANTIGONE: He that is dead will not accuse me of that.
CREON: He will, if you honour him no more than a traitor.
ANTIGONE: It was not a slave, but his brother, that died with him.
CREON: Attacking his country, while the other defended it.
ANTIGONE: Even so, we have a duty to the dead.
CREON: Not to give equal honour to good and bad.
ANTIGONE: Who knows? In the country of the dead that may be the law.
CREON: An enemy can't be a friend, even when dead.
ANTIGONE: My way is to share my love, not share my hate.
CREON: Go then, and share your love among the dead. We'll have no woman's law here, while I live.[1]

ANTIGONE: THEMES AND QUESTIONS

The role of principle in moral decision-making and action

Many of us believe that *principled behavior*, or the readiness to use moral principles to guide decisions and actions, is a central feature of a morally responsible life. We admire people who take a moral stand and take inspiration from their stories. At the same time we wonder why individuals choose some principles to defend and not others, what enables them to persist in the face of forces arrayed against them, and what consequences they are willing to endure to uphold a cherished ideal or deeply held belief.

Sophocles' *Antigone* offers us an opportunity to explore this terrain and **the role of principle in moral decision-making and action**. This timeless story is surprisingly modern, and as you read it you will certainly draw parallels not only with your own experiences but also with larger, societal concerns.

The challenge of right versus right

The clash between Antigone and her uncle, Creon, for example, represents the profound issue of two very different points of view on the nature of responsibility, and both positions have equally been called "moral." **What should we do in the face of deeply held moral beliefs that conflict with each other? How should we handle a challenge of "right" versus "right" with moral weight on *both* sides?**

These are not abstract questions, and, like the characters in the play, we will struggle to determine whether Creon's duties as head of state following a brutal civil war, which motivated his edict forbidding the burial of the rebel leader Polyneices, should outweigh Antigone's loyalty to her family and to the laws of the gods.

Action driven by moral principle

Both central characters suggest what behavior, driven by strong moral commitments, looks like. *Antigone* thus allows us to examine the **personal implications of being guided by strong moral beliefs**, and we will have to see whether we like the picture of human action driven by moral principle that emerges.

Moral alternatives

We will also want to look beyond the conflict to consider **moral alternatives**. One assignment question for this class asks you to imagine a way of resolving the Antigone–Creon situation – before it ends in tragedy. The aim of this exercise is to *practice* thinking about what such a resolution might look like: Who (in the cast of characters) would be involved, the actions that would be needed, and the compromises – if any – that might be necessary.

Leaders routinely face right versus right challenges of the kind described in *Antigone*, having to determine, for example, how an organization's actions will affect constituencies with different needs such as employees and shareholders. Appreciating the nature of right-versus-right challenges, and what might be done to resolve them, is thus a practical consideration, and one that may prove vital to you and your own exercise of leadership.

ASSIGNMENT

READING: *Antigone*, by Sophocles (in *The Theban Plays*).

1 Please consult the table of contents. Read the "Introduction," "The Theban Legend," "The Legend Continued," "The Legend Continued," and the play, *Antigone*.

2 How are Antigone and Creon different? How are they alike?

3 What *really* is the conflict between them?

4 Assuming you could, how would you resolve it? Be prepared to defend your position.

ANTIGONE: BACKGROUND

While we can find numerous modern parallels to the challenges and conflicts described in *Antigone*, we also can benefit from a deeper understanding of the world Sophocles lived in. This is particularly true of the political environment of Athens in the fifth century BCE and that city-state's experiment with democracy, the broader context of the play. Our analysis is also enhanced by appreciating the very different literary tradition that Sophocles was writing in, including the purpose and uses of dramatic productions like *Antigone*, details of how they were staged, and the tradition of tragedy that *Antigone* both contributed to and exemplifies.

Classical Greece and Athens in the fifth century BCE

Classical Greece was politically defined by the autonomous city-state. In addition, colonies of city-states, as well as competing alliances among them, often played an integral role in Greek politics. Nonetheless, Greece was united in what was generally viewed as a common language and culture; Greeks were well aware of the differences between their fellow Greeks – whether from their own city-state or not – and non-Greek "barbarians."

The first decades of the fifth century BCE saw the dramatic rise of the Athenian city-state at the expense of its traditional rival, Sparta, following Athens' successful leadership in a fierce war against the powerful Persian Empire. Over the century, Athens capitalized on its supremacy and became an unrivaled center of theater, philosophy, literature, and architecture. Dramatists such as Sophocles and Euripides, historians like Thucydides and Herodotus, and enlightened statesmen including Pericles all lived during this period, as did philosophers such as Socrates, whose insights laid the basis for those of Plato and Aristotle in the following century. Athens claimed to be a proud democracy – although, with only a small male citizenship and the institution of slavery, it was hardly a democracy by today's standards – and prided itself on its open political system.

In the last decades of the century, however, resentment of Athenian supremacy grew, and the Peloponnesian War, fought principally between Athens and Sparta, began. Athens was eventually defeated by Sparta in 404 BCE, and its democracy was temporarily overthrown.

Theater in Classical Greece

Staging and costumes

In contrast to most modern theaters, theaters in fifth-century Athens were roofless and open to the elements, as well as to all citizens. Instead of an elevated stage, the action took place on a wide circle of flat ground, the *orchestra*, around which, usually built into a hill, was stadium-like seating for the audience. Estimates of the number of seats in the largest theaters range between 15,000 and 30,000.[2] On the side of the *orchestra* not surrounded by seating was the *skene*, a building generally used as "backstage" – because it was decorated to illustrate the setting of the play; the modern usage of the words "scene" and "scenery" derives from the *skene*.[3]

In contrast to most modern productions, actors in these plays were heavily disguised, and their costumes included large masks. This element had a particular religious or mythical motivation: "A complete disguise was the external sign that the actor had given up his own identity in honour of the god, in order to let another being speak and act through him."[4]

Often there were fewer lead actors than lead characters, and actors would switch costumes in the *skene* in order to play different roles. There were no female actors, and female roles were therefore played by men.[5]

The audience comprised mostly male citizens, who had a break from work on festival days. Women, in smaller numbers, may have been present as both wives and courtesans. Children, resident aliens, ambassadors and foreign traders were also likely to have been in attendance.

Productions

Plays, using Athenian actors and choruses, were staged on annual religious holidays as a competition among playwrights, competition being a hallmark of Classical

Greek culture. The holiday was "a citywide festival, which was a religious ceremony and also a political occasion, a celebration of the imperial power and social cohesion of the Athenian people."[6]

Traditionally, three leading dramatists would each stage a set of three tragedies as well as a satyr play (a burlesque re-telling of a mythological tale) over the course of the three-day festival period. A high priest, as well as other priests and ranking officials, sat in the seats of honor; they, along with the acclaims of the audience, decided which competing poet would be awarded the coveted prize of victory.[7]

The meanings of Greek tragedy

Myth and religion

The world of the Classical Greeks has been described as a "Forest of Myths" – men and women would continually encounter images of myths on their jewelry, drinking cups, vases, public statues and wall paintings, as well as in every form of ceremony.[8] While the question of actual belief in the supernatural elements of the myths, including the pantheon of gods, was debated – indeed, philosophers as early as the sixth century BCE were ridiculing the belief in gods – the myths nonetheless served as the crux of Greek self-identity in lieu of a recorded pre-history.[9] For poets and playwrights, using mythology in their works was a means of both making their art broadly accessible and evoking the powerful images of the Greek world. Of the 293 plays from the fifth century that we know about, 68 were on the subject of the Trojan War (*circa* 1200 BCE), and the range of topics the others spanned was extremely narrow, limited to only a dozen familiar mythological stories and figures.[10]

Sophocles' *Theban Plays*, for example, a trilogy of which *Antigone* is the final installment, follows the family of Oedipus. It begins by telling the story of Oedipus' inability to escape fate – the prophecy that he would murder his father and marry his mother – in the first play, *Oedipus Rex*. The second play, *Oedipus at Colonus*, details the death of Oedipus and the civil war between his sons Eteocles and Polyneices for control of Thebes. The final play, *Antigone*, begins when order is restored in Thebes, the two sons of Oedipus having died in the civil war.[11] Oedipus and his family were well-known characters, being mentioned not only in the famous lyrics of Homer,[12] but also in other plays from Classical Greece, such as Aeschylus' play *Seven Against Thebes*, focusing on the civil war between Eteocles and Polyneices.

Myths were not only stories and tales, however; Greek mythology – and the pantheon of gods it featured – was the cornerstone of popular Greek religious belief. Myths provided answers to deep religious questions of creation, the afterlife, and the existence of evil and suffering; they also explained natural phenomena such as thunder and fire.

Evolving from religious observance, theatrical performances in Athens were performed during the *City Dionysia* springtime festival and the *Lenaia* winter festival,[13] both dedicated to the Greek god Dionysius, the patron deity of agriculture and theater. Dionysius also represented wine, civilization, and peace. In fact, Greek drama developed from peasant dances in honor of Dionysius, and aspects of its peasant dance origin still existed in the fifth century, for example, in the institution of the large Chorus and the circular *orchestra*.[14]

While all forms of theater referenced mythology, tragedy in particular drew its power from the audience's understanding of the supernatural. "The Greek saw himself in relation to the world around him, a world which existed for his benefit, but left him at the mercy of a number of contrary and unpredictable forces." The theater was a place where these forces could, through the agency of masked actors, be represented as heroes and gods. It was therefore a forum whereby both the playwrights and the audience could "contemplate the vicissitudes of life and seek guidance over major issues."[15]

This dynamic within Greek tragedy has been explained by a noted scholar of Greek thought:

> What is true [in Tragedy] is that a part, great or small, of the action . . . is considered to proceed from causes beyond the control of the characters . . . But the finest and most profound tragic effect comes when the poet is not content merely to set forth external events, nor even the fact of guilt, but exhibits also the moral attitude of his protagonist toward events and toward his own actions. He answers the call of honor, come what may; he endures what fate or the gods send. His act may have caused his downfall, but his will remains noble; he learns by suffering; and there may be a final vindication of the sufferer, though of an unexpected kind. Such tragedy, though lapsing now and again into traditional lament and pessimism, is penetrated by the feeling of fifth century Greece that life is a game played for high stakes, in which man may nobly win, or at worst, may nobly lose. The greatest Greek drama, in other words, rests on the interplay between fate and character, between what man can not change and what remains within his power.[16]

Family

Tragic theater often portrayed drama within families, revealing the particular importance attached to family in Classical Greece. Many myths, whether they concerned gods, demigods, or humans, described intra-family struggles.

The Greek philosopher Aristotle, in giving general advice to tragic poets, wrote, "When it is in the family relationships that violence occurs, as for example when murder or some similar action is committed or planned by brother against brother, son against father, mother against son or son against mother – this should be the objective."[17]

The *Theban Plays* clearly illustrates this theme, with the first play (*Oedipus Rex*) focused on acts of patricide and incest; the second play (*Oedipus at Colonus*) centered on a civil war between Oedipus' sons and their father's curse that the brothers should both die by each other's sword; and the third play (*Antigone*) being an exploration of the deep bonds of family loyalties. While the characters and settings vary among the plays, the narrative strain of one family's conflicts serves to unite both the trilogy as well as the myth itself.

BACKGROUND BIBLIOGRAPHY AND FURTHER READING

Knox, Bernard. *Word and Action: Essays on the Ancient Theater*, Baltimore, Md: Johns Hopkins Press, 1979.

> See especially Chapter 1 for an in-depth discussion of Greek myth and religion, and its relation to Greek theater.

Rehm, Rush. *Greek Tragic Theatre*, London: Routledge, 1992.

> Provides excellent insight into the "Performance Culture" of Athens, and vividly describes performances and productions in Classical Greece.

Simon, Erika. *The Ancient Theatre*, London: Methuen, 1972.

> See the chapter on "Ancient Greek Theatre" for a detailed discussion on the architecture and painting of theaters in Classical Greece, as well as on costumes and performances.

Walton, Michael J. *The Greek Sense of Theatre: Tragedy Reviewed*, London: Methuen, 1984.

> See Part 1 for a useful discussion on the reactions of the audience to Greek theater, specifically to tragedy.

Wiles, David. *Greek Theatre Performance: An Introduction*, Cambridge: Cambridge University Press, 2000.

> Provides a comprehensive analysis of Greek theater, including discussions on myth, ritual, politics, and gender, as well as on the production itself.

SOPHOCLES: BIOGRAPHY

Along with Aeschylus and Euripides, Sophocles remains known as one of the three great dramatists of Classical Athens. Born in 496 BCE in Colonus, a village near Athens, to a wealthy and well-regarded family,[18] Sophocles lived most of his life in Athens. But he appears to have maintained a connection with the village, which he used as the setting for his tragedy *Oedipus at Colonus*. In that work, he wrote about his village (through the voice of the Chorus):

> Here in our white Colonus, stranger guest,
> Of all Earth's lovely lands the loveliest,
> Fine horses breed and leaf-enfolded vales
> Are thronged with sweetly-singing nightingales.[19]

He was well educated, and at the age of sixteen was chosen to lead a dance celebrating the Athenian victory at Salamis, a major battle in the war against the formidable Persian Empire. Indeed, throughout his life, Sophocles was deeply involved in the life, politics, and religion of Athens, living, as he did, through the golden age of that city. E. F. Watling, in his widely read introduction to the Theban plays, wrote, "He lived through a cycle of events . . . without parallel in intensity of action and emotion, and of lasting significance in the procession of human achievement."[20] Sophocles was an associate of the enlightened ruler Pericles, and later in life, well after his reputation as a dramatist was clearly established, he served as an Athenian general, a treasurer of tribute money, and a priest, and was elected to a government advisory committee.[21]

Sophocles' career as a playwright began with a single stunning success. In 468 BCE he defeated the veteran dramatist Aeschylus, thirty years his elder, in the competition held at the Dionysian springtime festival in Athens. In the words of one scholar:

> The rivalry was not between two works, but between two styles of tragic art, and the subject chosen by the young poet, together with the desire to encourage his first attempt, was sufficient to outbalance the reputation of the great antagonist, whose verses lacked the air of freshness and youth that hung around the poetry of Sophocles.[22]

The "freshness" which Sophocles brought to the stage was a result of his innovations, first in regard to stage painting, but second, and perhaps more important, in the nature of the dramas themselves.

For instance, until Sophocles, Greek tragedy commonly used only two actors (who changed roles as needed) in addition to the Chorus; Sophocles added a third actor in his plays, allowing him to increase the number of characters, widen the possibilities for interactions, and thereby deepen and extend the dramatic conflict.[23] Indeed, Sophocles is known for his dramatic portrayal of conflict: "His particular contribution to dramatic structure is the staging of conflict, in particular conflict between opposing forces rigid in attitude and uncompromising in action."[24]

Seven of Sophocles' plays have survived in their entirety: *Ajax, Antigone, Trachinian Women, Oedipus Rex, Electra, Philoctetes,* and *Oedipus at Colonus.* In addition, a large part of a satyr play – an amusing and satirical rendition of a well-known dramatic story – has also survived. Based on the records, it appears that, in total, Sophocles wrote approximately 123 dramas for the festivals, and won as many as twenty-four victories.[25]

Sophocles lived for ninety years, and died in 406 BCE, just before the final defeat of Athens by Sparta in the Peloponnesian War.

AUTHOR BIBLIOGRAPHY

Bates, Alfred (ed.), *The Drama: Its History, Literature and Influence on Civilization,* Vol. 1, London: London Publishing Company, 1906, online: http://www.theatrehistory. com/ancient/sophocles001.html (accessed December 7, 2006).

Sophocles, *The Theban Plays,* translated by E. F. Watling, New York/London: Penguin Books, 1947.

"Sophocles." *Encyclopedia Britannica Online,* 2006 (accessed February 3, 2006).

Walton, Michael J. *The Greek Sense of Theatre: Tragedy Reviewed,* London: Methuen, 1984.

Watling, E. F., "Introduction," in Sophocles, *The Theban Plays,* New York/London: Penguin Books, 1947, pp. 7–22.

NOTES

1 Sophocles, "Antigone," in *The Theban Plays*, translated by E. F. Watling, New York/London: Penguin Books, 1947, p. 140.
2 Michael J. Walton, *The Greek Sense of Theatre: Tragedy Reviewed*, London: Methuen, 1984, p. 34.
3 Erika Simon, *The Ancient Theatre*, London: Methuen, 1972, pp. 2–8.
4 Ibid., p. 10.
5 Ibid., pp. 6, 10.
6 Bernard Knox, *Word and Action: Essays on the Ancient Theater*, Baltimore, MD: Johns Hopkins Press, 1979, p. 3.
7 Simon, op. cit., p. 5.
8 David Wiles, *Greek Theatre Performance: An Introduction*, Cambridge: Cambridge University Press, 2000, p. 17.
9 Ibid.
10 Knox, op. cit., p. 9.
11 *Antigone* was produced by Sophocles first, then came *Oedipus Rex*, and finally *Oedipus at Colonus*, Sophocles' final play before his death.
12 Homer was a legendary poet credited with composing *The Iliad* and *The Odyssey*, two landmark poetic compilations of Greek epic and myth.
13 Wiles, op. cit., p. 31.
14 Simon, op. cit., p. 3.
15 Walton, op. cit., p. 29.
16 William Chase Greene, *Moira: Fate, Good, & Evil in Greek Thought*, Cambridge, MA: Harvard University Press, 1944, pp. 91–92.
17 Quoted in Knox, op. cit., p. 21.
18 "Sophocles." *Encyclopedia Britannica Online*, 2006 (accessed February 3, 2006).
19 Sophocles, op. cit., p. 92.
20 E.F. Watling, "Introduction," in Sophocles, *Ibid.*, p. 7.
21 *Encyclopedia Britannica Online*, op. cit., see also Alfred Bates (ed.), *The Drama: Its History, Literature and Influence on Civilization*, Vol. 1, London: London Publishing Company, 1906, pp. 106–112, online: http://www.theatrehistory.com/ancient/sophocles001.html (accessed December 7, 2006).
22 Ibid.
23 *Encyclopedia Britannica Online*, op. cit.
24 Walton, op. cit., p. 103.
25 *Encyclopedia Britannica Online*, op. cit.

Chapter 6

Blessed Assurance

The challenge of a moral dilemma

ONE VERY OLD WOMAN seemed to peek from every door. Toothless, blue-black, her shy grin looked mischievous, a small head wrapped in the brightest kerchief. At some doorways, her hands might be coated with flour. At others she held a broom or some white man's half-ironed white business shirt. She wore male work boots four sizes too large, the toes curled up like elf shoes. Sometimes she smoked a pipe (this was in the Forties). Her long skirt dragged the floor, pulling along string, dustballs. She asked, "What they want now. You ain't the one from before – you a young one, ain't you?" and she chuckled at me. I smiled and swallowed.[1]

. . .

One month into the job, nobody knew my name. I'd stayed "Assurance." And my clients still looked pretty much alike to me. Maybe it sounds bad but, hey, they *were* alike. People started having names when I deciphered the last collector's rotten handwriting. One morning, it yielded like a busted code. Then the ladies began standing out from one another. Oh, man, I couldn't believe some of the tallies!

"Vesta Lotte Battle, 14 Sunflower Street – commenced payment on policy #1, Mar. 2, 1912, four policies complete, collected to date: $4,360.50."[2]

. . .

My ninth week on the job, all clients permanently broke down into themselves. There was the one missing two fingers, the one who always tried to give me geranium clippings for my mom, the plump one in the bed, the pretty young one in the wicker wheelchair, the old one in her metal wheelchair who wore a cowgirl hat, the one with the wig, the one who told the same three easy riddles each week, the one, the one.

. . .

My rounds sure felt easier when people had the decency to stay blended. Now I started worrying over payer and nonpayers too. You know how it is, once a crowd splits into separate faces, nothing can ever mash them back into that first safe shape.[3]

BLESSED ASSURANCE: THEMES AND QUESTIONS

Moral awareness

We generally assume that we will recognize a moral challenge when we are faced with one. We hope that the boundaries will be evident and the choices to make are obvious. But privately we may wonder: Will we really know? What is it that we will perceive and see? What will alert us that this is a situation we should pay attention to? What should we do in response? These are central issues that characters, most notably the protagonist, Jerry, confront in *Blessed Assurance*.

Blessed Assurance: A Moral Tale, which concludes Allan Gurganus' collection of stories, *White People*, introduces a narrator, Jerry, whom we listen to as an adult who's recounting a pivotal experience in his youth (around 1950 in a southern US state). Jerry tells us that a summer job he held at the age of nineteen – regularly collecting literally nickels and dimes from African-American citizens that would eventually pay for their funerals – was unforgettable. As an adult forty years later, he remains haunted by those events and the people he encountered, but he does not tell us precisely why. Indeed, he suggests that he himself does not know why this long-ago episode continues to be so important to him. And yet it was clearly a *moral* challenge to him, even if he cannot pinpoint it or articulate its boundaries – or determine whether he did the right thing.

For a long time it is not even clear to Jerry that he faced a moral challenge. We watch him as he struggles to master his new job, and we are given a rare opportunity to try to identify the point at which an individual's perception of their situation changes – the point at which they are first struck by **moral awareness**. Jerry's struggles can provide provisional answers to commonsense questions that relate to our own lives: **What does this moment of moral awareness look like?** Do we know it at the time, or only afterwards? Most importantly, in what ways does moral awareness affect us? Does moral insight make our lives easier? Or harder?

A moral dilemma

We will find that, even after Jerry appears to have a new view of his situation, the road to action for him is by no means clear. In fact, Jerry faces a situation with **competing obligations and choices that seem to contradict each other.** As readers we witness how Jerry attempts to sort through the conflicts inherent in his situation and the decisions he eventually did make (and didn't make) – in both his youth and maturity. Through Jerry's decisions we can explore **what action in the face of a moral dilemma looks like.** A **moral dilemma** is a *type of* right versus right challenge that is irreconcilable. What happens when we aspire to fulfill mutually exclusive moral obligations and duties? What should we do in this circumstance? And, because we know we face internal conflict, what should we expect and how will we feel?

Future impact of moral decisions

Jerry's story is also **a retrospective narrative** – a telling of early events from the vantage point of forty years of intervening life and history. But his story is not just about the past. We often wonder whether the actions we take today will affect us in the future. **How long is the shadow that moral decisions cast into the future?** Jerry's story allows us to begin to answer this question, to lay out the stakes of decision-making so we can appreciate the risks and impact of our actions beyond, possibly well beyond, the time frame of the immediate moment.

ASSIGNMENT

READING: *Blessed Assurance: A Moral Tale*, by Allan Gurganus (from *White People*).

1 How do you assess the business model used by Windlass Funerary Eventualities, Inc., the insurance company Jerry worked for?

2 How would you describe Mrs. Battle's character?

3 What is the nature of her and Jerry's relationship?

4 Do you agree with all of the actions Jerry took? Why? Why not?

5 Jerry looks back on his early decisions with regret. Review the shape that Jerry's life has taken, and then be prepared to weigh in on this argument, by agreeing, or mounting a defense of the ways in which Jerry might have been changed, for the better, by his actions.

BLESSED ASSURANCE: BACKGROUND

Blessed Assurance takes place in the American South in the late 1940s. It describes relationships between Jerry, its 19-year-old white protagonist, and the African-American residents of "Baby Africa," as the part of town that they live in was called. You may want to know more about the life and times it depicts. Background materials here will provide you with a deeper understanding of the story's context. They include a brief history of race relations in the United States, a description of society and culture in the American South, and, because the story has at its center a business built on weekly saving for a funeral, religious practices in the region among African-Americans and Southern whites.

Race relations in the United States: A brief overview

Slavery prior to the Civil War

In 1776, when America's Declaration of Independence was signed, there were an estimated 500,000 Africans held in slavery within the original thirteen colonies, a majority of whom lived in the southern states of Virginia, the Carolinas, and Georgia, as well as in the "border states" of Maryland and Delaware. In the South, slaves made up an estimated 40 percent of the population, and, in the view of many (but certainly not all) Southern and Northern whites, were necessary for the economic well-being of the Colonies.[4]

The Constitutional Convention of 1787, which drafted a permanent constitution uniting the thirteen former colonies, averted an early conflict over the role of slavery in the Union by enshrining within it a compromise on the issue based on notions of property. For purposes of representation and taxation, slaves were to be counted as three-fifths of a person. The slave trade was to continue at least until 1808, when Congress could abolish it (and at which time it overwhelmingly did).[5] In return for agreeing to return fugitive slaves, Northern states received concessions in trade and commerce. Through these compromises, an early crisis was averted, but at a price: Southern states continued to view slavery as a right of individual states, which intertwined the issue of slavery with an even larger and in some ways more divisive question: Was there to be a strong federal government with broad powers, or was America to be a union of relatively independent states?

The Civil War and reconstruction

The physical and economic expansion of the United States created new tensions over slavery and "States' Rights" for which the constitutional compromises in themselves proved inadequate. New compromises, commonly over the designated territories to which slavery could spread, were reached throughout the first half of the nineteenth century, although these took the form of temporary resolutions rather than permanent solutions. The efforts at compromise were severely hindered by the Supreme Court's decision in the Dred Scott case (1857), which ruled territorial compromises to be unconstitutional: Slavery was to be allowed in all United States territories, and blacks – even those who were free – could not be citizens of the United States.

The Civil War (1861–1865), fought between the North and the breakaway Southern slaveholding states from Texas to Virginia, was the culmination of tensions over States' Rights, in which the issue of slavery played a key role. With President Abraham Lincoln's "Emancipation Proclamation" (1863) the war increasingly became a moral imperative to abolish slavery as an institution, once and for all.

Consequently, when the North emerged victorious, efforts at "reconstruction" focused not only on reintegrating the South into the Union, but also on reconstituting the political, economic, and social framework on which Southern slaveholding society had been based. New constitutional amendments outlawed slavery and sought to guarantee the civil and political rights of African-Americans, while the military occupation of the South installed African-Americans in high positions of power such as Senators and Representatives, and even, in the case of Louisiana, a Governor. Meanwhile, Southern resentment – although by no means monolithic – festered over what was seen as a harsh Northern "imperial" rule, and the overturning of Southern society. Violent racist groups such as the Ku Klux Klan, ostensibly seeking to reclaim a Southern way of life, began to gather strength.

Segregation and the Jim Crow laws

As the Southern states were reintegrating into the Union, the gains of Reconstruction were increasingly reversed.[6] The so-called Jim Crow laws, named after a popular stage depiction of an uneducated rural black man, were passed across the South, limiting the political involvement of African-Americans, relegating them to second-class citizens in the social sphere, and segregating them from white education, which in effect limited their possibilities for advancement. Segregation was upheld numerous times by the Supreme Court, which ruled in 1896 that segregation did not violate equality – African-Americans could be "separate but equal." Segregation was not overturned by the Supreme Court until the 1950s, and strong legislation arising from the Civil Rights movement did not take effect until a decade later.

Society and culture in the American South

Post-reconstruction

Southern blacks and whites after the Civil War had both largely become share-croppers, agricultural tenants on the property of a landlord with whom they shared their crops.[7] Blacks were commonly restricted to this arrangement during and after Reconstruction because of institutional and racist measures aimed at tying them to the land, while whites increasingly turned to sharecropping because of the sharp economic decline in agriculture and in the profitability of cotton, the principal crop of the American South. Many white and black communities came to participate in a common way of rural life, dedicated to church, the community store, and the crop cycle. The Jim Crow laws and segregation were in many cases the only arrangement that kept whites – often equally destitute and having no better education for their own children – a step ahead of blacks on the socioeconomic ladder.

Mechanization and urbanization

From the 1920s onwards, and gaining momentum through the 1940s, the mechanization of agriculture increasingly undermined the economic rationale of share-cropping, and sharecroppers were ultimately even encouraged to move off the land by the larger plantation owners.[8] Both whites and African-Americans moved internally within the South to newly urbanized areas. Urbanization began as a gradual process, originating with mechanization and the growth of mill towns,[9] and accelerated in response to World War II (1939–1945), during and after which cities in the South grew three times as fast as comparable cities in the North.[10]

Societal effects

In the perception of some (but not all) Southern whites, a way of life was being lost during the first decades of the twentieth century, and especially after World War II. Even though jobs were plentiful in mill towns and in the new industries brought by the war, the profound economic and demographic shifts in this traditionally agrarian society "moved many politicians and writers to build, or build upon, a tradition of deep and encompassing cultural nostalgia that supplanted any engagement with ongoing cultural change or racial equality."[11] Race relations in newly urbanized areas, uncharted territory for most whites and blacks alike, were defined by Jim Crow laws, especially in places where races were bound to rub shoulders such as public transportation, public facilities, and restaurants.

Over time, Southern regions of the United States became increasingly economically isolated from the rest of the country. After World War II, in America's post-war and post-Depression economic boom, the relative socioeconomic backwardness of the South could no longer be overlooked, especially when influential African-American leaders in the North, bolstered by black participation in the war, increasingly agitated for change. Court decisions and executive orders from the federal government, which were slowly chipping away at the edifice of segregation, spurred many nostalgic and alarmist Southern whites into violent racial confrontations. Lynch mobs and organized white militias like the Ku Klux Klan and the White Citizens Council had become an important influence in the South, even if they weren't necessarily representative of the majority of white Southerners' desires.

The "Great Black Migration" and Southern black communities

Economic changes set in motion by the gradual obsolescence of sharecropping following World War II resulted in the "Great Black Migration," then the largest internal migration in American history, which saw a steady stream of five million African-Americans between 1940 and 1970[12] seeking employment in Northern cities such as Detroit, Chicago, and New York. There, the promise of gainful employment, upward mobility, and a somewhat less segregated society proved highly attractive.

The great migration North also had the effect of sorely testing family and community bonds in African-American society, and those who remained in the South often faced a hand-to-mouth existence in communities (like Gurganus' "Baby Africa" of *Blessed Assurance*) that were usually situated adjacent to, yet segregated from, white towns and cities. Prospects for advancement were extremely limited. The few residents with education could teach in the black school systems, preach in local churches, or operate small businesses within local communities; the majority, without education or opportunity to broach larger spheres of economic possibilities, could often only find work as domestic servants for white households, or as day laborers on existing agricultural "plantations."[13] These black townships often lacked the benefits and bare necessities found in the nearby white communities such as clean water, sewers, and electricity.

Payment on installment

In such communities, where residents had virtually no capital and no credit, a common method of purchasing expensive goods and services was paying in small weekly installments. These payments, as well as the company employees who collected them, were not unusual across America, especially in poorer areas – both white and black – where many, using this method, were able to buy otherwise prohibitively expensive consumer goods. Property, automobiles, furniture, and encyclopedias, among many other products, could be purchased "on the installment plan."

Religious practice in the American South

The hereafter

The American South was, and still is, a deeply Protestant Christian society, and this defining characteristic has been shared by both black and white communities. The notion of personal redemption, a cornerstone of Christian practice and theology, has been a particularly strong theme in Southern churches, black and white alike.

While sharing in this religious milieu, African-Americans also established their own religious identity based on cultural heritage, segregation of church services, and class differences. The result has generally been a more emotionally expressive, interactive religious service, which, although possibly having roots in West African tradition, was also originally a means of empowerment. "Shouting is about identity. Shouting is about power. It is about expressing that which, for so long, one could not without the threat of severe punishment."[14] Not only was emotional expressiveness a means of empowerment *vis-à-vis* society, but it was also an expression of conviction about an anticipated spiritual redemption.

Such manifestation was an attitude towards religious practice that white society – mostly its upper crust – found to be highly unusual, despite the religious values they had in common. Nevertheless, the notion of a "Great Hereafter," shared by many Christians, regardless of color or origin, created an affinity for a devotion to salvation that would come in another life.

African-American funerals: "Homegoings"

African-American funerals also were – and to a lesser extent continue to be – distinct. Originally, slaveholders left funeral services almost entirely to the slaves themselves, and for this reason there are continuities between black funeral services and West African funerary rituals.[15] African-American funerals were not only distinct in their origin, but also, because of the experience of slavery, noted for their spiritual orientation referring to "home."

Death was "Goin' home," and consequently, unlike white funerals, which often were restrained, reserved, and mournful, black funerals were hopeful, celebratory, and occasions where joyful and spontaneous displays of emotion were expected. W. E. B. DuBois, a highly influential black activist and scholar at the turn of the twentieth century, observed the spiritual and redeeming elements in Southern black funerals. "Losing the joy of this world," he wrote, Southern African-Americans "eagerly seized upon the offered conceptions of the next," since they lived a life "under sorrow and tribulation until the Great Day when He should lead His dark children home."[16]

An individual could commonly be expected to plan his or her funeral well in advance, hoping for the most uplifting send-off possible. In the twentieth century, the first successful business people in Southern black society, men and women alike, were owners of funeral homes, who were afforded great respect as pillars of the community. Not only did they provide funerals, a service which white funeral homes were typically unwilling to offer to black citizens; they also offered insurance, counseling, and even investment advice. These funeral homes continued the efforts of nineteenth-century burial associations, which allowed individuals to pay a weekly fee of several pennies for the cost of their funeral to be covered completely, guaranteeing that they would be "put away nicely."

BACKGROUND BIBLIOGRAPHY AND FURTHER READING

Daniel, Pete. *Standing at the Crossroads: Southern Life since 1900*, New York: Hill & Wang, 1986.
    An overview of the politics, society, and race issues which defined the American South.

DuBois, W. E. B. *The Souls of Black Folks*, Boulder, CO: Paradigm, 2004.
    Written in 1903 by a leading African-American proponent of civil and political rights, this survey provides an excellent depiction of African-Americans at the turn of the century.

Hall, Robert, and Carol Stack (eds), *Holding on to the Land and the Lord: Kinship, Ritual, Land Tenure, and Social Policy on the Rural South*, Athens, GA: University of Georgia Press, 1982.
    A collection of anthropological and historical essays covering a broad range of topics, including family, the rural economy, and religion.

Jenkins, McKay. *The South in Black and White: Race, Sex, and Literature in the 1940's*, Chapel Hill, NC: University of North Carolina Press, 1999.
    An attempt to uncover the underlying cultural and intellectual milieu of the American South during this decade.

Lemann, Nicholas. *The Promised Land: The Great Black Migration and How It Changed America*, New York: Vintage Books, 1992.
    Analyzes the origins of the Great Black Migration, as well as the political, social, economic, and even personal changes that accompanied it.

McIlwain, Charlton. *Death in Black and White: Death, Ritual, and Family Ecology*, Cresskill, NJ: Hampton Press, Inc., 2003.
    A scholarly yet accessible anthropological and historical examination of African-American funerary practices.

Parrish, Peter. *Slavery: History and Historians*, New York: Westview Press, 1989.
    An analytical assessment of slavery itself as well as the historiography of slavery in America.

ALLAN GURGANUS: BIOGRAPHY

Allan Gurganus, a white American, was born in Rocky Mount, North Carolina, in 1947.[17] "It was the kind of town where if I was misbehaving on the street, people I had never met before would come up and say, 'You have the Gurganus nose, and I know exactly who your grandparents are, and they would be ashamed of your setting off firecrackers, and put that down this instant.' And we obeyed."[18] His mother was a schoolteacher, and, in his own words, his "father's family were landowners, farmer-merchants ... It was also a very religious family."

A conscientious objector to the Vietnam War – an untenable position in his conservative hometown – Gurganus was eventually forced to enlist in the war effort when he was 18. He chose to join the Navy, where, by his own estimate, he read 1,200 books aboard the USS *Yorktown*, and authored countless letters home for many of his shipmates. He spent three years in the Navy. In a 1989 interview with *The New York Times*, Gurganus emphasized that his experience in Vietnam helped shape his view of race relations in the South:

> There were people in the town with our name who were black people, but I somehow never made the connection until one day I saw this 18th-century document listing the number of slaves who had been owned by people with my own name. I made a connection between the slaves and my own circumstances, because I had been drafted against my will to fight in Vietnam. And the helplessness of the slaves and the despair of being corralled and being shipped by boat to a territory I didn't feel I belonged in to do work for people I had no respect for, made me feel a tremendous identification with the slaves that my great-grandparents had owned.[19]

After leaving the Navy, Gurganus turned to writing, and graduated from Sarah Lawrence College. He studied under the well-known American writers Stanley Elkin and John Cheever, and achieved his first major success at the age of twenty-six when he had a short story published in *The New Yorker*, a high achievement for a writer of any age.

Gurganus has written two novels, *Oldest Living Confederate Widow Tells All* (1989) set in the South during the Civil War, and *Plays Well With Others* (1997) about the artistic and gay communities of New York City at the outbreak of the HIV/AIDS epidemic. He also published a collection of short stories, *White People,* in 2000, and a collection of four novellas in *The Practical Heart* (2002). The title novella in that collection won a National Magazine Prize when it was featured in *Harper's* magazine.

Besides writing, Gurganus has also taught at Stanford University, Duke University, Sarah Lawrence College, and the Iowa Writers' Workshop. He was inducted into the American Academy of Arts and Sciences and the Fellowship of Southern Writers.

AUTHOR BIBLIOGRAPHY

"Allan Gurganus – Biography", online: http://www.allangurganus.com/bio.php (accessed December 7, 2006).

"An Author and His Protagonist Have Their Roots in the South," *The New York Times*, August 14, 1989, online: http://www.nytimes.com/books/97/11/16/home/gurganus-roots.html (accessed December 7, 2006).

NOTES

1 Allan Gurganus, "Blessed Assurance: A Moral Tale," in *White People*, New York: Vintage Contemporaries, 1990, p. 197.
2 Ibid., p. 200.
3 Ibid., pp. 210–211.
4 See Peter Parrish, *Slavery: History and Historians*, New York: Westview Press, 1989.
5 Ibid., p. 20.
6 Pete Daniel, *Standing at the Crossroads: Southern Life since 1900*, New York: Hill & Wang, 1986, p. 28.
7 Ibid., p. 7.
8 Nicholas Lemann, *The Promised Land: The Great Black Migration and How It Changed America*, New York: Vintage, 1992, pp. 3, 48.
9 Daniel, op. cit., pp. 43, 102.
10 McKay Jenkins, *The South in Black and White: Race, Sex and Literature in the 1940s*, Chapel Hill, NC: University of North Carolina Press, 1999, p. 30.
11 Ibid., p. 12.
12 Ibid., pp. 20–21.
13 Lemann, op. cit., p. 309.
14 Charlton McIlwain, *Death in Black and White: Death, Ritual and Family Ecology*, Creskill, NJ: Hampton Press, 2003, p. 84.
15 Ibid., pp. 30–31.
16 "Of the Faith of the Fathers," Chapter 10 in W. E. B. DuBois, *The Souls of Black Folks*, Boulder, CO: Paradigm, 2004, pp. 101–110.
17 "Allan Gurganus: Biography" online: http://www.allangurganus.com/bio.php (accessed December 7, 2006).
18 "An Author and His Protagonist Have Their Roots in the South," *The New York Times*, August 14, 1989, online: http://www.nytimes.com/books/97/11/16/home/gurganus-roots.html (accessed December 7, 2006).
19 Ibid.

Chapter 7

Things Fall Apart

The challenge of new principles

OKONKWO WAS CLEARLY CUT OUT for great things. He was still young but had won fame as the greatest wrestler in the nine villages. He was a wealthy farmer and had two barns full of yams, and had just married his third wife. To crown it all he had taken two titles and had shown incredible prowess in two inter-tribal wars. And so although Okonkwo was still young, he was already one of the greatest men of his time. Age was respected among his people, but achievement was revered. As the elders said, if a child washed his hands he could eat with kings. Okonkwo had clearly washed his hands and so he ate with kings and elders.[1]

. . .

As the palm wine was drunk one of the oldest members of the *umunna* rose to thank Okonkwo:

"If I say that we did not expect such a big feast I will be suggesting that we did not know how openhanded our son, Okonkwo, is. We all know him, and we expected a big feast. But it turned out to be even bigger than we expected. Thank you. May all you took out return again tenfold. It is good in these days when the younger generation consider themselves wiser than their sires to see a man doing things in the grand, old way . . . You may ask why I am saying all this. I say it because I fear for the younger generation, for you people." He waved his arm where most of the young men sat. "As for me, I have only a short while to live, and so have Uchendu and Unachukukwu and Emefo. But I fear for you young people because you do not understand how strong is the bond of kinship. You do not know what it is to speak with one voice. And what is the result? An abominable religion has settled among you. A man can now leave his father and his brothers. He can curse the gods of his fathers and his ancestors, like a hunter's dog that suddenly goes mad and turns on its master. I fear for you; I fear for the clan." He turned again to Okonkwo and said, "Thank you for calling us together."[2]

THINGS FALL APART: THEMES AND QUESTIONS

The challenge of new principles

Whether we view ourselves as individuals with moral values we have worked long and hard to clarify, or as novices just starting out on this journey, we nonetheless believe that the search for moral principles to guide our lives is personal – something that we by and large control. Of course we acknowledge our debt to our families, to our communities, and to the traditions that have influenced us. But most of us still expect a relatively clear field of play when it comes to determining our own beliefs.

Yet we might wonder what would happen if, instead of having the freedom of personal choice, we had thrust into our midst individuals, and then, later, whole groups, who asserted the superiority of their worldview and moral beliefs. How would we respond? Would we be curious, open-minded, eager to engage with those who think very differently from us? Would we flatly assert the primacy of our own views, beliefs, and traditions? What options would we have, and which would we take?

We can, through our imaginations, enter into these questions – **the challenge of new principles** – through *Things Fall Apart*, Chinua Achebe's famous novel about the Umuofia, an Ibo clan of Nigeria at the turn of the twentieth century, the time of the coming of the Christian missionaries and the British colonial authorities.

Culture, belief, and choice

Our protagonist is the "great man" Okonkwo, and for nearly two-thirds of the novel we will examine the actions he takes to follow the ways of the clan. Achebe creates a detailed picture of life among the Umuofia – a life governed by its own rules, beliefs, and traditions that create predictable patterns of behavior and established methods of handling inter- and intra-village conflict.

Achebe's description of the clan's mores includes practices that challenge contemporary Western notions of right and wrong, raising the question of **how culturally and historically bounded our beliefs might be at any time,** and we will find ourselves forced to come to terms with how we respond to the life of the Umuofia in its entirety. We also will be asked to consider the variations in practice that exist within and across villages, and, in particular, to examine how much room for interpretation there is in the clan's beliefs, **whether nuanced reasoning and limit-setting on personal action is permitted, expected, or forbidden.**

Popularly called "Roaring Flame," Okonkwo has a nearly ungovernable temper, and a complicated family history that affects his outlook: motivating him to great achievements, but also burdening him with constant worries that he will follow the path of his father. The novel thus allows us to examine **the interplay between history, the self, and belief,** to think about how our own situations may influence and shape our attitudes, goals, and behavior.

Beliefs in changing times

The introduction of the missionaries and colonial authorities is gradual, a haze on the horizon that comes into greater focus with the arrival, first, of a single missionary, and then, over time, with the imposition and expansion of colonial rule.

This is a true clash of civilizations, confronting us, like Okonkwo and the Umuofia, with some of the hardest questions we will ever face: **Do universal ethical principles exist? How might I know whether my own beliefs and principles have such universal validity?**

Just as Achebe describes the Umuofia in all its complexity, he invites our examination of individual missionaries and British colonial figures, providing us with an opportunity to draw our own conclusions about the strengths and inherent worth of the forces confronting the Umuofia.

Strategies for action

We are increasingly aware that we live in a world of multiple beliefs, and of competing claims for different value systems and ways of life. As individuals, and as future leaders, we know we will have to devise our own approaches to the various forms that belief and social systems can take. So we will look with particular interest at the **strategies for action** that are mounted both by Okonkwo and other members of the clan, and by the missionaries. **How are proponents of beliefs expected to navigate a changing terrain?** Are any of these strategies more successful than the others? Would we choose one of them for ourselves, and, if so, which would it be?

ASSIGNMENT

READING: *Things Fall Apart,* by Chinua Achebe.

1 How would you describe the evolution of Okonkwo's character through the story?

2 How do you assess his actions?

3 How would you describe the evolution of Umuofia's culture?

4 What can we learn from this story?

5 What kind of moral challenge is this?

THINGS FALL APART: BACKGROUND

Things Fall Apart presents a compelling and complex portrait of the Umuofia, the clansman Okonkwo, and the challenges to the clan and its way of life posed by the missionaries and British colonial authorities. Many who read this book find themselves wanting to know more about the strands that Achebe so skillfully weaves together. These are described in the following background materials; they focus on three topics: British colonialism in Africa; village life in pre-colonial West Africa – including familial, economic, political, and religious practices; and missionary activities in the nineteenth century. Together, these materials will enhance your appreciation of the novel and your ability to analyze the characters and groups and their actions.

The British Empire

Extent and early history

The British Empire controlled, at various times, vast amounts of territory and sea lanes in and around Ireland, North America, the Caribbean, India, Hong Kong, Australia, Egypt and the Middle East, as well as in West, East, and South Africa. The Empire, which can be traced to the sixteenth century, proved highly resilient: only after World War II (1939–1945) did the economic, social, and political burdens of Empire prove too great to bear. Today the British Commonwealth, an association of independent nations that recognize the British crown as their sovereign, serves, along with some isolated British possessions such as Gibraltar, as the last vestiges of this once mighty imperial power.

With its strong naval forces and merchant marine system, England was well placed in the sixteenth century to capitalize on opportunities offered by so-called New World discoveries. This position was greatly strengthened following the defeat of the Spanish Armada by English naval forces in 1588, which allowed England to replace Spain as the preeminent naval power in the Atlantic. The founding of North American colonies quickly followed, as did increasing rivalry with the French and the Dutch.

Colonies were often founded and enlarged for reasons of personal gain, and of adventure, or in some cases by those wishing to escape religious persecution. Yet the overarching ideology of Empire was commonly based on reasons of trade and positioning *vis-à-vis* other European powers. This combination of motivations often proved hard to disentangle, given the early existence of royally sanctioned monopoly companies such as the British East India Company, founded in 1600, to trade in tea and spices.

The distinctions between trade and geopolitics became especially blurred once the Industrial Revolution began in earnest around 1750, creating opportunities for manufacturing exports and the requirements of importing raw materials, both of which were crucial to England's industrializing economy. The African slave trade, which the British dominated in the eighteenth century, was meant to ensure human resources in the colonies and to guarantee the profitability of this "Triangular Trade" in the Atlantic – a trade of slaves, raw materials, and manufactured goods. Empire in the Atlantic was delivered a severe blow with the success of the American Revolution, which began in 1776. Nonetheless, the Empire proved adaptable enough to continue without a devastating loss in power and prestige.

Meanwhile, the British East India Company had expanded its trade operations on the Indian subcontinent, and near the end of the seventeenth century had been given the right to mint its own money, provide for its own defense (through mostly locally conscripted soldiers), and engage in its own foreign relations. The company's robust and aggressive nature helped it prevail over the Portuguese and the French, and then to expand at the expense of local rulers who increasingly opposed it. Indeed, another motivation of colonial expansion became the protection and security of already existing colonies. The Cape of Good Hope in South Africa, for example, was annexed at the end of the eighteenth century in order to secure a safe passage to India.

British colonialism in Africa

Before the end of the eighteenth century, the Atlantic slave trade had confined British involvement in West Africa to coastal ports; the trade, which began around 1530, led neither to colonization nor to new commercial opportunities.[3]

In 1807, Britain outlawed the international slave trade for a combination of reasons: a glutted and declining sugar market (the staple crop of British plantations in the West Indies), drastic economic changes that began favoring the free market over mercantilist ventures, and a politically charged domestic environment in which moral opposition to the slave trade was rife and vocal.[4] Suppressing the slave trade and encouraging alternative trades in raw materials, such as palm oil, which could benefit Britain's industry and economy, heightened Britain's involvement in West Africa to serve its political and economic goals.

At the same time, motivated by the assurance of land, British colonists began arriving at the Cape Colony in South Africa in 1820. Confrontations with the Boers (a Dutch-speaking settler group), as well as with indigenous peoples such as the Kaffirs, forced the colony's security perimeters and frontiers to expand, such as when Zululand was annexed in the aftermath of the devastating Zulu wars (ending in 1879), won only by Western military technology. When diamonds and gold were discovered in abundance, mining created its own dynamic, increasing both settler immigration and penetration into the frontiers, exemplified by the diamond magnate Cecil Rhodes's creation of Rhodesia. A similar process of cascading motivations and goals took place in West Africa.

The final decades of the nineteenth century saw the emergence of what has been called the "New Imperialism," in which vast tracts of land worldwide were brought under European control. As industrialization spread across Europe, Britain had by this time lost its intrinsic competitive advantage as progenitor of the Industrial Revolution. Nations such as France and the newly unified nation-states of Italy and Germany now clamored to compete with Britain (and with each other) for power, trade, and prestige.[5] It was this rivalry that ultimately caused the "Scramble for Africa," a fierce competition among European powers to control, administer, and exploit the resources of large swaths of the African coast and interior, often at the expense of local rulers and indigenous political systems.

Village life in pre-colonial West Africa

Family and the local economy

In pre-colonial West Africa – until the last decades of the eighteenth century – the basic economic and social unit was the immediate family living in villages, which in turn were collected in "towns" often named for ancestors. For the Ibo (alternatively spelled Igbo)-speaking peoples of modern-day Nigeria, the subject of Chinua Achebe's novel, towns – village groupings such as *Umuofia* – tended to be the most extensive source of identity to which an individual ascribed.[6] Social and political structures were similar across Ibo towns, although there did exist a great deal of diversity in specific customs and arrangements.

Family and clan structures generally provided important connections within villages and between them. Within the villages, individual families would commonly own a compound, a designated area where husband and wife (or wives) lived in separate houses, the children living with their mother. Within the compound livestock was grazed, spirits were worshipped in personal shrines, and crops were grown. These crops included the yam, a vegetable that required painstaking attention but was highly prized for its yield. Other agricultural products proved equally as important. The palm tree, for instance, was put to numerous applications, including the production of palm wine, palm oil, and the use of its fronds for walls and roofs.

These were overwhelmingly agricultural societies, and therefore working the land, which took place largely at the family level, was the single most important economic activity. Success in agriculture was rewarded: Wealthy, respectable and successful heads of households could attain much-coveted titles such as the *Ozo* title, affording them highly valued social privileges.

Politics and society

Politically, there existed an intricate system of institutions in which the clan – called the *umunna* – and the voice of elders generally predominated.[7] Clans were important units within villages and across them, and the eldest members of a clan were commonly its leaders, serving on local councils.[8] Usually, a clan traced its lineage to a single ancestor, and sometimes a clan had common lands and cults. Births, marriages, and funerals were celebrated communally at this level.

Life in the village was defined not only by immediate and extended family, but by other connections as well. Each male member belonged to an age group, a collection of men born in the same year, and this group was responsible for common duties which changed according to age and seniority. A group would work together to perform menial tasks when young; maintain law and order, fight, and engage in public works when adults; and participate in government and decision-making when elders. Public participation was therefore virtually ensured. Community life centered on the market, where families, clans, and even members of different villages would not only engage in trade, but also participate in community-wide civic and religious functions.

Life in West Africa was therefore predominantly communal and family-oriented, its central values based on hard work and clan responsibilities. The local groups – the family, the clan, the village, and the town – maintained a constant importance throughout an individual's life. Thus the saying of the Ibo that "The proud man will go alone."[9]

Belief and worship

In Ibo belief, there is, above all, the Supreme Being, *Chukwu,* or Great Spirit (also known by other names indicating his other supreme properties). While *Chukwu* is supreme and completely benevolent, he is also mysterious, nebulous, and thus not considered directly approachable except in the most extreme circumstances.[10] More directly involved with humankind are the spirits, which, although inferior to *Chukwu,* are still in possession of great powers; it is to them that supplications and sacrifices are commonly offered. These spirits are highly varied. Some are inherently kind, some inherently evil. Some have special significance, such as the yam spirit, the thunder spirit, water spirits, which attach spiritual meaning to rivers and lakes, and the Earth Spirit (*ani* or *ala*) which has dominion over law and custom. In addition, each individual has his or her own personal spirit, or *Chi,* to which worship is occasionally directed; a "good" *Chi* will intercede on its person's behalf, while a "bad" *Chi* will allow its person to suffer harm. Sacrifice and prayer, on the levels of the individual, the village, or even the entire town, are the essence of these spirit cults.

Ancestors, too, although not spirits, are deserving of worship and sacrifice because from their position in the afterlife they are still members of the family, and are certainly just as interested in it as those still living in the flesh. They are, for instance, invited to dine with the family.[11] Funeral rites, meant to ensure that a departed family member succeeds to the afterlife, are therefore extremely important. Disregarding customs and laws, which the ancestors upheld or established, is considered to be a great offense to them; and thus the ancestor cult, along with the Earth Spirit, is the guardian of the social, moral and legal order.[12]

Law and custom, tradition, etiquette and religion, all go by the same name; all are included in the word *omenani,* literally, "what happens on the land."[13] Planting and harvesting, hunting, forests, caves, market days, feasts, births, marriages, deaths, medicinal charms, healers, social titles – all are imbued with deep spiritual meanings. Humanity itself is given great significance and great power, which in effect means that every object, action, and occurrence is imbued with a notion of great responsibility. The beloved palm wine, for instance, has been held in Ibo society to be both a beverage and a libation; and, indeed, sacrifice of all types has played a crucial role in Ibo worship. Even human sacrifice, although traditionally rare, was not unknown in exceptional circumstances. A French anthropologist, writing in the 1970s about indigenous African beliefs, has argued that the individual "affirms himself through the feeling of his own power, and denies himself by giving himself away."[14]

Missionary activities in the nineteenth century

Moral justification

Christian missionaries in the nineteenth century followed on the heels of British colonial expansion into the region; missionary activity in West Africa was based on guilt about the African slave trade, which Britain had dominated throughout much of the eighteenth century.[15] Although slavery was not outlawed in Britain until 1807, Sierra Leone and its main port of Freetown were settled by freed black slaves beginning in 1787 under the watchful eyes of the British. Missionary activity began soon after, spearheaded by those who had championed the abolition (of slavery) movement. That ending slavery and bringing the Christian gospel to Africa were twin goals could be seen in the names of missionary societies, such as the London-based Society for the Extinction of the Slave Trade and the Civilisation of Africa.[16] African missions, from their forward bases in Sierra Leone, were seen as a form of atonement,[17] and missionaries struggled against slavery throughout the century.

Missionaries and colonists

Although American Protestant missionaries had no colonial intentions, and some Catholic missions, such as those in King Leopold's Congo,[18] operated to the chagrin of their home countries, there was a good deal of convergence between colonists and missionaries in both interests and personnel in certain instances.

This was particularly true of Anglican missions. An impoverished class of poor clergy in Victorian England became the rank-and-file of Anglican missionary societies, especially as they existed in colonial towns. Because of the increased social mobility they found there, Anglican missionaries could become colonial administrators, or even, as in West Africa, merchants in palm oil, which ultimately replaced slaves as a primary export. Well-educated clergy well versed in contemporary engineering and medicine also led pioneering missions into the continent's interior; they were as enthusiastic about the building of railroads, for instance, as were the colonists. Their aim was not only to penetrate and survive the interior, but also to demonstrate to indigenous people the connection between a belief in Christ and the benefits of civilization.[19]

Constructing schools and hospitals, a primary activity of missionaries, did indeed advance literacy and education as well as general health, and Chinua Achebe, the son of an Ibo missionary-school teacher, was himself a beneficiary of these institutions. British missionaries could therefore be just as much promoters of the Victorian gospel of progress, a true product of their time, as they were believers in and preachers of the timeless gospel of Christ.[20]

The belief in progress

Indeed, while colonialism and missionary activity often existed as separate enterprises, they both drew strength from the same cultural milieu. This was the Age of Exploration in which the efforts of adventurous explorers mapping the presumed unknown were admired and romanticized. Newspapers and learned organizations alike extolled the exploits of those who began to seek the source of the River Niger soon after Freetown was established; and, similarly, those who sought to identify the source of the Nile later in the century were afforded heroic status. Religious missions existed within this framework. David Livingstone, "the Greatest Missionary,"[21] was also one of the most intrepid explorers of the century, "among the high heroes of Victorian adventure."[22]

The Victorian English belief in the nature of progress meant that whether it was spreading religion, laying railroads, or extending the authority of the British Crown through British colonies, the white man – and a British white man in particular – by virtue of his superior technology and civilization, had a "civilizing mission" or a "White Man's Burden." There was therefore nothing that would be deemed hypocritical in Livingstone's statement that "I go back to Africa to make an open path for commerce and Christianity."[23]

Perceptions of Africa

An unbridled belief in progress also had another side. Darwin's scientific theories of evolution had become popularized (and misconstrued); what some colonists and missionaries found in Africa was confirmation of an "evolutionary superiority" of the white race, resulting in a condescending, if not hostile, attitude towards "natives."[34] Few dispatches in the latter part of the nineteenth century from Africa reported on the cultural or artistic achievements of Africans; rather, their visual arts and crafts were often dismissed as little more than idolatry. The nineteenth century missionaries, colonists, traders, and explorers who made their way to Africa therefore came, in the words of historians of the colonial experience, "puffed up with the virtue of emancipating black slaves – but with the conception of Africans only as slaves, porters, or eunuchs in harems."[35] Increasingly, with presumed Western civilizational and technological superiority in mind, the relationship came to be defined along the lines of the British poet Hilaire Belloc's satirical ditty: "Thank God, that we have got/The Maxim gun, and they have not."

BACKGROUND BIBLIOGRAPHY AND FURTHER READING

Arinze, Francis. *Sacrifice in Ibo Religion*, Ibadan: Ibadan University Press, 1970.
    A detailed exploration of the rituals surrounding sacrifice in Ibo-speaking groups, as well as the meanings behind them. Also provides an in-depth description of the belief system itself, as well as of Ibo society.

Foy, Yvonne, and Roy Lewis. *Painting Africa White*, London: Weidenfeld & Nicolson, 1971.
    A highly informative record of European activities in Africa in the nineteenth century, as well as a useful account of how Europeans perceived Africa at the height of colonialism.

Ilogu, Edmond. *Igbo Life and Thought*, Onitsha: University Publishing Company, 1985.
    A short treatment of Ibo society, customs, and beliefs, written by a Christian African missionary.

Isichesi, Elizabeth. *The Ibo People and the Europeans*, London: Faber & Faber, 1970.
Documents the effects on Ibo society of European penetration into West Africa from slavery through colonialism.

Moorhouse, Geoffrey. *The Missionaries*, London: Eyre Methuen, 1973.
Provides important insights as to the backgrounds of European and American missionaries (of all denominations) who went to Africa in the nineteenth century. Also gives an account of David Livingstone's travels.

Ohadike, Don. *Anioma*, Athens, OH: Ohio University Press, 1994.
Details the history of a particular Ibo-speaking group.

Zahan, Dominique, translated by K. E. Martin and L. M. Martin. *The Religion, Spirituality, and Thought of Traditional Africa*, Chicago, IL: University of Chicago Press, 1979.
An ambitious anthropological work which attempts to elucidate the "Animating Principle" of African spiritual life.

The BBC (British Broadcasting Corporation) has a helpful collection of maps and scholarly articles on the expansion and decline of the British Empire: http://www.bbc.co.uk/history/british/empire_seapower/ (accessed December 7, 2006).

CHINUA ACHEBE: BIOGRAPHY

Chinua Achebe (pronounced CHIN-you-uh ah-CHAY-bee) is one of Nigeria's best-known writers, and one of the most highly esteemed African writers in the English language. In the words of one literary critic, his "careful and confident craftsmanship, his firm grasp of the material and his ability to create memorable and living characters place him among the best novelists now writing in any country in the English language."[26]

Albert Chinualumogu Achebe was born in 1930 in Ogidi, Nigeria, which was, until 1960, a colony of Great Britain. He was born into an ethnically Ibo evangelical Protestant family, his father being a teacher in a missionary school. Although Achebe studied English writers, including Dickens, Shakespeare, and Conrad, he realized after graduating from high school in 1947 that "he was forsaking his African roots by identifying with the white man – not the African, who was often portrayed in such literature as a savage."[27] Having always been attracted to indigenous culture and festivals, he dropped his British name "Albert" and took his indigenous name, "Chinua."

Once he had enrolled in the University College in Ibadan, he increasingly became frustrated by English-language literature about Nigeria which he saw as patronizing, superficial, and inaccurate, ultimately persuading him to try his own hand at writing while an undergraduate.[28] He chose to write in English, a language he saw as a tool, not as an enemy, in order to repossess the language – to help Nigeria, in his words, "regain belief in itself and put away the complexes of the years of denigration and self-abasement."[29]

After graduating with a BA in 1953, he traveled through Africa and America, worked briefly as a teacher, joined the Nigerian Broadcasting Company, and during the 1960s was the director of external services in charge of the Voice of Nigeria.[30] It was also during this period that he wrote many of his novels, participating in a Nigerian "Renaissance" in which Nigeria witnessed, in the words of a scholar on the subject, "the flourishing of a new literature which has drawn substance both from traditional oral literature and from the present and rapidly-changing society."[31]

Things Fall Apart, published in 1958, was his first novel. The book won high acclaim, and established his reputation as a writer. It has since been translated into over fifty languages. After writing a collection of short stories and a children's book, he published three more novels during the 1960s: *No Longer at Ease* (1960), *Arrow of God* (1964), and *A Man of the People* (1966); the last, written six years after Nigeria's independence, lamented the failures of Nigeria's infant democracy.

Nigeria, an ethnically and religiously divided country in which the Ibo are only one of many groups competing for influence, descended into civil war in 1967, when the Ibo-dominated eastern region of the country seceded from the federal government, proclaiming itself the independent Republic of Biafra. Achebe, by then a leading novelist in Nigeria, supported the Ibo cause, serving as the Biafran Minister of Information and traveling to foreign capitals to publicize the Biafran struggle. Nigerian troops ultimately regained control of the region in 1970, after an estimated one million civilians in Biafra had died from food shortages.[32]

Following the war, Achebe found it difficult to write long fiction, although he did publish numerous collections of poetry, short stories and essays, as well as children's books. Only in 1988 did he author another novel, *Anthills of the Savannah*, which was also well received. Beginning in the 1970s, Achebe began teaching at the University of Nigeria as well as overseas at the universities of Massachusetts and Connecticut. He became the director of several publishing companies, and founded a leading Nigerian literary journal. In 1990, Achebe was paralyzed in a car accident in Nigeria; he has been receiving therapy in the United States where he has taught at Bard College, "a reluctant refugee," in his own words.[33]

Achebe has made no effort to conceal the overriding message of his writings. In a short autobiographical sketch, he writes:

> I am a political writer. My politics is concerned with universal human communi-
> cation across racial and cultural boundaries as a means of fostering respect for
> all people. Such respect can issue only from understanding. So my primary con-
> cern is with clearing the channels of communication in my own neighborhood
> by hacking away at the thickets that choke them.[34]

He finishes by explaining his mission:

> So the problem remains for Africa, for black people, for all deprived peoples
> and for the world. And so for the writer, for he is like the puppy in our proverb:
> that stagnant water in the potsherd is for none other but him. As long as one
> people sit on another and are deaf to their cry, so long will understanding and
> peace elude all of us.[35]

AUTHOR BIBLIOGRAPHY

"(Albert) Chinua(Iumogu) Achebe, 1930–", *Biographical Resource Center*, Farmington Hills, MI: Thomson Gale, 2006.

Bigelow, Barbara Carlisle (ed.), "Chinua Achebe," *Contemporary Black Biography*, Vol. 6, Detroit, MI: Gale Research Inc., 1994, pp. 1–5.

"Chinua Achebe," *African Biography*, 1999. Reproduced in *Biography Resource Center*, Farmington Hills, MI: Thomson Gale, 2006, online: http://galenet.galegroup.com/ezp1.harvard.edu/servlet/BioRC (accessed December 12, 2006). Document number: K2421000001.

"Chinua Achebe," *Books and Writers*, online: http://kirjasto.sci.fi/achebe.htm (accessed February 9, 2006).

Schlager, Neil and Lauer, Josh (eds), "Achebe, Chinua," *Contemporary Novelists*, Detroit, MI: St James Press, 2001, pp. 1–4.

NOTES

1 Chinua Achebe, *Things Fall Apart*, New York: Anchor Books, 1994, p. 8.
2 Ibid., p. 166–167.
3 Roy Lewis and Yvonne Foy, *Painting Africa White*, London: Weidenfeld & Nicolson, 1971, p. 82.
4 "Colonialism, Western." *Encyclopedia Britannica Online*, 2006, online: http://www.search.eb.com/eb/article-9106074 (accessed December 11, 2006).
5 Ibid. See also "Introduction," in Daniel Headrick, *The Tools of Empire: Technology and European Imperialism in the Nineteenth Century*, Oxford: Oxford University Press, 1981.
6 Francis Arinze, *Sacrifice in Ibo Religion*, Ibadan: Ibadan University Press, 1970, p. 2. What we now refer to as "tribes" – large groups with a common language and set of traditions – did not necessarily constitute the essential unit of identification. The Ibo were certainly one such linguistic group, among whom there seems to have been very little overarching sense of "tribal" affiliation.
7 Elizabeth Isichesi, *The Ibo People and the Europeans*, London: Faber & Faber, 1970, p. 72.
8 Don Ohadike, *Anioma*, Athens, OH: Ohio University Press, 1994, pp. 70–72.
9 Arinze, op. cit., p. 5.
10 Ibid.
11 Ibid., p. 19.
12 Edmund Ilogu, *Igbo Life and Thought*, Onitsha: University Publishing Company, 1985, pp. 8–11.
13 Arinze, op. cit., p. 30.
14 Dominique Zahan, translated by K. E. Martin and L. M. Martin, *The Religion, Spirituality, and Thought of Traditional Africa*, Chicago, IL: University of Chicago Press, 1979, p. 5.
15 Lewis and Foy, op. cit., pp. 58–59.
16 Geoffrey Moorhouse, *The Missionaries*, London: Eyre Methuen, 1973, p. 21.
17 Lewis and Foy, op. cit., pp. 58–59.
18 Leopold, King of Belgium, ruled the Congo as a personal domain.

19 Ibid., pp. 61, 74–75.
20 For instance, David Livingstone. See Moorhouse, op. cit., pp. 128–131.
21 Ibid., p. 111.
22 Lewis and Foy, op. cit., p. 57.
23 Moorhouse, op. cit., p. 131.
24 Lewis and Foy, op. cit., p. 3.
25 Ibid., p. 4.
26 Quoted in "(Albert) Chinua(lumogu) Achebe, 1930–," *Biographical Resource Center,* Farmington Hills, MI: Thomson Gale, 2006.
27 "Chinua Achebe," *African Biography,* 1999. Reproduced in *Biography Resource Center,* Farmington Hills, MI: Thomson Gale, 2006, online: http://galenet.galegroup.com/ezp1.harvard.edu/servlet/BioRC (accessed December 12, 2006). Document number: K2421000001
28 Ibid.
29 Quoted in *Biographical Resource Center,* op. cit.
30 "Chinua Achebe," *Books and Writers,* online: http://kirjasto.sci.fi/achebe.htm (accessed February 9, 2006).
31 Quoted in *Biographical Resource Center,* op. cit.
32 *African Biography,* op. cit.
33 *Biographical Resource Center,* op. cit.
34 Quoted in Neil Schlager and Josh Lauer (eds), "Achebe, Chinua," *Contemporary Novelists,* Detroit, Mich.: St James Press, 2001, pp. 1–4.
35 Ibid.

Moral Reasoning

Moral Reasoning Module Map

Central theme	Text and setting	Storyline	Preparation
Reasoning from moral theory	*Trifles,* by Susan Glaspell Early twentieth-century rural America	Two friends must decide whether to help a farm wife accused of murdering her husband	Play: 11 pages
	"Moral Theories," from *Principles of Biomedical Ethics,* Tom L. Beauchamp and James F. Childress		Text excerpts: 30 pages
Reasoning from personal perspective	*The Sweet Hereafter,* by Russell Banks Contemporary America	Four individuals respond in the aftermath of a school bus accident	Novel: 260 pages
Reasoning from a moral code	*The Remains of the Day,* by Kazuo Ishiguro Britain between world wars	A butler reckons with the consequences of a life in service to a British lord	Novel: 240 pages
Reasoning from multiple moralities	*A Man for All Seasons,* by Robert Bolt Sixteenth-century England	Sir Thomas More looks for a way to reconcile duty to his king, his religion, his family, and himself	Play: 180 pages Movie: 2 hours

Chapter 8

Moral Reasoning Preview

An auto mechanic was called early one morning to the scene of a wreck on a state highway. Arriving at the isolated, wooded spot, he could see immediately what had happened: A large flatbed truck had gone off the highway and hit a tree head-on. On impact, its load of steel had torn loose and slid forward through the back of the cab, pinning the driver helplessly inside. The cab was on fire, in danger of exploding at any minute.

As he arrived, so did a police car. And as the trooper ran to the open cab window, the mechanic could hear the driver inside screaming, "Shoot me! Shoot me!" It was obvious that the trooper could not lift that load of steel and free the driver. So, with the flames growing in intensity, the trooper slowly removed his service revolver from his holster. Then he paused, reconsidered, and slid the revolver back into his holster. And then, amid the driver's screams, he removed it a second time, paused, and put it back once again.

It was at that point in this agonized struggle that the mechanic saw the officer do a remarkable thing. Running back to his cruiser, he grabbed a small tetrachloride fire extinguisher. It was hardly enough to quell the fire. But it was large enough to spray in the driver's face and put him to sleep, which is what he did.

Shortly afterward, the cab exploded.

What was going on in that trooper's mind?

Rushworth Kidder, How Good People Make
Tough Choices, pp. 57–58.

Understanding moral reasoning

How do people reason morally?

When faced with a moral challenge, we act, or consciously or unconsciously decide not to. Yet just as the author above inquired, "What was going on in that trooper's mind?" we may also wonder how we make these essentially practical decisions. Do people reason when they confront moral challenges and attempt to resolve them? Is reasoning in the face of moral challenges different from regular reasoning? Does the complexity of a situation – its moral stakes, for instance – affect our ability to reason? Above all, how do people articulate and justify the rationales for their decisions and actions from a moral point of view?

The view from philosophy and religion

Moral reasoning – how we seek to analyze, assess, and determine to act upon a moral challenge – has been addressed by philosophers for thousands of years. Aristotle, for example, believed that ethical and moral decision-making was a practical exercise for philosopher and practitioner alike. In expounding his ethical theories, Aristotle noted that virtue is "concerned with choice ... this being determined by a rational principle, and by that principle by which the man of practical wisdom would determine it."[1]

Confucius, the Chinese philosopher who straddled the sixth and fifth centuries BCE, similarly advocated practical moral reasoning. He emphasized elevating the moral stature of his disciples, and led by example through the practical decisions he made as Minister of Justice in the Chinese province of Lu.

Many individual philosophers have since sought to craft guidelines for moral reasoning based on particular ethical philosophies – "moral theories," four of which we will examine briefly below, and then through an assigned reading for this module.

Organized religion has also traditionally provided distinct moral imperatives and moral worldviews, often based on the relationship between people and a god or gods. The Ten Commandments of the Judeo-Christian tradition, for instance, are commonly seen as establishing specific ethical principles. Islam similarly developed ethical guidelines based on the holy book the Koran, the sayings and actions of the prophet Muhammad, and the consensus of Islamic scholarship. In fact, all religions and human organizations have provided, explicitly or implicitly, assumptions about what is, and is not, morally acceptable. Attempts to make sense of moral challenges – how to think through them and act upon our insight – are as old as human society.

The view from science

Over the past few decades, neurology – the scientific study of the brain – has confirmed through scientific experimentation that moral reasoning is in fact a complex cognitive task.

Work done with fMRI tests – neural imaging scans used to determine activity in the brain – has shown that, in responding to narratives of certain types of moral challenge, activity is heightened across various regions of the brain, including those regions that facilitate emotion, as well as those that facilitate reasoning.[2] Studies have also been conducted on patients who, often because of head injuries, have lost their ability to make sound ethical judgments, despite retaining their intelligence (measured by IQ tests) and their ability to think abstractly.[3] Moral reasoning is thus a multifaceted exercise involving heart as well as mind.

Neuroscientists, cognitive psychologists, biologists, and linguists are all working to explain the mechanisms that we use to reason morally. For example, biologist Marc Hauser, author of *Moral Minds: How Nature Designed Our Universal Sense of Right and Wrong*,[4] has hypothesized that our ability to reason morally is an evolved capacity. Hauser asserts that we each naturally possess a "moral grammar" – an instinctual understanding of fundamental moral beliefs such as prohibitions against murder or treating others as we would like to be treated – that has created a capacity for nearly instantaneous response to moral challenges, and has proved essential in developing humans' ability to live cooperatively with each other.

Reasoning processes

This module, another group of four readings, provides us with the opportunity to observe moral reasoning in action. We will be introduced to protagonists who, in dealing with morally challenging situations of varying degrees of scope and complexity, rely on very different kinds of reasoning processes.

Reasoning through moral challenges

Having been introduced to a variety of moral challenges in the previous module, we are now in a better position to address moral reasoning as a route into making sense of these situations.

Rushworth Kidder, for example, argues that understanding the differences among types of moral challenge helps us morally reason in three ways: First, it allows us to understand that "however elaborate and multifaceted, dilemmas can be reduced to common patterns," thus assuring us that dilemmas are, in fact, manageable problems; second, it allows us to get to the heart of moral dilemmas by allowing us to move beyond extraneous detail; and, third, it allows us more easily to make the useful distinction between right versus wrong and right versus right dilemmas.[5] Furthermore, as will be borne out by the material in this module, recognizing the existence of a moral challenge is almost always the first step in making sense of it.

Reasoning from moral codes

Sociologists and anthropologists typically hold that societies socialize their young people with accepted norms of morality. In doing so, they propagate a so-called moral code – a worldview and associated belief system that define the boundaries of right and wrong and imply behavior that fits within these limits.

Moral codes take many forms. They can be incorporated into the customs and traditions of a society, formally legislated through a legal code, or held as sacred through the beliefs and practices of an organized religion. They can be general to a society at large, or more specific to certain groups. The military, for example, has a professional code of ethics, as do medical practitioners. Communities, families, and even circles of friends may have their own moral expectations.

At the same time, individuals also often develop their own sense of right and wrong, or their own definitions of concepts such as justice and honor. Conceivably, an individual could be beholden to several, possibly conflicting, moral codes based on his or her different roles, responsibilities, group affiliations, and personal beliefs.

Moral codes can serve as a useful benchmark from which to reason about moral challenges, and in Kazuo Ishiguro's novel *The Remains of the Day* we will be able to observe the process and consequences of reasoning from a moral code.

Reasoning from moral theories

In addition to moral codes, philosophers have supplemented our "ethical toolbox"[6] with different moral theories, that is, frameworks we may use in navigating the many ethical questions posed by moral challenges. As we reason about such problems, these different moral theories can serve as touchstones for ways to think through and resolve them. Along with the first work of fiction in this module – Susan Glaspell's short play *Trifles* – we will take an in-depth look at four fundamental moral theories through a supplementary reading:

- *"Utilitarianism,"* a consequence-based theory, contends that "utility" should be the major principle in ethics, meaning that actions may be considered right or wrong according to the balance of value and disvalue – value being measured in total happiness or pleasure – they bring. This moral theory was popularized by the nineteenth-century English philosopher and political economist John Stuart Mill, drawing from earlier writings of David Hume, Jeremy Bentham, and others who looked at the connections between morality and society.
- *"Kantianism,"* an obligation-based theory, posits that one must act out of obligation; that is, one must *intend* what is morally required. Likewise, one should never commit to taking an action unless he or she is willing to see that action made a universal law. "Kantianism" is named after the eighteenth-century German philosopher Immanuel Kant, who popularized its principles.
- *"Liberal Individualism,"* a rights-based theory, defines "rights" as claims that individuals or groups can justifiably make on other individuals or segments of society; rights are valued because they protect members of society against "oppression, unequal treatment, intolerance, arbitrary invasion of privacy, and the like."[7]
- *"Communitarianism,"* a community-based theory, contends that ethical decisions should focus primarily on nurturing and strengthening the common good

and communal life. Developed as a reaction against the perceived excesses of liberal individualism and capitalism, this approach suggests that individuals' moral obligations derive largely from their social role, and they are encouraged to promote traditional practices and social cooperation.

Stages of moral reasoning

Although we may make use of moral codes and moral theories in navigating a moral dilemma, the question remains: What actually goes on in a person's mind as he or she attempts to reason through a moral challenge?

Lawrence Kohlberg, as well as other developmental psychologists who have adopted his six stages of moral development, argues that moral reasoning is a process manifested differently at various points in people's development. For example, a young child who bases her behavior on punishments and rewards would provide a very different rationale for her moral choices than would an adult whose moral development has evolved into a more nuanced appreciation of others in relation to herself.

For Kohlberg and others who have studied this area, moral reasoning in its highest stage of development is characterized by three elements: First, an attitude of sympathy towards other people; second, the ability to reason from other people's perspectives and stand in their shoes (what he calls "moral musical chairs"); and, third, "universalizability" – the recognition that acceptable moral judgments should be consistent across similar cases, and, ideally, should be consistent in a single case among actors with different perspectives.[8]

In Russell Banks's novel *The Sweet Hereafter*, the actions and rationales of major actors in a community-wide tragedy are examined separately, affording us a unique opportunity to see how different people reason about the same event from multiple perspectives.

Overview of readings in this module

The four texts in this module will allow us to examine the advantages, limitations, and pitfalls of different modes of moral reasoning:

- **Reasoning from moral theory.** *Trifles* will vividly illustrate a pair of protagonists facing an immediate moral dilemma. In conjunction with a reading on four moral theories, Susan Glaspell's short play can be assessed and discussed through each of these ethical lenses, allowing us to understand better the process of reasoning from moral theory.
- **Reasoning from personal perspective.** *The Sweet Hereafter* will present a community tragedy through the eyes of several different participants, allowing us to experience first-hand the process of reasoning from different personal perspectives.
- **Reasoning from a moral code.** *The Remains of the Day* will follow a protagonist, a butler, adhering to a particular – and unusual – moral code and worldview.

It will afford us the unique opportunity to witness a character who, in fact, explicitly reasons from that perspective.

- **Reasoning from multiple moralities.** Robert Bolt's play *A Man for All Seasons* (and the accompanying film adaptation) follows the grave challenge faced by the English lawyer and political insider Sir Thomas More as he attempts to navigate competing moral codes, clashing moral theories, and multiple perspectives all at once. His struggle, and ultimate decision, will draw together all the elements of this module in portraying the utility and the complexity of moral reasoning that can accommodate multiple moral perspectives that lead in different directions.

NOTES

1 http://classics.mit.edu/Aristotle/nicomachaen.2.ii.html (accessed December 13, 2006).

2 Joshua Greene and Jonathan Haidt, "How (and Where) Does Moral Judgment Work?" *Trends in Cognitive Science,* 2002, vol. 6, no. 12, pp. 517–523.

3 See also Antonio Damasio, *Descartes' Error: Emotion, Reason, and the Human Brain,* New York: Quill, 1994, pp. 3–19.

4 Marc D. Hauser, *Moral Minds: How Nature Designed Our Universal Sense of Right and Wrong,* New York: Ecco, 2006.

5 Rushworth Kidder, *How Good People Make Tough Choices: Resolving the Dilemmas of Ethical Living,* New York: Fireside, 1995, pp. 22–23.

6 This is a phrase used by Anthony Westin, author of *A 21st Century Ethical Toolbox,* Oxford: Oxford University Press, 2001, to describe the resources we have available in excavating moral challenges.

7 See Tom L. Beauchamp and James F. Childress, *Principles of Biomedical Ethics,* Oxford: Oxford University Press, 2001, p. 355.

8 Lawrence Kohlberg, Dwight Boyd, and Charles Levine, "The Return of Stage 6: Its Principle and Moral Point of View," in Thomas Wren (ed.), *The Moral Domain,* Cambridge, MA: MIT, 1990, pp. 165–169.

Chapter 9

Trifles

Reasoning from moral theory

COUNTY ATTORNEY: And what did Mrs. Wright do when she knew that you had gone for the coroner?

HALE: She moved from that chair to this one over here (*pointing to a small chair in the corner*) and just sat there with her hands held together and looking down. I got a feeling that I ought to make some conversation, so I said I had come in to see if John wanted to put in a telephone, and at that she started to laugh, and then she stopped and looked at me – scared. (*The* COUNTY ATTORNEY, *who has had his notebook out, makes a note*) I dunno, maybe it wasn't scared. I wouldn't like to say it was. Soon Harry got back, and then Dr. Lloyd came, and you, Mr. Peters, and so I guess that's all I know that you don't.

COUNTY ATTORNEY: (*Looking around*) I guess we'll go upstairs first – and then out to the barn and around there. (*To the* SHERIFF) You're convinced that there was nothing important here – nothing that would point to any motive.

SHERIFF: Nothing here but kitchen things.

(*The* COUNTY ATTORNEY, *after again looking around the kitchen, opens the door of a cupboard closet. He gets up on a chair and looks on a shelf. Pulls his hand away, sticky.*)

COUNTY ATTORNEY: Here's a nice mess. (*The women draw nearer.*)

MRS. PETERS: (*To the other woman*) Oh, her fruit; it did freeze. (*To the* LAWYER) She worried about that when it turned so cold. She said the fire'd go out and her jars would break.

SHERIFF: Well, can you beat the woman! Held for murder and worryin' about her preserves.

COUNTY ATTORNEY: I guess before we're through she may have something more serious than preserves to worry about.

HALE: Well, women are used to worrying over trifles.[1]

TRIFLES: THEMES AND QUESTIONS

How we reason

All of us tend to leap, without effort, from perception to interpretation and sense-making. These leaps help us shape the chaos that surrounds us into recognizable patterns and comprehensible events; without the leaps, we would be unable to function. **But, to become skilled in moral reasoning, we first have to become aware of** *how we reason*, that is, of how we take in data from the world around us and draw conclusions about what we see, understand, and believe. *Trifles*, a tiny play – only eleven pages long – will help us with this process.

Trifles presents us with two characters, Mrs. Peters and Mrs. Hale, who must decide what actions to take regarding Mrs. Wright, a neighbor who is in jail, accused of having killed her husband. The two women have been brought by their husbands to the Wright home to secure some personal items Mrs. Wright has asked for. Mr. Peters is the town sheriff and Mr. Hale was the first to become aware of the murder; the two men, along with the county attorney, are searching the house, the presumed crime scene, for evidence that would shed light on Mr. Wright's murder and Mrs. Wright's involvement in it.

We'll work hard to appreciate the choices Mrs. Hale and Mrs. Peters face and to understand the decisions they make. This will not be easy. We'll know less than we might want to know about the murder, about the relationship between Mr. and Mrs. Wright, and even of the opinions of Mrs. Peters and Mrs. Hale, who, like all of the characters in the play, say very little. We'll have to make some assumptions about the situation and to draw our own conclusions. So, as we analyze Mrs. Hale's and Mrs. Peters's choices and decisions, we'll be able to take a careful look at our own reasoning processes – to think about *how* we think.

How to reason morally

We'll then take our analysis of the characters' actions and judge them, asserting our own opinions of whether Mrs. Peters and Mrs. Hale are *morally justified* in acting as they did. How are we to decide? What definition should we use for "moral"?

Four moral theories

Our second reading presents four different moral theories that we might think about as **categories for reflection and choice**, giving us a variety of perspectives to use. The reading is from a handbook on biomedical ethics, written for doctors and nurses, medical researchers, hospital administrators, and health-policy specialists who face daily decisions with moral stakes as they treat patients, conduct research, deliver service, and debate public policy.

The four theories are illumined through a particular moral challenge.[2] Each theory is used to describe a different way of reasoning through the situation, and we will see that the emphasis of moral analysis and judgment shifts markedly from one theory to the next.

The theories pose practical questions: **Will my action produce morally good** *consequences*? (Utilitarianism, or consequence-based theory). **Does my action allow me to fulfill basic** *duties or obligations*? (Kantianism or obligation-based theory). **Do I need to consider the** *rights* **of people whom my decision affects?** (Liberal individualism or right-based theory). **How does my decision affect the interests of the** *community* **of which I am part?** (Communitarianism or community-based theory).

An exercise in moral reasoning

Usually when we debate we draw on arguments of various kinds, moving freely from one rationale to the next to make as complete an argument as possible. Instead, this assignment asks you to do something unusual, which is to justify your assessment of whether the two women's actions were moral or not using *just one* of the four moral theories. In other words, you should prepare to "make your case" arguing from the standpoint of consequences, or duty, or rights, or community. Each theory can be used to support the actions taken by Mrs. Hale and Mrs. Peters – or to criticize what they did.

The purpose of this assignment is to enable you to experience what it feels like to think through your judgment with the rigor that comes from following a single strand of logic – one particular way of deciding whether an act is moral or not. We're not looking to make you a lifelong convert to any of the moral theories; in fact, you will find that each has strengths and weaknesses. But you will find the opportunity to exercise your reasoning along a single moral pathway highly useful, creating greater confidence in your abilities to use moral reasoning and to recognize it when others use it as well.

ASSIGNMENT

READINGS: *Trifles*, by Susan Glaspell. Excerpts from Chapter 8, "Moral Theories," from *Principles of Biomedical Ethics*, by Tom L. Beauchamp and James F. Childress, found in Appendix 1 (pp. 181–212).

1 The four moral theories in the reading represent fundamental categories for moral reflection and decision-making. Be prepared to summarize each of them briefly.

2 Do you approve or disapprove of the actions taken by the two women in *Trifles*? Using *just one* of the four moral theories, make a case for either justifying or criticizing what they did. Be prepared to defend your case in class.

TRIFLES: BACKGROUND

Trifles is set in an unidentified town in rural America, early in the twentieth century, when, for example, "party line" phones, shared among neighbors to reduce the cost of phone service, were just becoming popular. The treatment of Mrs. Wright and the options available to Mrs. Hale and Mrs. Peters were strongly influenced by prevailing attitudes and laws. The following background materials will help you understand the status of women at the time Susan Glaspell, the playwright, describes.

Women in the United States in the nineteenth century

Throughout the nineteenth century, women in the United States had few legal or political rights. With the exception of some sparsely populated territories and states along America's western frontier such as Wyoming,[3] women were almost universally denied the right to vote or to hold office. At various times, groups of women did organize politically to support a diverse array of goals – such as women's rights, education, universal suffrage, the abolition of slavery, the ten-hour work day, temperance movements,[4] improving conditions for the mentally ill, and, in the South after the Civil War (1861–1865), memorial societies for Confederate soldiers.[5]

Even so, their ability to participate in the public sphere remained largely circumscribed. Throughout much of the United States women could not bring lawsuits, practice as lawyers, or serve on a jury. Even in Wyoming, where jury service was allowed, women who were interested in serving on a jury met harsh resistance in threats, ridicule, and abuse, and husbands who declared that they "would never live with their wives again if they served on the jury."[6] The Seneca Falls Convention of 1848, a landmark women's rights gathering, therefore declared without much exaggeration that women were "civilly dead"[7] – a condition that would, in effect, be perpetuated for decades.

Even in the domestic sphere, women had virtually no rights. The law made a husband the "master" of his wife, able to deprive her of her liberty and, if he desired, to beat her. A husband owned all of his wife's property – including any wages she earned.[8] In the case of divorce, it was understood that the man would retain custody of his children. As the delegates at the Seneca Falls Convention wrote: "Legally, she ceases to exist . . . All that she has becomes legally his, and he can collect and dispose of the profits of her labor as he sees fit . . . If he renders life intolerable, so that she is forced to leave him, he has the power to retain her children."[9]

The fight for women's rights

By the turn of the century – roughly the setting of *Trifles* – women's rights activists had cause for optimism, even if many of the restrictions on women were still firmly in place and progress was slow. For example, the birthrate throughout the century had decreased by 40 percent, household technology had increased in efficiency, public school education was expanded, and the school day lengthened; all of these developments enabled women to spend increasingly less time bearing and caring for children and their households, therefore allowing a significant segment of middle-class women to "develop interests outside the domestic sphere."[10]

In addition, women's colleges and co-educational colleges were slowly gaining acceptance; by 1900, five thousand women graduated with a bachelor's degree – Susan Glaspell graduated from Drake University in Des Moines in 1899[11] – and many of these women became champions of the women's rights cause.

Finally, the end of the century saw a drastic increase in paid female labor, especially in domestic service. Increasingly, activists convinced working women that the ballot would be a useful way of improving their bargaining power.[12]

In the first decade of the twentieth century, female suffrage expanded further in western states, such that by the presidential election of 1912 four million women could vote in nine western states – a bloc that could not be ignored; and, indeed, national politicians such as Woodrow Wilson and Theodore Roosevelt reached out to it.[13] *Trifles*, written and performed in 1916, was penned at a time of the growing visibility and even militancy in the now well-organized women's rights movement; it was certainly a time when the issue of gender was one of major discussion and controversy.

World War I (1914–1918), which the United States entered in 1917, gave the movement its final push, as women took over factory work and critical jobs on the home front. Ultimately, "[t]he successful campaign was not an overtly feminist one, but instead quietly emphasized women's wartime patriotism and rightful citizenship."[14] A similar outcome took place in other nations, with Austria, Canada, Ireland, Poland, the United Kingdom, Germany, Luxembourg, and the Netherlands granting universal suffrage soon after the war.[15]

In 1920, the Nineteenth Amendment to the US Constitution was ratified, granting women the right to vote; women also won other legal rights including control over property and wages, and the right to custody of their children in the case of divorce.[16] Nonetheless, the extension of legal rights was only the beginning, as institutional and even legal discrimination against women continued for decades.

BACKGROUND BIBLIOGRAPHY AND FURTHER READING

Ben-Zvi, Linda. *Susan Glaspell: Her Life and Times*, Oxford: Oxford University Press, 2005.
    A comprehensive biography of Susan Glaspell, including details of the political, cultural, and intellectual environment in which she wrote.

Ross, Susan Deller. *The Rights of Women*, Carbondale, IL: Southern Illinois University Press, 1993.
    A publication of the ACLU, provides insights into the historical lack of rights accorded to women. See especially the introduction.

Scott, Anne and Andrew M. *One Half the People: The Fight for Universal Suffrage*, Philadelphia, PA: J. B. Lippincott Company, 1975.
    Details the development of the women's rights movement in America from the seventeenth

century until 1920. Contains many useful primary documents which were published on the issue of women's rights.

Seneca Falls Convention, "Declaration of Sentiments," online: http://www.closeup.org/ sentimnt.htm (accessed December 7, 2006). Also in Scott, op. cit., pp. 50–60.

The document passed by the landmark convention on women's rights held in Seneca Falls, New York. Contains the assertion that: "The history of mankind is a history of repeated injuries and usurpations on the part of man toward woman, having in direct object the establishment of an absolute tyranny over her."

Weatherford, Doris. *A History of the American Suffragist Movement*, Santa Barbara, CA: ABC-CLIO, 1998.

A narrative of the women's rights movement from the seventeenth century until 1920. Includes a useful timeline, as well as primary documents.

SUSAN GLASPELL: BIOGRAPHY

Susan Glaspell was born in Davenport, Iowa, in 1876,[17] only thirty years after Iowa became a state, yet also at a "time when the United States was rushing determinedly into the next century."[18] Glaspell was raised on, and clung to, tales of early pioneer life in the Midwest[19] "The Middle West", she wrote, "must have taken strong hold of me in my early years, for I've never ceased trying to figure out why it is as it is."[20]

Glaspell graduated from the Davenport public schools, and afterwards wrote a society column for a local newspaper. In one of the last columns she authored before embarking to Des Moines, Iowa, for her college education at Drake University, she wrote, concerning the accusation that the "new women" who went to college were "sexless exponents of higher education," that: "If I believed this, I would be compelled to . . . burn down all the women's colleges in the land."[21] While at Drake, Glaspell occupied herself with both oratory and writing short fiction. She graduated with a bachelor's degree in 1899, at a time when very few women were studying in higher education.

After graduating, Glaspell remained in Des Moines, where she continued to write short fiction and succeeded in having numerous stories published in mass-market magazines. Additionally, she worked as a columnist and a reporter for local newspapers, eventually covering a court case on which *Trifles* would later be based. Accused in the case was the wife of a man who had been killed with an axe while in bed. Although originally the crime had been blamed on robbers, suspicions turned on the wife when the murder weapon was discovered in the home, and as neighbors began hinting at a history of trouble within the family. Glaspell later wrote, "When I was a newspaper reporter out in Iowa, I was sent down-state to do a murder trial, and I never forgot going into the kitchen of a woman locked up in town. I had meant to do it as a short story, but the stage took it for its own."[22]

In 1913, having published two novels – *The Glory of the Conquered*, and *The Visioning*[23] – Glaspell married a former professor of English literature, "Jig" Cook. Together, they moved to Provincetown, on the tip of Cape Cod, Massachusetts, and spent winters in the artistic scene of Greenwich Village in New York City. In Provincetown, in a tiny wooden building, they established the "Provincetown Players," a small theater group that would become best-known for producing the works of Eugene O'Neill, one of the greatest American dramatists.[24] The Provincetown Players also performed numerous plays of Glaspell's, including *Trifles* – the first play she wrote entirely on her own.

After Jig died in Greece in 1924, Glaspell authored a memoir commemorating his life, titled *The Road to the Temple*. She soon after married Norman Matson in 1925, with whom she co-wrote a full-length play in 1927 that would later be staged on Broadway.[25] In 1930 she wrote *Alison's House*, a play that was awarded the Pulitzer Prize for drama. Also in this period she wrote two of her best regarded novels, *Brook Evans* and *Fugitive's Return*, the former being made into a film by Paramount pictures under the title *The Right to Love*.[26]

Divorced in 1931, Glaspell published nothing until 1939. In the last decade of her life she published four more novels – *Ambrose Holt and Family*, *The Morning Is Near Us*, *Norma Ashe*, and *Judd Rankin's Daughter* – before her death from pneumonia in Provincetown in 1948.

AUTHOR BIBLIOGRAPHY

"About Susan Glaspell," The Susan Glaspell Society, online: http://academic.shu.edu/glaspell/aboutglaspell.html (accessed January 16, 2005).

Ben-Zvi, Linda. *Susan Glaspell: Her Life and Times*, Oxford: Oxford University Press, 2005.

Gainor, J. *Susan Glaspell in Context*, Ann Arbor, MI: University of Michigan Press, 2004.

Gioia, Dana, and X. J. Kennedy. "Biography: Susan Glaspell," in "Student Resources," *Literature: An Introduction to Fiction, Poetry and Drama*, online: http://occawlonline.pearsoned.com/bookbind/pubbooks/kennedycompact_awl/chapter21/objectives/deluxe-content.html (accessed January 15, 2005).

NOTES

1   Susan Glaspell, "Trifles," in *Plays by Susan Glaspell*, Cambridge: Cambridge University Press, 1987, pp. 37–38.
2   A father, confronted with the choice of whether to donate a kidney to his daughter, asks a doctor to lie by declaring him medically unfit for the procedure.
3   Before achieving statehood in 1890, the territory of Wyoming was organized in 1869 with a provision for women's suffrage. In 1893 the state of Colorado passed an amendment introducing women's suffrage, followed by Idaho and Utah in 1896.
4   Groups opposing the use and sale of alcohol.
5   Anne and Andrew M. Scott, *One Half the People: The Fight for Universal Suffrage*, Philadelphia, PA: J. B. Lippincott Company, 1975, pp. 7–8.
6   Quoted in Doris Weatherford, *A History of the American Suffragist Movement*, Santa Barbara, CA: ABC-CLIO, 1998, p. 101.

7   For the full text of the Seneca Falls Convention's "Declaration of Sentiments," see online: http://www.closeup.org/sentimnt.htm (accessed December 7, 2006).

8   Susan Deller Ross, *The Rights of Women*, Carbondale, IL: Southern Illinois University Press, 1993, p. xiii.

9   Quoted in Weatherford, op. cit., p. 41.

10 Scott, op. cit., p. 27.

11 Linda Ben-Zvi, *Susan Glaspell: Her Life and Times*, Oxford: Oxford University Press, 2005, pp. 35–36.

12 Scott, op. cit., p. 28.

13 Weatherford, op. cit., p. 195.

14 Ibid., p. 224.

15 Ibid., p. 225.

16 Ross, op. cit., p. xiii.

17 Ben-Zvi, op. cit., p. 22.

18 Ibid., p. 4.

19 The "Midwest" refers to the north-central area of the United States, which includes Iowa, Ohio, Illinois, Kansas, Nebraska, Indiana, Missouri, Michigan and Wisconsin. It is sometimes referred to as the "breadbasket" of the country.

20 Ibid., p. 5.

21 Quoted in Ben-Zvi, ibid., p. 33.

22 Quoted in Ben-Zvi, ibid., p. 41.

23 "About Susan Glaspell," The Susan Glaspell Society, online: http://academic.shu.edu/glaspell/aboutglaspell.html (accessed January 16, 2005).

24 Dana Gioia and X. J. Kennedy, "Biography: Susan Glaspell" in "Student Resources," *Literature: An Introduction to Fiction, Poetry and Drama*, online: http://occawlonline.pearsoned.com/bookbind/pubbooks/kennedycompact_awl/chapter21/objectives/deluxe-content.html (accessed January 15, 2005).

25 J. Gainor, *Susan Glaspell in Context*, Ann Arbor, MI: University of Michigan Press, 2004, p. 243.

26 "About Susan Glaspell.," op. cit.

Chapter 10

The Sweet Hereafter

Reasoning from personal perspective

Mitchell Stephens, Esquire, the lawyer:

"They do that, work the bottom line; I've seen it play out over and over again, until you start to wonder about the human species. They're like clever monkeys . . . They calculate ahead of time what it will cost them to assure safety versus what they're likely to be forced to settle for damages when the missing bolt sends the bus over a cliff, and they simply choose the cheaper option. And it's up to people like me to make it cheaper to build the bus with the extra bolt, or add the extra yard of guardrail, or drain the quarry . . . That's the only way you can ensure moral responsibility in this society. Make it cheaper."[1]

Dolores, the bus driver, translating for Abbott, her husband:

"What Abbott said was: The true jury of a person's peers is the people of her town. Only they, the people who have known her all her life, and not twelve strangers, can decide her guilt or innocence. And if Dolores – meaning me, of course – if she has committed a crime, then it's a crime against them, not the state, so they are they ones who must decide her punishment too. What Abbott is saying, Mr. Stephens, is forget the lawsuit. That's what he's saying."[2]

Nichole, a survivor:

"It just wasn't right – to be alive, to have had what people assured you was a close call, and then go out and hire a lawyer; it wasn't right. And even if you were the mother and father of one of the kids who had died, like the Ottos or the Walkers, what good would it do to hire a lawyer? . . . [T]o be the mother and father of one of the kids who had survived the accident, even a kid like me, who would spend the rest of her life a cripple, and then to sue – I didn't understand that at all, and I really knew it wasn't right. Not if I was, like they said, truly lucky."[3]

> *Dolores, reflecting on Billy, eyewitness and father of two children killed:*
>
> "I didn't know what to think of how Billy had changed since the accident. He scared me; but mostly he made me sad. He had been a noble man . . . now he was ruined. The accident had ruined a lot of lives. Or, to be exact, it had busted apart the structures on which those lives had depended – depended, I guess, to a greater degree than we had originally believed. A town needs its children for a lot more than it thinks."[4]

THE SWEET HEREAFTER: THEMES AND QUESTIONS

Reasoning from personal perspective

We've all experienced situations in which what appears to be moral to one person does not appear that way to another. What causes these differences in perception, opinion, and judgment? How might individual differences shape how we each think about an incident that has occurred and how we decide to respond? To answer these questions, we would want to examine closely the histories of different characters and to hear their thoughts as they experience the same event, to learn where these differences come from and how they are realized in decisions and actions.

Russell Banks provides us with just this kind of path into the lives and decisions of others in his powerful novel *The Sweet Hereafter*. Banks tells the story of a horrific school bus crash in a small town called Sam Dent in upstate New York. Fourteen children die; one is left paralyzed. The text is written from the standpoint of four characters, with each chapter narrated by a single one. Dolores Driscoll is the school bus driver; through her we "witness" the crash and will attempt to discover her feelings about it and how they lead to some surprising actions. Billy Ansel, another narrator, is the father of twins who die in the accident and a local hero who uses his business fixing cars to rehabilitate other veterans, like him, of the Vietnam War. Mitchell Stevens, a lawyer and the third narrator, comes to Sam Dent prepared to bring a lawsuit on behalf of the crash's victims – those injured, and the parents of children who died. The last character is Nichole Burnell, the paralyzed teenager who must decide what role she will play in the impending lawsuit.

We will follow the action of the novel as each character relates it. As we do, we will be able to appreciate **the multiplicity of perspectives that accompany any event and the actions that surround it**, and to consider how important it may be to develop a method for **confronting and testing differences in perspective** as part of moral reasoning.

Moral theories in use

We will also want to scrutinize the reasons that the characters provide for their actions, looking for evidence of **moral theories in use** – the often unconscious appeal many of us make to different moral justifications for our decisions. Do the characters make arguments based on the consequences that their decisions will have for individuals, for families, or even for the town as a whole (a utilitarian point of view)? Do they appear to be driven by the need to make good on perceived moral duties and responsibilities? Do they want to protect their own or someone else's rights? And how do their beliefs about what the town of Sam Dent might need to help its citizens recover from the accident motivate their decisions (communitarianism, or reasoning based on community values and cohesion)?

Each one of these represents a different moral viewpoint. *The Sweet Hereafter* presents a convincing portrait of how real people, caught up in an event that affects them all, use moral reasoning in their decision-making. It also raises the question of **how hard we may have to listen to ourselves and to others to find the basis on which moral arguments are being made.**

Moral reasoning and the law

The characters don't announce their moral arguments; like most of us, they weave them seamlessly into other positions and perspectives. One of these is that of the law. In *The Sweet Hereafter* we will be able to **explore how legal reasoning is different from moral reasoning, and the ways in which a legal approach to a problem is, and is not, helpful.** The dimensions of the problem facing the town of Sam Dent include questions of how to determine accountability and apportion blame for the accident, how to handle compensation if any should be required, how to reconcile individuals to loss, and even how to heal a grieving community.

We will test the law for its ability to accomplish these moral objectives, as well as for its ability to resolve more narrow questions such as whether legal liability and compensation from economically viable parties should be sought, and whether these actions will have any deterrent effect in Sam Dent or in other communities.

Moral reasoning and emotion

Any story that centers on a school bus accident would be bound to surface painful reactions from people touched by the event, particularly those who need to make decisions on how to respond to it in one form or another. As Dolores, Billy, Mitchell Stephens, and Nichole consider what has happened and what they believe they must do, we will be able to examine the ways in which emotion is woven into the experience of, and reaction to, moral problems. We will also have the opportunity to consider **how rational moral reasoning really is,** and, more specifically, to ask **what role emotions play (and should play) in moral reasoning.**

ASSIGNMENT

READING: *The Sweet Hereafter,* by Russell Banks.

1   Do you think the community of Sam Dent benefited from not pursuing the lawsuit? Why or why not?

2   How would you explain the choices and actions taken by Dolores, Billy, Nichole, and Stephens?

3   You will find evidence of the moral theories discussed in the *Trifles* class in the rationales provided by the four characters. Be prepared to discuss examples you have identified of reasoning based on consequences, duty, rights, or community.

THE SWEET HEREAFTER: BACKGROUND

The Sweet Hereafter was inspired by a newspaper article Banks read about a school bus accident and the town's involvement with lawsuits in its aftermath. It raises questions of fact for us that are answered in the following materials – questions such as how common such accidents are, and what regulations are used to prevent them. We also may want to know more about the US legal system of civil litigation and enough about the Vietnam War to appreciate the context of the novel; both of these topics are also taken up in the materials that follow.

School buses and school systems

The image of the long, boxy, yellow school bus has become a symbol of American public education. Around 440,000 public school buses operate each year across the United States, traveling more than 4 billion miles. School buses transport 24 million children daily to and from school or school-related activities[5] out of approximately 50 million students who are enrolled in elementary school or high school.[6] In the decentralized public education system that exists in the United States, locales such as cities, towns, and townships are in charge of administering their own school systems. Providing school buses as a means of transportation for pupils is therefore the responsibility of local school boards, which either hire school bus drivers directly or use larger companies that provide school bus services under contract. While these companies will often have central garages and terminals for their vehicles, private bus drivers in some cases have the choice of garaging and maintaining the bus themselves, taking the vehicle home or parking it in a convenient area.[7]

Bus drivers

Whether working directly for a school system or for a contracting company, school bus drivers typically drive one or two routes in the morning and afternoon during which they pick up and drop off pupils at their homes (or a nearby location). Some drivers also take students on mid-day or after-school field or athletic trips.

Since bus drivers often drive the same daily routes, they typically come to know, and build relationships with, the pupils they transport, as well as, in some cases, their parents. The bus driver is a familiar face to those students who ride the bus to school and back.

Drivers are expected by both parents and the school district to be alert in preventing accidents, to maintain order on the bus, and to exercise particular caution when pupils are getting on or off the vehicle. Often, however, school bus drivers have never driven a vehicle larger than an automobile before their employment, and are therefore required to obtain a commercial driver's license, receive between one to four weeks of driving instruction, and attend classroom training on state and local laws and policies, safe driving practices, driver–pupil relations, first aid, the needs of disabled students, and evacuation procedures.[8]

School bus safety

Of all types of motor vehicles, school buses are required to meet the most stringent federal motor vehicle safety standards,[9] and everything from the weight of the seat cushions, to the spacing of the seats, to the height of the seat backs, is designed with safety in mind. (Even the absence of seat belts on many school buses is based on research showing that on a school bus they may in fact cause more injuries than they prevent.) Traffic laws, such as the requirement that motorists stop on both sides of the road for a school bus in the middle of picking up or unloading passengers, are meant to reinforce school children's safety.

Statistically, school buses are the safest motor vehicles on American roads. From 1989 through 1999, school buses were 87 times safer than automobiles, light trucks, and vans for children aged 5 through 18 traveling during school transportation hours.[10] Indeed, whereas passenger cars experience, on average, 1.5 fatalities for each 100 million vehicle-miles traveled (VMT), school buses experience only 0.2 fatalities for the same 100 million VMT.[11]

In the decade from 1989 to 1999, 10 passengers on average were killed each year in school bus crashes, and most of these fatalities occurred in "non-survivable situations" where the vehicle itself was tremendously damaged. Between 1990 and 2000, only 6 passengers on average were killed each year in crashes, most occurring in a moving collision involving a large bus, or a rollover involving a van-sized bus.[12] While fatalities have been rare, in the decade between 1990 and 2000 there were over 289,000 school bus crashes, causing over 10,000 incapacitating injuries, and over 78,000 non-incapacitating or suspected injuries among passengers.[13] Meanwhile, in 2002 alone, there were 21,434 occupant fatalities in car and light truck crashes, and nearly 2.7 million injuries.[14]

Civil litigation

In a criminal trial in the United States a public prosecutor accuses a defendant of violating criminal law; in a civil case, however, a private party – not a public prosecutor – accuses a defendant of violating a civil obligation. Civil cases may involve the violation of a statute, a regulation, a contract, or a principle of the common law (i.e., the law developed through the courts). One class of civil cases is based on the law of torts. A tort is an infraction of a non-contractual obligation or legal duty, resulting in physical, emotional, or monetary damage to the person to whom the duty is owed.[15] Torts include, for example, negligence, misrepresentation, libel, assault, and other wrongful acts.

When a defendant is found liable in a civil case, the plaintiff is typically awarded monetary damages. Even in cases of "wrongful death," monetary damages can be awarded – based not just on expenses such as medical bills and funeral costs, but also on the victim's pain and suffering and, in some cases, the loss of the "pleasure of living."[16] Valuing human life – as well as pain and suffering – in monetary terms is controversial and difficult, although various methodologies are used to develop specific calculations in actual lawsuits.

Individuals and corporations can both be held liable in civil suits, and the liability of one does not assume or preclude the liability of the other. For example, a corporation can be held liable without any of its employees being held personally liable if there is a finding that the corporation's "collective knowledge" was sufficient to prove the requisite knowledge and intent to establish culpability.[17] If, however, a corporation takes certain precautions as a matter of policy, an employee may be found liable for his or her actions on behalf of the corporation without the corporation itself being held liable. Indeed, employees can rarely escape liability based on a defense of "just following orders."[18] In some cases, a corporation and an individual employee may both be held liable. School boards as well as school employees (including bus drivers) have in the past been sued for negligence and found liable for damages, including harm done to pupils.[19]

Jurisdiction and procedure

Civil cases are heard in civil courts, and selecting the local, state, or federal jurisdiction depends on the amount of the claim or the specific nature of the case. In the United States, the right to a trial by jury is guaranteed under federal and state laws even for civil trials. If both plaintiff and defendant agree, however, this right may be waived in favor of a so-called bench trial, that is, a trial presided over and adjudicated only by a judge. Bench trials are often preferred if a case involves purely a legal matter involving no factual dispute.

Frequently, a lawsuit may be settled "out of court" before a verdict has been delivered or even before the trial has begun. Settling out of court, whether by arbitration or by mediation, or because the plaintiff accepts a defendant's offer, commonly occurs so one or both parties can avoid either a costly trial and legal fees or a verdict that may damage one or both parties' reputation and credibility.

Negligence

In a negligence suit, the injured party, i.e., the plaintiff, accuses the defendant of creating an unreasonable risk of harm. The plaintiff must show that the defendant breached his or her duty to exercise "reasonable care."[20] A rule of "Strict Liability" may also be applied to some cases, for example those involving harm done by animals, abnormally dangerous activities, or faulty and dangerous products.[21] Strict liability does not require that the responsible party be "blameworthy" for the negligence.

Plaintiffs in trials of negligence will typically seek monetary damages, which a jury or judge, depending on the type of trial, can award. One type of monetary award may be for compensatory damages, which are meant to equal the value of harm done by the defendant, whether quantifiable (such as medical bills) or unquantifiable ("pain and suffering"). Another award may be for punitive damages, which are meant to punish and deter the defendant. Finally, a nominal damage might be awarded, i.e., a token amount that nonetheless signifies the defendant's responsibility.[22]

Legal culture in the United States

The United States is known for its litigious culture. A colorful variety of seemingly frivolous cases have gained media attention, reinforcing this perception – for instance, a case involving a spilled cup of McDonald's coffee. In that case, the plaintiff was awarded compensatory as well as punitive damages for being served coffee which, experts testified, was served at temperatures capable of causing third-degree burns.[23]

Lawsuits, however, are often used to effect change, especially where governmental jurisdiction is fragmented or muddled (as in school districts), and standards are therefore difficult to legislate or enforce. Courts can call attention to certain issues through high-profile cases. Civil courts, especially those with large jurisdictions, have consequently been seen in certain instances as a "policy avenue," and, in fact, landmark civil decisions have affected everything from consumer law, to race relations, to abortion, to the outcome of the 2000 presidential election.

A brief note on the Vietnam War

In 1961, President John F. Kennedy began committing US advisors to aid the anti-communist South Vietnamese forces in the Vietnamese Civil War against the North Vietnamese Army and the guerilla Viet Cong forces. President Lyndon B. Johnson drastically escalated the American commitment, with over 500,000 American troops stationed in Vietnam by 1968. By the time President Richard M. Nixon succeeded in extricating US forces from the region in 1973, 58,148 Americans had been killed and around 304,000 wounded out of more than 2.5 million who served in the war. Vietnam was an especially unpopular war, and spawned a large protest movement in the United States.

At the time of the Vietnam War, all American men were subject to a military draft (which evolved into a lottery system), but there were numerous exemptions along with various deferments for college (and graduate school) attendance and certain occupations. In consequence, the military ranks comprised a preponderance of comparatively poorer and less-educated troops. Regardless of background, however, a significant number of veterans suffered physically and psychologically as a result of their battlefield experiences. Ambivalence about – even hostility towards – the troops themselves only magnified the difficulty they faced in readjusting to civilian life.

RUSSELL BANKS: BIOGRAPHY

Russell Banks was born in 1940 in Newton, Massachusetts, into a (self-defined) working-class family, and was raised in both eastern Massachusetts and New Hampshire. In his own words:

> I have a less obstructed path as a writer to get to the center of [working-class] lives. Part of the challenge of what I write is uncovering the resiliency of that kind of life, and part of it is demonstrating that even the quietest lives can be as complex and rich, as joyous, conflicted and anguished, as other, seemingly more dramatic lives.[24]

His characters and stories not only draw on his economic background; they also reflect heavily on his childhood surroundings. Many of his novels and stories take place in economically depressed small towns of New England and northern New York State.

As a child, Banks was recognized as having artistic talent, especially in the visual arts. Nearing the age of twenty, he began reading more serious literature, "and out of a desire to essentially imitate what I was reading, I began to write, like a clever monkey."[25] His writing was shaped, he explained, by "reading the American classics like [Mark] Twain who taught me at an early age that the ordinary lives of ordinary people can be made into high art."[26]

The first in his family to go to college, Banks attended Colgate University for less than a year, and later graduated Phi Beta Kappa[27] from the University of North Carolina at Chapel Hill. In college during the 1960s, he was a dedicated political activist in the civil rights movement, as well as in the anti-Vietnam War movement.[28] A committed poetry and fiction writer after graduating, he worked as a plumber, a shoe salesman, and a window trimmer before he could ultimately support himself as a writer.

Throughout the 1960s and early 1970s Banks published several collections of poetry, and in 1975 his first novel, *Family Life,* as well as a collection of short stories, *Searching for Survivors,* were printed. He has since written nine other novels in rapid succession: *Hamilton Stark* (1978), *The Book of Jamaica* (1980), *The Relation of My Imprisonment* (1984), *Continental Drift* (1985), *Affliction* (1990), *The Sweet Hereafter* (1991), *Rule* of the Bone (1995), Cloudsplitter (1998), and The Darling (2004). Four collections of his short stories were also published during this time.

The Sweet Hereafter, Banks's seventh novel, was inspired by actual events. He writes that he developed the idea when he read:

> [A] newspaper clipping describing the aftermath of a school bus accident in a Mexican-American small town in the south of Texas, in the late [19]80s. It was not so much the accident itself as the report in the newspaper of the effects on the families of the tragedy and of the lawsuits that many of the families pursued. It tore the community apart. It was that that I decided was worth a novel.[29]

His works, widely translated, have appeared across Europe and Asia. In addition, two of his novels – The Sweet Hereafter and Affliction – have been adapted to feature-length films. The Sweet Hereafter, directed by Canadian director Adam Egoyan and developed in close collaboration with Banks, won prestigious awards at the 1997 Cannes film festival.[30]

Banks has received numerous prizes and awards for his works, including the Literature Award from the American Academy of Arts and Letters. One literary critic has claimed that Russell Banks is "the most important living white male American on the literary map, a writer we, as readers and writers, can actually learn from, whose books help and urge us to change."[31]

Since becoming a well-known author, Banks has taught at several colleges and universities, including Columbia University, Sarah Lawrence College, University of New Hampshire, New York University, and Princeton.[32] He currently lives in upstate New York.

AUTHOR BIBLIOGRAPHY[33]

"Russell (Earl) Banks," Contemporary Authors Online, Farmington Hills, MI: Thomson Gale, 2006 (accessed February 14, 2006).

"Russell Banks Biography," HarperCollins Publishers, online: http://www.harpercollins. com/global_scripts/product_catalog/author_xml.asp?authorid=479 (accessed February 14, 2006).

Time.com, Transcript of Live Chat with Russell Banks, March 4, 1998, online: http://www. time.com/time/community/transcripts/chatttr030498.html (accessed February 14, 2006).

NOTES

1 Russell Banks, The Sweet Hereafter, New York: HarperPerennial, 1991, p. 91.
2 Ibid., p. 151.
3 Ibid., p. 171.
4 Ibid., pp. 235–236.

5   National Highway Traffic Safety Administration (NHTSA), "School Bus Safety Fact Sheets," online: http://www.nhtsa.dot.gov/people/injury/buses/GTSS/factbus.html (accessed September 26, 2005).

6   Based on the 1999 US Census, online: http://www.census.gov/prod/2001pubs/p20-533.pdf (accessed September 26, 2005).

7   US Department of Labor, "Occupational Outlook Handbook", online: http://www.bls.gov/oco/ocos242.htm (accessed September 26, 2005).

8   Ibid.

9   NHTSA, "School Bus Safety Fact Sheets," op. cit.

10 Ibid.

11 NHTSA, "Report to Congress: School Bus Safety: Crashworthiness Research," April 2002, online: http://www-nrd.nhtsa.dot.gov/departments/nrd-11/SchoolBus.html (accessed September 26, 2005).

12 Ibid., p. 7.

13 Ibid., p. 6.

14 NHTSA, "Motor Vehicle Traffic Crash Injury and Fatality Estimates," May 2003, p. 8, online: http://www-nrd.nhtsa.dot.gov/pdf/nrd-30/NCSA/Rpts/2003/809-586.pdf (accessed September 29, 2005).

15 Christopher Bruner and Lynn Paine, "Negligence: A Legal Perspective," unpublished note, Boston, MA: Harvard Business School Publishing, 2005, pp. 1–3.

16 Carlos Gonzales and Michael Wheeler, "Note on the Value of Life," Harvard Business School Case Number 9–902–152, Boston, MA: Harvard Business School Publishing, 2002, pp. 2–3.

17 For example, if a bank customer withdraws over $10,000 through different transactions with different bank tellers, this should trigger a federal bank reporting requirement. If it does not, no single teller can be held liable, although the bank, which would have "collective knowledge" of this event, could be. See Lynn Paine and Michael Santoro, "Note on Individual and Corporate Liability", Harvard Business School Case Number 9–305–049, Boston, MA: Harvard Business School Publishing, 2004, p. 1.

18 Ibid., pp. 1–2.

19 For example, Cole v. Warren County R-III School District and John Bass, 23 S.W.3d 756 (Mo.Ct.App. 2000).

20 Bruner and Paine, op. cit., pp. 1–3.

21 Ibid., p. 4.

22 Ibid., pp. 4–5.

23 Gerlin, Andrea, "A Matter of Degree: How a Jury Decided That a Coffee Spill Is Worth $2.9 Million: McDonald's Callousness was Real Issue, Jurors Say, in Case of Burned Woman," *The Wall Street Journal*, September 1, 1994, p. A1.

24 *Contemporary Authors Online*, Farmington Hills, MI: Thomson Gale, 2006.

25 Time.com, Transcript of Live Chat with Russell Banks, March 4, 1998, online: http://www.time.com/time/community/transcripts/chatttr030498.html (accessed February 14, 2006).

26 Ibid.

27 Phi Beta Kappa is a prestigious honors society.

28 Time.com, op. cit.

29 Ibid.

30 "Russell Banks Biography," HarperCollins Publishers, online: http://www.harpercollins.com/global_scripts/product_catalog/author_xml.asp?authorid=479 (accessed February 14, 2006).

31 Quoted in *Contemporary Authors Online*, op. cit.

32 HarperCollins Publishers, op. cit.

33 The background information to *The Sweet Hereafter* is complete as included in this text; Chapter 10 has no annotated Bibliography and Further Reading section.

Chapter 11

The Remains of the Day

Reasoning from a moral code

IT IS MY IMPRESSION THAT OUR generation was the first to recognize something which had passed the notice of all earlier generations: namely that the great decisions of the world are not, in fact, arrived at simply in the public chambers ... Rather, debates are conducted, and crucial decisions arrived at, in the privacy and calm of the great houses of this country. What occurs under the public gaze with so much pomp and ceremony is often the conclusion, or mere ratification, of what has taken place over weeks or months within the walls of such houses. To us, then, the world was a wheel, revolving with these great houses at the hub, their mighty decisions emanating out to all else, rich and poor, who revolved around them. It was the aspiration of all those of us with professional ambition to work our way as close to this hub as we were each of us capable. For we were, as I say, an idealistic generation for whom the question was not simply one of how well one practiced one's skills, but *to what end* one did so; each of us harboured the desire to make our own small contribution to the creation of a better world, and saw that, as professionals, the surest means of doing so would be to serve the great gentlemen of our times in whose hands civilization had been entrusted.[1]

. . .

"I've been doing a great deal of thinking, Stevens. A great deal of thinking. And I've reached my conclusion. We cannot have Jews on the staff here at Darlington Hall."

"Sir?"

"It's for the good of this house, Stevens. In the interests of the guests we have staying here. I've looked into this carefully, Stevens, and I'm letting you know my conclusion."

"Very well, sir."

"Tell me, Stevens, we have a few on the staff at the moment, don't we? Jews, I mean?"

> "I believe two of the present staff members would fall into that category, sir."
>
> "Ah." His lordship paused for a moment, staring out of this window. "Of course, you'll have to let them go."
>
> "I beg your pardon, sir?"
>
> "It's regrettable, Stevens, but we have no choice. There's the safety and well-being of my guests to consider. Let me assure you, I've looked into this matter and thought it through thoroughly. It's in all our best interests."[2]

THE REMAINS OF THE DAY: THEMES AND QUESTIONS

An agent's duties

As we think about the kinds of moral challenges we will face in the future, we naturally turn to our lives at work. Whether we consider our role from the standpoint of industry, or of the law, or of economics, a worker is frequently characterized as someone who acts as an "agent" to a "principal," that is, as a "subordinate" who is expected to support the activities of a supervisor. Here, for example, is a definition of the relationship from a US legal text for accountants:

> Agency is a relationship between two parties, a *principal* and his *agent*. In this relationship there is an agreement that one party, the agent, will act to perform work or services as the representative of and under the control of the other, the principal. More simply put, the agent is someone who represents another person, called a principal.
>
> The agency relationship is *consensual.* That is, it is created by the mutual agreement or assent of the parties . . .
>
> Four elements must be present to create an agency relationship. First, there must be a manifestation by the principal that the agent will act for the principal. Second, the agent must agree to act for the principal. Third, the agent must be subject to the principal's direction and control . . . [C]ontrol is crucial and distinguishes agency from other relationships similar in appearance. And finally, the parties must be legally competent to be principal and agent.[3]

Even the most senior organizational leaders typically have bosses – principals whose interests they serve: CEOs serve as agents of their firm's board of directors, who represent the interests of shareholders and of the corporation; university presidents report to supervising boards; and so on. Since nearly all of us will serve as an agent at some point in our work life, it makes sense to understand the role of agent and the kind of challenges and moral reasoning that may be required of individuals who are expected to serve the interests of others.

The Remains of the Day provides us with an opportunity to dive deeply into the agent's role. In an interview, Kazuo Ishiguro, the novel's author, explained his decision to write a book on the experience of Stevens, a butler: "I chose the figure [of a butler] deliberately, because that's what I think most of us are. We're just butlers. It is something I feel about myself and many of my peers ... If you acquired certain abilities, your duty was to put them toward something useful. But for most of us the best we can hope for is to use our rather small skills in serving people and organizations that really do matter."[4]

The Remains of the Day is a retrospective narrative set in England, largely during the period between World Wars I and II, when Stevens, the butler, serves Lord Darlington, a private citizen who is gravely concerned about what he perceives as the unfairness of the Treaty of Versailles to the defeated Germans. The novel traces Stevens's reflections on his life with Lord Darlington, reflections that are stimulated many years later by a vacation – a motoring trip – that he takes at the behest of his new "master," an American who has purchased Darlington Hall.

Through Stevens, we, too, can consider what life as an agent may require. We follow the decisions he makes in serving Lord Darlington, the challenges he faces in serving his new master, and his attempts to come to terms with the impact of these decisions on his own life and on the lives of others.

A professional life

Butlering is the center of Stevens's life, and as a committed professional he spends a great deal of time attempting to define "what a great butler is." His reflections on his role and attempts to act consistently with it raise important questions for us: **How does a central passion or professional mission give meaning to our life?** What are the positive effects of attempting to meet ideals of professional conduct? Are there any negative effects or consequences we should be alert to?

Reasoning from a moral code

Stevens's dedication to the interests of Lord Darlington is clear throughout the novel, and we will watch as he translates this dedication into a set of principles that he uses to guide his decisions. In fact, The Remains of the Day presents us with **a protagonist who has a clearly thought out moral philosophy**, a comprehensive worldview that links his professional life to a larger and (to him) moral purpose. This philosophy is tested at critical moments in the novel, and we are able to explore how **the role of agent** and **duties to a principal can conflict with other obligations and commitments.**

Stevens tries to make sense of how this philosophy has shaped his life, and we will do our own accounting to determine whether Stevens's worldview, system of beliefs, and reasoning have led to sound and defensible decisions. Stevens's philosophy will also help us explore our understanding of **a moral code** and the **impact such fixed systems might have on the act of reasoning through individual situations.**

ASSIGNMENT

READING: *The Remains of the Day*, by Kazuo Ishiguro.

In an article in the *LA Times* in 1989, Kazuo Ishiguro said: "I chose the figure [of a butler] deliberately, because that's what I think most of us are. We're just butlers. It is something I feel about myself and many of my peers ... If you acquired certain abilities, your duty was to put them toward something useful. But for most of us the best we can hope for is to use our rather small skills in serving people and organizations that really do matter."

1   How does Stevens think about *butlering*?

2   How would you characterize his relationship with Lord Darlington?

3   What lesson does this story suggest to you about moral reasoning – and, in particular, about the challenges of agents?

The Remains of the Day: BACKGROUND

The period between World Wars I and II was a time of complex political maneuvering, and you will find yourself wanting to know more about the Treaty of Versailles, the status of the countries which fought in World War I, and British fascism – all of which are described in the materials that follow. Butlering – Stevens's occupation – also has a rich history, described below, that encompasses the "Great Houses" of England, the organization of workers who supported these establishments, and the particular role of butler.

Europe and Britain after World War I

The Treaty of Versailles

The Treaty of Versailles, signed in 1919, officially ended World War I, a bloody conflagration among European powers – and, since April 1917, the United States – which had begun in 1914. With the military defeat of Germany and its allies, the major victors – the United Kingdom, France, and the United States – agreed on a treaty that would require Germany to accept full responsibility for the war (an assertion that still remains historically contentious), pay heavy reparations, drastically reduce and restrict its military forces, and surrender European territory as well as overseas colonies.

The treaty represented a compromise among these so-called Big Three powers. While the United States, under President Woodrow Wilson, aimed for a stable European order ideally based on notions of national self-determination and a League of Nations, the French, under Prime Minister Georges Clemenceau, sought reparations from and revenge against Germany and a reversal of the military victories Germany had won over France since the last half of the nineteenth century. Britain, meanwhile, under Prime Minister Lloyd George, remained more cautious: Although Britain lost many soldiers in the war and did expect to extract reparations from Germany, it also was wary of France, its major colonial rival, and hoped that a non-threatening Germany could be economically revived as a counterweight to perceived French ambitions.

Ultimately, this compromise did not succeed in either satisfying or completely emasculating Germany, although it did have the effect of crippling the German economy throughout the 1920s and 1930s. This situation was easily exploited by ultranationalist movements such as the Nazi Party, which railed against the treaty's harsh terms.

The British Union of Fascists

As a whole, Britain opposed the growth of the German Nazi Party and was only reluctantly willing to compromise with its leader, Adolf Hitler, in the hopes of achieving a lasting peace. Nevertheless, a political faction did exist in Britain that praised the policies and character of leaders such as Germany's Hitler and Italy's Benito Mussolini, and incited violence against Jews, communists, and political opponents. This movement, the British Union of Fascists, was founded in the early 1930s by the aristocratic politician Oswald Mosley.

Like many aristocrats, Mosley and his wife had strong family connections and sympathies with Germany dating back to the nineteenth century,[5] and indeed the movement was supported by a core group of mostly aristocratic and military figures. Arguably, the movement operated on fertile soil: This was also an era in which privileged classes, fearing a repeat of the Russian Revolution of 1917 in their own countries, became increasingly suspicious of growing labor militancy and communist movements, and began to lose faith in the efficacy of democracy.[6]

British fascism was a comparatively small movement, and had little support even among the upper classes. However, the Union of British Fascists only truly became a fringe movement once war with Germany seemed imminent at the end of the 1930s. Previously in the decade, Mosley and his faction had received support and accolades from some mainstream institutions such as the *Daily Mail* newspaper, and the charismatic Mosley was even praised by playwright George Bernard Shaw.

Domestic service in Britain

The "Great Age of Servants"

The Victorian and Edwardian eras (approximately the 1830s until the onset of World War I in 1914) were the "Great Age of Servants" in Great Britain. According to the Official Census in 1891, the servant class was among the largest segments of the working population: 1,386,167 females and 58,527 males were indoor servants in private homes at a time when the total population of England and Wales was approximately 29 million.[7] These domestic servants included butlers, footmen, cooks, nurses, governesses, housemaids, and nannies.[8] Even at the turn of the twentieth century, the Duke of Portland's Great House at Welbeck Abbey employed – in its kitchen alone – a steward, a wine butler, an under-butler, a groom of chambers, and numerous footmen, pageboys, chefs, bakers, kitchen maids, porters, and odd-job men, among others.[9]

Domestic servants were not just a luxury of the aristocracy, and in fact the majority of domestic servants were employed by the middle classes. In many cases, female servants (as opposed to male servants) were not considered a luxury at all, but rather a necessity in a time before many modern household conveniences.

For instance, houses in the nineteenth century rarely had indoor plumbing, and hot water therefore needed to be transported in buckets from the coal-fired heating ranges in the kitchen to the bathrooms for bathing and washing. The heating ranges themselves were far from straightforward; not only were they dirty, but they also required constant maintenance.[10] In another example, the electric washing machine did not supplant labor-intensive laundry washing until well into the twentieth century.[11]

Another reason for the "necessity" of domestic servants had to do with the insecurities of the middle classes, and the social desire to mimic the aristocracy:

> Women of the Victorian and Edwardian middle classes regarded a life of complete idleness as being essential to maintaining their position in life. If they put a piece of coal on the fire, lifted a duster or answered a doorbell, they were "letting their husbands down."[12]

Upstairs and downstairs life

Domestic servants lived apart from their employers, although generally under the same roof, with different below-ground entrances and staircases and living quarters in sparsely furnished attic rooms. They typically existed in a completely separate social sphere from that of their employers. Expected to go almost unnoticed, servants, for example, were unable to participate in conversations with employers unless directly addressed. An ideology of strict class hierarchy fed this system. As *The Footman's Guide*, an instruction manual for footmen and butlers published in 1847, cautions: "Providence having placed some portion of mankind in superior, and some in inferior, situations, the rules of society have settled that a corresponding deference in their address and behavior are due from the latter to the former."[13] The "class system" since the nineteenth century has never been a formally structured or enforced arrangement, but rather a set of assumptions and attitudes about one's place that spanned all the socioeconomic classes. Even to this day, the role of class remains a politically charged topic in Britain.

Those servants lucky enough to work in the so-called Great House of an aristocrat were in turn considered the aristocracy of domestic servants. Indeed, the downstairs world of the servants was, even within the same house, equally hierarchical, with upper servants such as the butler, the valet and the housekeeper eating in separate rooms from the lower servants.[14] There was also a clear, if complex, distinction between men's work and women's work.[15] Servants could advance their position through promotion from an upper servant, or by seeking better employment in another household with the help of character references from their former employers. Equally, however, if a servant was fired, or left without such a letter, he or she would be hard-pressed to find new employment. Maids who became pregnant could expect instant dismissal, and would often then face a life in the dismal workhouses or, worse, in prostitution.[16]

Decline of domestic service and the great houses

As World War I approached, the British institution of domestic service was slowly being eroded. Technological advances were making staff members redundant, and, with the establishment of universal education, the horizons of the next generation of potential servants were expanding. Ultimately, World War I sent men to the front and women into the factories and into positions formerly reserved for men; the labor base of domestic service was therefore greatly reduced,[17] and the social upheavals of the war made the return of a servant class nearly impossible. Finally, in the aftermath of World War II, which ended in 1945, huge inheritance taxes were levied on large estates in order to help finance the rebuilding of war-torn Britain. The upkeep of Great Houses became unaffordable for many in the aristocracy,[18] and since then quite a few of these large country residences have been converted to public use.

The butler

Responsibilities and prestige

As opposed to female servants, the service of whom was ubiquitous in middle-class and aristocratic households alike during the "Great Age of Servants," male servants such as footmen, valets (personal servants), and butlers were a luxury as well as a mark of prestige for their employers. Male servants could advance along a clearly defined career path, usually starting as a "hall boy," moving through the ranks of footman, ultimately to become a butler.[19]

The butler was the foremost position in a traditional household staff (see Table 11.1), supervising the cook, the housekeeper, the under-butlers, the housemen, the maids, and other household staff, as well as in some cases the house's budget and expenses – a truly managerial position requiring little in the way of direct physical labor.[20] For example, while a butler would typically announce a visitor, it was the footman who traditionally would open the door.

Table 11.1 Traditional organization of a household staff[21]

	The butler	
Head chef[22]		Head housekeeper
	1st footman	
	[2nd footman]	
	[3rd footman]	
1st assistant		1st assistant
[2nd assistant]	Valet	[2nd assistant]
		Laundry maids
Kitchen maids	Chauffeur	House maids
		Parlor maids
Scullery maids	Gardener	Seamstress

Source: From the International Guild of Professional Butlers online: http://www.butlersguild.com/guests/general/organizational_chart.html (access October 7, 2005).

Note: Often the chef will acquiesce to the butler on administrative matters and in regard to house standards only. Food issues were commonly discussed directly between the chef and employer.

Although addressed by their employers only by their last name, butlers were addressed by fellow servants as well as tradesmen with the title Mister. Indeed, butler was a position of noted accomplishment and prestige, steeped in traditions and proudly associated with the greatest houses of England. As the International Guild of Professional Butlers explains, revealing the pride of place felt by those in butlering: "Although manservants have been employed all over the world as long as one cares to remember, it was the British Butler who transformed this profession into a form of art and thus became the standard in this field."[23]

Rise and decline of the English butler

The rise of the butler paralleled a gradual and, after World War I, sharp decline in the pageantry and number of great houses' domestic staff. Originally a position overseeing the wine cellar and ale casks, the *bouteillier* (bottler) in medieval times was not accorded a high position, and even in the eighteenth century ranked below the clerk of the stables, the clerk of the kitchen, the manager of the estate, the house steward (manager of all domestic affairs), the valet, the confectioner, the chef and the baker among others. As positions were consolidated, the butler acquired, in addition to the original roles of the *bouteillier*, the managerial roles of the house steward, as well as the roles of the valet in matters of personal assistance where valets did not exist (and increasingly they did not).[24] Thus, around the time of World War I, a butler was effectively the chief of staff in prestigious households.

However, after the world wars, as great houses drastically shrank in wealth and staff, and the institution of domestic service languished, butlers increasingly were forced to take a more active role. As household staffs became increasingly ana-chronistic, a butler was often the only living-in staff member that remained, respon-sible now for all aspects of running and maintaining the house. "The commanding office of butler which had demanded so much respect before World War II was diluted as the size of staffs declined and the range of duties expected of him multiplied."[25]

Before World War II, there were over 30,000 butlers in Britain, today there may be only 2,000 worldwide, the majority of whom serve houses outside England – mostly in the United States and the Middle East.[26]

BACKGROUND BIBLIOGRAPHY AND FURTHER READING

Allen, Christopher and Kimberley Burton Allen, *A Butler's Life: Scenes from the Other Side of the Silver Salver*, Savannah, GA: Frederick Beil, 1997.
The autobiography of a modern butler.

Dawes, Frank. *Not in Front of the Servants: A True Portrait of Upstairs Downstairs Life*, London: Century Hutchinson, 1989.
A history of domestic service in England in the nineteenth and twentieth centuries based on the recollections of former servants.

Greer, Herb. "The Patricians and Their Notorious Party," *The Wall Street Journal*, May 16, 2000, p. A 24.
Provides a short overview of the British fascist movement, as well as its aristocratic connections.

Griffiths, Gareth and Samuel Mullins. *"Cap and Apron": An Oral History of Domestic Service in the Shires, 1880–1950*, Cambridge: Leicestershire Museums, Art Galleries and Record Service, 1986.
A description of "great houses" from the point of view of former domestic servants. Contains transcriptions of actual interviews.

Sambrook, Pamela. *The Country House Servant*, Stroud: Sutton Press, 1999.
Describes the life of female servants in England.

Williams, James. "The Footman's Guide: containing plain instructions for the footman and butler, for the proper arrangement, and regular performance of their various duties, in large or small families," 4th edition (London, 1847?) in *The Making of the Modern Economy*, Thomson Gale, 2005 (available as an e-resource on http://library.harvard.edu)
A thorough job manual for a male domestic servant in the nineteenth century. Also gives great insights into the "ethos" of the profession.

In addition, the website of the International Guild of Professional Butlers gives fascinating insights into the profession of butlering, past and present http://www.butlersguild.com/ (accessed December 7, 2006).

KAZUO ISHIGURO: BIOGRAPHY

Kazuo Ishiguro was born in 1954 in Nagasaki, Japan, and moved with his family to England at the age of five when his father, who was an oceanographer, began work with a British research project in the North Sea. His residence in England was meant to be temporary, and even into his adolescence the family spoke of returning to Japan. Nonetheless, they remained in England, and despite being raised in a "Japanese style" household, Ishiguro was given, in his words, a "very typical middle-class southern English upbringing."[27]

Before enrolling at the University of Kent to study English and Philosophy, Ishiguro spent time as a grouse-beater (a job associated with bird hunting) for the Queen Mother at a castle in Scotland, and also hitchhiked around North America. After graduating with honors in 1978, he engaged in social work for a year on behalf of the homeless in London.[28]

At the time, Ishiguro was aiming to be a professional musician. He recalled:

> I served my creative apprenticeship for writing in the form of songs.
> I wrote over a hundred songs. I don't think it's such a jump from
> songs to stories . . . By the time I had moved toward the end of my
> songwriting period I had found a style . . . To some extent, that is
> the style I have stuck with as a writer.[29]

In 1979 he enrolled in a Master's program in creative writing at the University of East Anglia, and by the time he completed his degree in 1980 he had already published several stories and negotiated a contract for his first novel in advance of its completion. "After years of total failure as a musician," he mused in an interview, "as soon as I had a go at writing, all my stories sold."[30]

His first two novels, *A Pale View of Hills* (1982) and *An Artist of the Floating World* (1986), were set in Japan and involved Japanese characters. They were well received and critically acclaimed, the former novel receiving an award from the Royal Society of Literature, and the latter novel capturing the prestigious Whitbread Book of the Year Award. He feared, however, "getting cast in this role as a Japanese correspondent in residence in London,"[31] especially since he had been raised in the United Kingdom. He lamented, "I sometimes feel that if I had written a book like Kafka's *Trial*, people would say to me, 'What a strange judicial system the Japanese have.'" Therefore, in writing *The Remains of the Day* (1989):

> I made the conscious decision to do the next book away from Japan,
> and I felt a great sense of liberation. There was a part of me that
> wanted to find out if my acceptance was conditioned on the fact that
> I was acting as a mediator to Japanese culture. I wanted to see if

people could appreciate me purely as a novelist as opposed to a Japanese novelist.[32]

The Remains of the Day won the prestigious Man Booker Prize, one of the highest awards in fiction. The award is given each year by a panel of literary critics, writers, and academics to the best novel from any British Commonwealth country and the Republic of Ireland.[33] The Booker Prize confirmed Ishiguro as "one of the foremost British writers of his generation."[34] In 1995 he received the Order of the British Empire, "the order of chivalry of British democracy,"[35] for his service to literature.

The Remains of the Day was adapted into a feature-length film in 1993, starring Anthony Hopkins and Emma Thompson. Since then, Ishiguro has published three other novels: *The Unconsoled* (1995), *When We Were Orphans* (2001), and *Never Let Me Go* (2005). His work has been translated into twenty-eight languages.[36]

AUTHOR BIBLIOGRAPHY

"Kazuo Ishiguro," *Contemporary Authors Online*, Farmington Hills, MI: Thomson Gale, 2005.

"Kazuo Ishiguro", *Writer*, 2001, vol. 114, no. 5, pp. 24–28.

Krider, Dylan. "Rooted in a Small Place: An Interview with Kazuo Ishiguro," *Kenyon Review*, 1998, vol. 20, no. 2, pp. 146–155.

Richards, Linda. "Kazuo Ishiguro," *January Magazine*, October 2000, online: http://www.januarymagazine.com/profiles/ishiguro.html (accessed December 8, 2006).

Sim, Wai-chew. "Kazuo Ishiguro," *Review of Contemporary Fiction*, 2005, vol. 25, no. 1, pp. 80–115.

NOTES

1 Kazuo Ishiguro, *The Remains of the Day*, New York: Vintage International, 1988, pp. 115–116.
2 Ibid., pp. 146–147.
3 Sidney M. Wolf, *The Accountant's Guide to Corporation, Partnership, and Agency Law*, New York/Westport/London: Quorum Books, 1989, p. 183.
4 Kazuo Ishiguro, interviewed by Patricia Highsmith, *LA Times*, October 1, 1989.
5 "The Patricians and Their Notorious Party," *The Wall Street Journal*, May 16, 2000, p. A 24.
6 Ibid.
7 Frank Dawes, *Not in Front of the Servants: A True Portrait of Upstairs Downstairs Life*, London: Century Hutchinson, 1989, p. 15.

8 Ibid., p. 15.
9 Ibid., p. 16.
10 Ibid., p. 25.
11 Pamela Sambrook, *The Country House Servant*, Stroud: Sutton Press, 1999, p. 5.
12 Dawes, op. cit., p. 29.
13 James Williams, "The Footman's Guide: Containing plain instructions for the footman and butler, for the proper arrangement, and regular performance of their various duties, in large or small families," London, 1847?, in *The Making of the Modern Economy*, Thomson Gale, 2005, p. 86 (available as an e-resource on http://library.harvard.edu).
14 Samuel Mullins and Gareth Griffiths, *"Cap and Apron": An Oral History of Domestic Service in the Shires, 1880–1950*, Cambridge: Leicestershire Museums, Art Galleries and Record Service, 1986, p. 36.
15 Sambrook, op. cit., p. 7.
16 Dawes, op. cit., p. 18.
17 Ibid., pp. 28–30.
18 Christopher Allen and Kimberley Burton Allen, *A Butler's Life: Scenes from the Other Side of the Silver Salver,* Savannah, GA: Frederick Beil, 1997, p. xii.
19 Ibid.
20 Ibid.
21 Online: http://www.butlersguild.com/guests/general/general_information.html (accessed October 7, 2005).
22 Allen and Allen, op. cit., p. xii.
23 Mullens and Griffiths, op. cit., p. 35.
24 Allen and Allen, op. cit., p. xii.
25 Quoted in Wai-chew Sim, "Kazuo Ishiguro," *Review of Contemporary Fiction*, 2005, vol. 25, no. 1, pp. 80–115.
26 Ibid.
27 "Kazuo Ishiguro," *Writer*, 2001, vol. 114, no. 5, pp. 24–28.
28 Dylan Krider, "Rooted in a Small Place: An Interview with Kazuo Ishiguro," *Kenyon Review*, 1998, vol. 20, no. 2, pp. 146–155.
29 Ibid.
30 Ibid.
31 See online: http://www.themanbookerprize.com/about/ (accessed December 7, 2006).
32 "Kazuo Ishiguro," *Contemporary Authors Online*, Farmington Hills, MI: Thomson Gale, 2005.
33 See online: http://www.royal.gov.uk/output/page498.asp (accessed October 7, 2005).
34 *Writer*, op. cit.

Chapter 12

A Man for All Seasons

Reasoning from multiple moralities

ROPER:	Arrest him.
ALICE:	Yes!
MORE:	For what?
ALICE:	He's dangerous!
ROPER:	For libel; he's a spy.
ALICE:	He is! Arrest him!
MARGARET:	Father, that man's bad.
MORE:	There is no law against that.
ROPER:	There is! God's law!
MORE:	Then God can arrest him.
ROPER:	Sophistication upon sophistication!
MORE:	No, sheer simplicity. The law, Roper, the law. I know what's legal not what's right. And I'll stick to what's legal.[1]

. . .

MORE:	. . . The Apostolic Succession of the Pope is – . . . Why it's a theory, yes; you can't see it; can't touch it; it's a theory. . . . But what matters to me is not whether it's true or not but that I believe it to be true, or rather, not that I *believe* it, but that *I* believe it . . .[2]

. . .

MORE:	. . . My lord, when I was practicing the law, the manner was to ask the prisoner before pronouncing sentence, if he had anything to say.
NORFOLK:	. . . Have you anything to say?
MORE:	Yes . . . To avoid this I have taken every path my winding wits would find. Now that the Court has determined to condemn me, God knoweth how, I will discharge my mind . . . concerning

> my indictment and the King's title. The indictment is grounded in an Act of Parliament which is directly repugnant to the Law of God. The King in Parliament cannot bestow the Supremacy of the Church because it is a Spiritual Supremacy! And more to this the immunity of the Church is promised both in Magna Carta and the King's own Coronation Oath!
>
> CROMWELL: Now we plainly see that you are malicious!
>
> MORE: Not so, Master Secretary! . . . I am the King's true subject, and pray for him and all the realm . . . I do none harm, I say none harm, I think none harm. And if this be not enough to keep a man alive, in good faith I long not to live . . . I have, since I came to prison, been several times in such a case that I thought to die within the hour, and I thank Our Lord I was never sorry for it, but rather sorry when it passed. And therefore, my poor body is at the King's pleasure. Would God my death might do him some good . . . Nevertheless, it is not for the Supremacy that you have sought my blood – but because I would not bend to the marriage![3]

A MAN FOR ALL SEASONS: THEMES AND QUESTIONS

A man of conscience

What would we be willing to give up for the sake of our convictions? Many of us have considered this question, sometimes running through what-if scenarios involving moral challenges that we or others have faced. While powerful as a means of reflection, these mental exercises sometimes lack crucial specifics – the details of what is at stake and of how people can end up in a situation where self-sacrifice may be required.

A Man for All Seasons, Robert Bolt's powerful play (and movie), tells the story of the historic conflict between Henry VIII and Thomas More, a sixteenth-century lawyer, Chancellor of England, renowned intellectual, and passionate churchman. The conflict rests on weighty questions: Who has the authority to determine whether a marriage (and hence its heirs) is legitimate? Can a King declare himself to be the head of the [Catholic] Church in England? If so, where might the authority to make this declaration come from?

The questions raised by the play are also personal, in fact, intensely personal. **Whom do we aim to satisfy when we act according to our conscience?** Is it selfish to take such a stand, particularly when the results will affect others, some quite negatively? How should we navigate conflicts between our personal views and the duties we owe to others? These are important questions for people who intend to lead lives that *they themselves* will regard as morally responsible. **In the mix of our moral duties, where do we place our duty to ourselves?**

Reasoning from multiple moralities

More's conflict will help us consider what moral reasoning looks like when individuals are devoted to "multiple moralities" – modes of thinking that rest on different categories of moral commitment. In More's case these commitments are many: duties to his king and country; love for his wife and his daughter Margaret; steadfast belief in the rule of law; friendships with other members of Henry's court; deeply felt religious convictions. We will watch More as he attempts to think through the conflicts he faces among these different constituencies and beliefs; through More we will be able to examine **what moral reasoning looks like in someone who is attempting to accommodate a variety of moral perspectives.**

To the degree that More is successful, we will want to ask **what it is about him that enables him to hold to a multi-faceted view of morality,** especially when so many people seem to feel the need to reduce their moral commitments to a single principle, person, or belief.

Making good on multiple obligations

More's situation also enables us to consider how we might act in the face of multiple moral duties with high stakes and great risk. **How do people in such situations think about the situations they find themselves in? Do they try to escape, or do they rush with full force toward a situation in which they might lose everything? Are there options between these extremes?**

More's conflict with Henry lasted five years, ending with his death for treason – a judgment immediately condemned and for which nearly all of the parties involved were themselves killed by Henry during the years that followed. We will of course be concerned about More's end, but, even more so, with the path that got him there. **It is no simple task to aim for good consequences across multiple fronts.** We will see what we can learn from More about managing conflict and about moral reasoning, strategic decision-making, and the tactics of action.

ASSIGNMENT

READING: *A Man for All Seasons,* by Robert Bolt.
VIEWING: *A Man for All Seasons,* 1966, directed by Fred Zinnemann.

1 What was Thomas More willing to die for?

2 How did he reconcile that decision with his obligations as a husband and father? As a subject of Henry VIII? Do you agree with his reasoning? Why or why not?

A MAN FOR ALL SEASONS: BACKGROUND

The sixteenth century was a time of religious upheaval and political strife, and Thomas More's dispute with Henry VIII emerged from a confluence of events in Europe and England that are briefly described in the materials that follow. They cover topics that will help you better appreciate the nature of the divisions that More was caught up in, and the stakes for the many parties to the conflicts. The topics include: The "reformation" of the Catholic Church; the division of authority between Church and State in England; political tensions between England and Spain; and the "great matter" – the questions surrounding Henry VIII's marriage to Catherine of Aragon. You will also find a brief biographical note on Thomas More.

The Reformation in Europe

In the sixteenth century, the Roman Catholic Church experienced a profound doctrinal split, resulting in what became known as Protestantism, a branch of Christianity that, broadly, emphasized the individual's relationship to God in contrast to an institutional mediation provided by the Church. Significantly, the aim of "re-forming" the Church began almost at the outset of the 1,500-year-old religion itself; the simplicity of Jesus' life and message, as reported in the New Testament of the Christian Bible, seemed to collide with the notion of mediating institutions themselves and the Church in particular, which early on adopted the rational organizational model of Rome. The institution was periodically condemned as too worldly, too focused on its own political agenda, too interested in its own economic welfare, and thereby unfit to address matters of individual faith and behavior. The moral worth of the Church as an institution had been challenged on and off for centuries, although the authority of Rome ultimately prevailed.

By the early sixteenth century, however, Rome exhibited all the hallmarks of corruption. Popes, believed to be the successors of one of Jesus' own disciples, Peter, at times lived scandalous lives; positions within the Church hierarchy often went to the highest bidder; taxes levied on populations for Church-related expenses increased – in addition to those levied for secular, State-related purposes.

Meanwhile, other forces gathered storm. For example, the printing press, and its internet-like influence at the time, created an explosion of reading material to an increasingly literate population. The Church could no longer control the content of people's ideas, as it could when it had near-total influence on what people read. Trade and exploration – and the exposure to more global influences – triggered a questioning of ideas, which became housed in another institution, universities; and an array of individuals arose to challenge the status quo.

By the sixteenth century, the challenge to the Church had become sharper and, most important, more broadly publicized. Martin Luther, in his famous *Ninety-Five Theses* published in 1517, argued for the individuality of one's relationship to God, with faith – not action or ritual – as the key to Christian salvation. His ideas, which beyond calling for reform of the Church actually questioned its legitimacy altogether, were, for the time, almost instantly available and widely popularized, and consequently posed the greatest threat to the Church of all. The Church's purpose lay within its assumed legitimacy and authority of being the intercession between an individual and God; rites, rituals – the institution's entire rationale, organization, and practice – were predicated on playing that role.

Church and State in England

In Europe at the beginning of the sixteenth century, the separation between the secular and the religious was extremely ambiguous – where such a separation was even acknowledged to exist at all. The Church was present in an individual's life for all matters of life and death, and the ecclesiastical calendar ordered the lives of both individuals and communities throughout the year. Disease, including recurring bouts of plague, was held to be first and foremost a religious issue. In the lives of many, the Church held sway over many aspects of daily existence. It was in this general milieu that bishops across Europe had come not only to act as ecclesiastics, managing their dioceses' clergy, but also as secular lords, managing vast estates.[4] It was also in this milieu that the papacy not only ruled its own principalities in Italy, but also sought to influence and control European affairs; indeed, the belief that the papacy had both spiritual and temporal power was a fundamental element of the Catholic Church in this period.

In England, however, although the role of the Church in everyday life was probably no less than in the rest of Europe, the Church's power was circumscribed. Of all European kingdoms, England had the most well-developed institutions of monarchy and law in the sixteenth century. Magna Carta, issued in 1215, set the stage for a royally led government of broadened (although by no means popular) participation, which was to include institutions such as Parliament, offices of civil service such as the Lord Chancellor, and courts that lay outside ecclesiastical jurisdiction. Law was therefore well developed both in theory as well as in practice: Thomas More, for example, was a *practicing* lawyer.

Ecclesiastical and royal jurisdictions collided on many issues throughout the centuries before and after Magna Carta, but by the fourteenth century an accommodation was clearly being reached between King and Pope.[5] By the sixteenth century, in the appointment of bishops, the King would make his preference clear, and the Pope would commonly appoint the King's candidate. Where disagreements occurred, compromises could commonly be reached.[6] A bishop would therefore hold his land, like a lay lord, thanks to the King, and wield spiritual power thanks to the Pope. This was an arrangement that generally worked for both parties, safeguarding their individual spheres.

This relationship was still greatly ambiguous, however. By one estimate, the Church controlled one-third of all land in England at the beginning of the sixteenth century,[7] and the Church's leading office-holders, such as bishops, were often important civil servants. Cardinal Wolsey, who preceded Thomas More as Lord Chancellor, was at the same time a papal legate.[8] While the King successfully defended the kingdom's claim of superiority in matters of taxation and the courts,[9] as well as in the punishment of clergy, the Church remained ascendant in other matters. One preserve of the Church that would ultimately prove fateful for the course of the Reformation in England was the continuing dominance of Rome in ultimately deciding matrimonial cases.

Henry VIII and Catherine of Aragon

Marriage

Henry VIII ascended the English throne in 1509, and soon afterward married Catherine of Aragon, the daughter of King Ferdinand II and Queen Isabella of Spain. The marriage had been arranged by Henry VIII's father and predecessor, Henry VII, in order to maintain an alliance between England and Spain.

However, Catherine had previously been married to Henry VIII's brother Arthur, who died of an illness. Thus, a special dispensation (freedom from a prohibition) from the Pope had been necessary to safeguard the legitimacy of Catherine's marriage to Henry VIII, which would commonly be regarded as contrary to biblical tenets: "Thou shalt not uncover the nakedness of thy brother's wife."[10] Although Catherine insisted that her marriage to Arthur had not been consummated – a fact that would have eased the question of her new wedding's legitimacy – and although the contours of the prohibition could be interpreted in other ways,[11] the papal intervention was thought necessary in order to legitimate the marriage beyond a doubt.

The "Great Matter" and the politics of annulment

By the 1520s, Henry was gravely concerned about Catherine's inability to bear him a male heir – her pregnancies had consistently resulted in either miscarriages or the death of the child in infancy. Although she had successfully given birth to a daughter, Mary, Henry nonetheless continued to place great importance on a son. His father, Henry VII, had been the first Tudor king, having attained kingship through conquest amidst a civil war – the Wars of the Roses – which pitted the houses of York and Lancaster against each other. The Tudor accession, and the re-uniting of the two houses through Henry VII's marriage to Elizabeth of York, still looked precarious enough to Henry VIII to necessitate a male heir to secure succession.

Because of the circumstances surrounding their marriage, this issue became one of theology: Catherine's inability to produce a male heir was attributed to divine punishment for contradicting a biblical prohibition.[12] Although divorce was legally and religiously impossible, Henry hoped to be able to secure a papal annulment on these theological grounds. Papal annulments were frequent, and often quick, especially where royalty was concerned.

The process began in 1527, although it soon became clear that in this case a papal annulment would not be easy. Not only was the request provocative and even insulting to the Papacy, given its previous dispensation; it was also diplomatically fraught: Rome, and with it the Pope, had recently fallen under the control of Catherine's nephew, the Holy Roman Emperor, and the staunchly Catholic Spain would hardly support an annulment for fear, among other reasons, of "bastardizing" the Queen's daughter, Mary. Moreover, an apparently strong political faction supporting the Queen and the Pope existed at home.

The beginning of the English Reformation

Henry's haste to annul his marriage, and his impatience with the increasingly lengthy and difficult annulment procedure, was also fuelled by his love for the (allegedly) reformist-leaning Anne Boleyn.[13] Although Henry had previously been given the title "Defender of the Faith" by the Pope for his stance against Lutheranism, his impatience, and Anne Boleyn's influence over him in matters of religion, led ultimately to a more radical course when in 1529 he began to move against the Church's clerical and secular power in England.

THOMAS MORE: BIOGRAPHY

Born in or around 1477 to John More, a leading London lawyer, Thomas More was educated at top London schools and attended university for two years at Oxford before studying to become a lawyer himself. After a brief experiment in monastic life, More embarked on his legal career, soon becoming an under-sheriff of London – a judicial role. A skilled negotiator, he also led negotiations with foreign governments in matters of trade and foreign affairs.

At the same time, More befriended Continental thinkers such as Desiderius Erasmus, a leading Humanist who believed in reforming the Church from within, and returning to the Bible and the ideas of the early Church fathers. More also began a literary career, authoring an influential, though unfinished, *Life of Richard III;* and in 1516 he published *Utopia*, commonly regarded as his greatest work. Detailing a polity led by reason and, in so doing, critiquing the institutions and personalities in Europe at the time, the book established his reputation as a great thinker in the Humanist school.

In 1521, More was knighted, and Sir Thomas was brought directly into royal service as under-treasurer. During the 1520s he served as an advisor to Henry VIII, who was writing an attack on Martin Luther, and More himself leveled a scathing attack on Luther that was published in 1523 – the same year More became Speaker of the House of Commons.

When Cardinal Wolsey fell from power in 1529, More succeeded him as Lord Chancellor, a position which, besides involving duties as Speaker in the House of Lords, also oversaw the administration of the legal system and its courts. More continued in this role throughout Henry's lengthy annulment procedure and ultimately his split with Rome. More was arrested in 1534 for refusing to declare an oath to the new change in spiritual authority (although he was willing to acknowledge Henry's marriage to Anne Boleyn). After writing a tract on Christian thought, *A Dialogue of Comfort Against Tribulation*, in prison, More was tried and executed as a traitor in 1535.

Henry also dismissed formerly close advisors such as Cardinal Wolsey, the Lord Chancellor, who, because of his position as a clergyman, could ultimately not be reconciled to these new leanings. Instead of Wolsey, Henry appointed a layman as Lord Chancellor, a position that was often confined to clergymen: Thomas More. Henry also appointed the reformist cleric Thomas Cranmer as Archbishop of Canterbury (the highest clerical position in England); and Thomas Cromwell, a leading proponent of England's independence from Rome, became Henry's close advisor.

Together, Cranmer and Cromwell pushed reforms through both Parliament and the Church, allowing Henry officially to marry Anne Boleyn in 1533 and declare himself Supreme Head of the English Church – separate from Catholic Christendom – with the 1534 Act of Supremacy.

The Church in England under Henry VIII, although now independent of the Pope (now referred to as "The Bishop of Rome"), would maintain continuity with many of the theological traditions of Catholicism, and hardly went to the extremes of Lutheranism. Nonetheless, the Act of Supremacy was the first and central act in the creation of what would ultimately become an independent, Protestant-leaning Anglican Church.

TIMELINE OF RELEVANT EVENTS

1477/1478	Thomas More born in London
1485	Henry VII assumes power at the Battle of Bosworth Field, drawing the Wars of the Roses to a close
1491	Henry VIII born
1509	Henry VIII ascends the throne, marries Catherine of Aragon
1515	Thomas Wolsey, Archbishop of York, becomes Lord Chancellor
1516	Mary born to Henry VIII and Catherine
	More publishes *Utopia*
1517	Martin Luther publishes *Ninety-Five Theses*
1521	More brought into royal service as under-treasurer
1523	More publishes attack on Martin Luther, becomes Speaker of the House of Commons
1520–1527	Henry VIII begins to pursue "The King's Great Matter"
1527–1529	Appeals to Rome for an annulment fail
1529	Cardinal Wolsey ousted as Lord Chancellor
	More appointed new Lord Chancellor
1532	Thomas Cromwell becomes close advisor to Henry VIII
1533	Henry VIII marries Anne Boleyn
	Thomas Cranmer, the new Archbishop of Canterbury, declares first marriage annulled
1534	Act of Supremacy declaring Henry VIII head of English Church
	More arrested on charges of treason, imprisoned in Tower of London
1535	More tried and executed

BACKGROUND BIBLIOGRAPHY AND FURTHER READING

Ackroyd, Peter. *The Life of Thomas More*, New York: First Anchor Books, 1998.
  A thorough biography of Sir Thomas More.

Brigden, Susan. *New Worlds, Lost Worlds: The Rule of the Tudors 1485–1603*, New York: Viking, 2000.
  An in-depth look at politics and society in the age of the Tudors.

Carleton, Kenneth. *Bishops and Reform in the English Church: 1520–1559*, Rochester, NY: Boydell Press, 2001.
  Details the ambiguous position of bishops in sixteenth-century England.

Sandoz, Ellis (ed.). *The Roots of Liberty: Magna Carta, the Ancient Constitution, and the Anglo-American Tradition of Rule of Law*, Columbia, MO.: University of Missouri Press, 1993.
  A collection of essays which are useful in understanding the development of British political institutions, including the rule of law.

Solt, Leo, *Church and State in Early Modern England 1509–1640*, New York: Oxford University Press, 1990.
  Investigates the conflicts between "Church" and "State" in England throughout this period. Especially helpful for understanding the Henry VIII's split with Rome.

ROBERT BOLT: BIOGRAPHY

Robert Bolt was born near Manchester, England, in 1924, into a lower-middle-class family of chapel-going Methodists.[14] His father was a shopkeeper, and his mother was a teacher.[15] After working for a short time at an insurance company, Bolt served in the military during World War II both with the Royal Air Force and the Royal West African Frontier Force. He then attended the University of Manchester, where he studied history. Once he graduated, in 1950, Bolt became a school teacher in order to support himself while struggling as a playwright,[16] and, while teaching, he "honed his passionate love of history and language" and also produced his first play, for a children's nativity pageant.[17]

He quickly achieved stunning successes in the theater, producing *The Critic and the Heart* (1957) at the Oxford Playhouse, and also the comedy *Flowering Cherry*, which was performed in London in 1958 and on Broadway the next year, each production featuring a distinguished cast. Bolt achieved wide recognition as well as critical and financial success.[18]

Meanwhile, he was already writing his best-known play, *A Man for All Seasons,* which was produced in 1961 in London – an instant success – and in New York the next year, where it won five Tony Awards and the prestigious

New York Drama Critics' Award.[19] The literary critic J.C. Trewin called the play "one of the few contemporary portrait-plays likely to last."[20]

After *A Man for All Seasons*, Bolt turned to screenwriting for films when the well-known director David Lean commissioned him to write the screenplay for *Lawrence of Arabia* (1962), the epic story of the British soldier T. E. Lawrence who led an Arab revolt during World War I. The film, over three and a half hours long, remains a classic. Bolt followed up this success with two more screenplays, both of which won him Academy Awards: *Dr. Zhivago* (1965) and the screen adaptation of *A Man for All Seasons* (1966). Both were popular and critical successes.[21]

At the same time, Bolt was a well-known political activist on the left. In 1960 he joined the "Committee of 100," a group of British writers, artists, and other noted personalities who used civil disobedience to oppose the nuclear arms race. He was arrested in 1961 for a sit-in in Trafalgar Square in London, at a time when his *Lawrence of Arabia* screenplay was still a work in progress. Despite the risks his absence caused the film's production, he nonetheless initially refused to sign a pledge to keep the peace, which would guarantee his release from jail. Ultimately, however, film executives prevailed on him to sign the pledge. "This surrender, in total contrast to Sir Thomas More's refusal to save his life by signing a royal document, had, according to Bolt's friends, a profound effect on his life and self-confidence, and the guilt lasted for years."[22]

Bolt worked on several other films and plays until 1979, when, after open-heart surgery, he suffered a severe stroke, which left him paralyzed and speechless. However, he made a near-miraculous (although not total) recovery, and was able to complete the project he had been working on at the time of his stroke, a screenplay entitled *The Bounty*. The film was produced in 1984, starring Mel Gibson and Anthony Hopkins. He soon after penned (with great difficulty) the screenplay for *The Mission* (1986), starring Robert De Niro. The film, about the plight of native South American peoples at the time of the Portuguese and Spanish colonialism, won the prestigious Palme d'Or at the Cannes Film Festival.

When he died in 1995, Bolt was in semi-retirement, living with his wife, the actress Sarah Miles.

AUTHOR BIBLIOGRAPHY

Amidon, Stephen. "Robert Bolt: Obituary," *The Financial Times*, February 23, 1995, p. 27.

Calder, John. "Obituary: Robert Bolt," *The Independent*, February 23, 1995, p. 16.

Hawkins-Dady, Mark (ed.). "Bolt, Robert (Oxton)," *International Dictionary of Theatre*, Vol 2: *Playwrights*, Farmington Hills, MI: St James Press/Gale Research, 1994, pp. 110–111.

Lyall, Sarah. "Robert Bolt Is Dead at 70: Oscar-Winning Screenwriter," *The New York Times*, February 23, 1995, p. 10.

"Robert (Oxton) Bolt," *Contemporary Authors Online*, Farmington Hills, Mich: Thomson Gale, 2006.

NOTES

1   Robert Bolt, *A Man for All Seasons*, New York: First Vintage International Edition, 1990, p. 65.
2   Ibid., p. 91.
3   Ibid., pp. 159–160.
4   Kenneth Carleton, *Bishops and Reform in the English Church: 1520–1559*, Rochester, NY: Boydell Press, 2001, p. 1.
5   Leo Solt, *Church and State in Early Modern England 1509–1640*, New York: Oxford University Press, 1990, p. 3.
6   Carleton, op. cit., p. 7.
7   Solt, op. cit., p. 4.
8   Carleton, op. cit., p. 9.
9   Cases could usually only be appealed to the Papal Curia with the King's permission.
10 Leviticus 18:16. See Susan Brigden, *New Worlds, Lost Worlds: The Rule of the Tudors 1485–1603*, New York: Viking, 2000, p. 113.
11 For instance, Deuteronomy 25:5–10 speaks about the *obligation* of a man to marry his sister-in-law in the case of his brother's death.
12 Brigden, op. cit., p. 113.
13 Ibid., p. 114.
14 John Calder, "Obituary: Robert Bolt" *The Independent*, February 23, 1995, p. 16. Methodism is a Protestant denomination of Christianity. Founded in England in the eighteenth century, it soon after separated from the established Church of England, and took different forms in various (mostly English-speaking) countries. Methodism in Britain, although still somewhat hierarchical, is defined by the existence of ministers and preachers, as opposed to bishops, and worship is conducted in "Chapels."
15 "Robert (Oxton) Bolt" *Contemporary Authors Online*, Farmington Hills, MI: Thomson Gale, 2006.
16 Stephen Amidon, "Robert Bolt: Obituary," *The Financial Times*, February 23, 1995, p. 27.
17 Sarah Lyall, "Robert Bolt Is Dead at 70: Oscar-Winning Screenwriter," *The New York Times*, February 23, 1995, p. 10.
18 Calder, op. cit.
19 Amidon and Lyall, op. cit.
20 Quoted in *Contemporary Authors Online*, op. cit.
21 Ibid.
22 Calder, op. cit.

Moral Leadership

Moral Leadership Module Map

Central theme	Text and setting	Storyline	Preparation
Exercising authority	*The Prince,* by Niccolò Machiavelli Sixteenth-century Italy	A handbook of advice for new leaders	Handbook: 100 pages
Earning legitimacy	*The Secret Sharer,* by Joseph Conrad 1890s off the coast of Siam	A new captain's struggle to establish himself in his first command	Short story: 30 pages
Balancing benefits and harms	*Truman and the Bomb,* excerpts of historical and fictional accounts. Japan, World War II	US President Harry S. Truman's decision to use the atomic bomb and its consequences	Text excerpts: 16 pages
	Excerpts from *Just and Unjust Wars,* by Michael Walzer		Text excerpts: 110 pages
Taking a stand	*Personal History,* autobiography of Katharine Graham 1970s America, recalled	The leadership of *Washington Post* publisher Katharine Graham during the investigations of the "Pentagon Papers" and Watergate	Autobiography excerpt: 80 pages
	Excerpt from *A Good Life,* autobiography of Ben Bradlee		Autobiography excerpt: 14 pages
Assuming leadership	*American Ground: Unbuilding the World Trade Center,* by William Langewiesche Post-September 11th USA	How a small group of city bureaucrats and engineers came to manage the "unbuilding" of the World Trade Center	Historical account: 200 pages

Chapter 13

Moral Leadership Preview

TWO MONTHS after fire burned down his mill, [Malden Mills owner Aaron] Feuerstein the businessman was vying for time with Feuerstein the growing local and national phenomenon, the executive with a heart in an era of short-sighted profit-taking and callous disregard for workers.

Publicity over his decision to rebuild in battered Lawrence and to pay workers idled by the Dec. 11 fire had been unrelenting, and all good: Prime coverage on major networks, a gushing profile in *People* magazine, guest of President Clinton for the State of the Union Address. Strangers were sending him money; kids at a local McDonald's wanted his autograph.

But back at the mill – behind closed doors – his top managers in mid-February were grappling with what they saw as a harsher reality.

A third of the mill's 2,320 Lawrence workers were still out of jobs, but all were being paid. Feuerstein had put off limits any layoffs or consolidations to shave labor costs, but debts were mounting. And his remarks on "social responsibility" and a newfound eagerness to debate such issues were making managers nervous.

"Aaron," his top executive, Howard Ackerman, half-joked, "have we become a nonprofit organization?"

Everybody had an uneasy laugh. No, Feuerstein assured his managers, he was not running a nonprofit textile mill.

But he was not about to let go of the one positive thing to come out of the fire: Widespread recognition of Malden Mills as a special company.

More, he was growing into the role of famous person – and liking it. And the more he read and was exposed to the views of others, including US Labor Secretary Robert Reich, the more convinced he was that too much of corporate America had grown shortsighted and anti-worker.

"I think we're going to win in the long run because of this," he told his managers, noting his liberal pay and other pro-worker policies had won support for the rebuilding project from bankers, government officials, suppliers and many of his customers.

> But the short run was proving to be a nightmare. Behind the honors and headlines, Feuerstein the businessman was being forced to dig in hard.
>
> *The Boston Globe*, September 9, 1996

The challenge of moral leadership

After having examined moral challenges and moral reasoning in the previous two modules, we now have the opportunity to relate these insights directly to the subject of leadership. What is *moral* leadership? What does it look like? What distinguishes it from leadership in general, and even from effective leadership? After all, history is full of leaders who may have been effective as judged by their ability to mobilize people, resources, and ideas, yet are widely held to have been pursuing immoral goals or utilizing morally repugnant means to achieve their intended ends.[1]

One straightforward definition of moral leadership might be: Directing a morally acceptable or laudable cause, sustained by means that are also widely recognized to be moral. The Pulitzer Prize-winning psychiatrist Robert Coles wrote to this effect, saying that "moral leadership [is] intellect calling upon the energies of conscience, with the loyalty of others a signal that such a call has been contagiously successful."[2] By this measure, Ernest Shackleton, with his deep sense of responsibility and the overwhelming loyalty of his crew, was a widely successful moral leader.

However, one need not lead a team to survival in the face of near-certain death to exhibit moral leadership. Leaders confront moral challenges of various types and of varying levels of complexity on a regular basis – these challenges range from the difficult task of earning the right to be a leader, to the equally arduous task of navigating the resulting power imbalances with those being led. Leaders will face right-versus-wrong challenges, right versus right challenges, challenges posed by new principles, and so forth; how a leader reasons through and acts in these difficult situations will affect many more individuals than just the leader herself. This is what places the subject of leadership firmly within the moral domain; and, indeed, leaders, like Aaron Feuerstein in the opening vignette, are often judged – among other criteria – on the basis of the perceived morality of their actions.

Exercising authority

Studies of primates (such as chimpanzees and gorillas), as well as children and adults in laboratory settings, have demonstrated that conferring authority and establishing a hierarchy of roles is an innate group activity, especially when the group is required to make a coordinated effort at solving a problem.[3] "Authority provides orientation," writes Ronald Heifetz, instructor and author on the topic of leadership, "which in turn diminishes stress and provides a hub of cohesive bonding as each member develops some tie" with the leader. In humans, moreover, it has been shown that authority is not automatically conferred on a member who has a formal institutional claim on a top-ranking position; indeed, it can be attained by those without formal designation to a leadership role[4] – a phenomenon we will examine in *American Ground*, William Langewiesche's account of the "deconstruction" or cleanup of the World Trade Center site in New York following the September 11, 2001 terrorist attacks.

Although a naturally occurring phenomenon, and a beneficial one when exercised responsibly, the exercise of authority has moral significance. For example, how leaders obtain their authority and what they do with it – that is, what they do with the sometimes vast power and resources they have at their disposal – are more than just practical considerations; they are questions of a moral nature.

Machiavelli's *The Prince*, the first reading in this module, has served as a handbook for leaders and aspiring leaders for centuries precisely because it seeks to delineate the boundaries of when and how a leader should seek to act when exercising authority.[5] The first half of his treatise focuses on the often turbulent process of attaining power, while the second half provides more general advice on how to maintain it. Machiavelli's prescriptions offer a stark reminder of the moral responsibilities that leaders must navigate as they exercise their power.

Aside from considerations of power and the moral complications it may entail, leaders must also make constant decisions about the ends they seek and the means they use to obtain them. A later reading describing President Truman's decision to use the atomic bomb on Japan will vividly illustrate the wide-ranging effects that a leader's choices in exercising authority may have. In conjunction with excerpts from the political commentator Michael Walzer's *Just and Unjust Wars*, the account will allow us to examine the moral judgments that are applied to leaders' choices of various ends and means, and to the ways that they balance the harms they inflict and the benefits they confer on others.

Earning legitimacy

"Legitimacy" commonly refers to the perceived right of a person, group, or organization to exercise power based on a broad consensus among those over whom power is held. Leadership necessitates a connection between leaders, who assert their authority to lead, and followers; effective leadership is demonstrated when those who follow accept the legitimacy of the leader's assertion of authority. John W. Gardner, a seasoned author on the topic of leadership, prefers the word "constituent" over "follower" to illustrate vividly the nature of this relationship. "Leaders," he writes, "are almost never as much in charge as they are pictured to be, followers almost never as submissive as one might imagine."[6]

The authority to lead is a "conferred power to perform a service,"[7] and as such it can be given and taken away. When it is given, "constituents" do so as part of a two-way exchange. Although social scientists have offered various models to explain the exercise of leadership and authority,[8] authority is, in essence, based on a social contract between the leader and the led: "Given your know-how, I give you the power to make decisions to accomplish a service, and I'll follow those decisions as long as it appears to me that they serve my purposes."[9]

How does a new leader go about earning legitimacy? Max Weber, the late-nineteenth-century sociologist and philosopher, argued that a leader's legitimacy could have one of three sources: *rational-legal*, that is, a codified set of organizational rules and laws; *traditional*, that is, an uncodified and more amorphous consensus about "the way things have always been"; or *charismatic*, which derives from the personality and properties of the leader herself. In the modern world, although the traditional and charismatic elements are still essential, the rational-legal source of legitimacy has perhaps become most important.[10]

Another useful way of viewing legitimacy is to distinguish three overlapping types of legitimacy, any of which a leader may or may not possess. *Procedural legitimacy*, like Weber's rational-legal category, refers to the legal or institutional means by which a leader can be formally recognized; this may be by organizational appointment, through an election, following an established process of heredity, and so forth.

Technical legitimacy, a second type, flows from a leader's demonstrated capacity for leadership. Leaders who have technical legitimacy are viewed as being able to fulfill their end of the tacit social contract between leader and constituent. An individual may have full procedural legitimacy, but still be unable to lead because he lacks technical legitimacy – his constituents do not have faith in his abilities to lead them in the task at hand.

Finally, we might consider *moral legitimacy* to be equally important. Thucydides, the classical Greek historian, judged a historical leader by writing that: "His way of life made him objectionable to everyone as a person, and thus [the Athenian people] entrusted their affairs to other hands." Because leadership is based on a two-way relationship, leaders are indeed judged in the moral domain about the decisions they make while building and exercising their authority.

What does moral legitimacy look like, and what is its effect? In this module we will read Joseph Conrad's short story *The Secret Sharer*, in which the turbulent process of attaining legitimacy is colorfully depicted through an immediate moral challenge. We will also read selections from the autobiographies of Katharine Graham and Ben Bradlee, which will help illustrate the impact a leader's moral legitimacy can have on both the effectiveness and moral vision of an entire organization. Finally, *American Ground* will chart the process whereby, even without procedural legitimacy, both technical legitimacy and moral leadership can still nonetheless be demonstrated and attained.

Overview of readings in this module

The readings in this module allow us to understand the challenges inherent in all forms of leadership, especially in the twin tasks of exercising authority and earning legitimacy. They will afford us the opportunity to reason through several different leadership situations, enabling us to come away with a more nuanced understanding of what moral leadership is, what it looks like when practiced, and how it can be demonstrated:

- **Exercising authority.** *The Prince* will present a seemingly practical system of both attaining and exercising authority. Hotly debated and controversial since its original publication, the text will allow us to focus directly on power, how it is secured, maintained, and used.
- **Earning legitimacy.** *The Secret Sharer* will introduce a new sea captain's challenge, allowing us to ask important questions about how the actions of hierarchical leaders – those with procedural legitimacy, if nothing else – can qualify as moral leadership, and how practicing moral leadership can enhance a leader's overall legitimacy and credibility.
- **Balancing benefits and harms.** *Truman and the Bomb*, in conjunction with a selection of readings from the political science classic, *Just and Unjust Wars*, will allow us to examine the criteria by which leaders are judged, and how these judgments relate to the leader's legitimacy and perceived leadership and decision-making capabilities.
- **Taking a stand.** The autobiographical episodes from the lives of Katharine Graham and Ben Bradlee will allow us to understand just how important moral legitimacy is for a leader, especially one who must take a stand in the face of forces that are much more powerful than she. These fascinating readings will also illustrate the effect that moral leadership can have on an entire team and organization.
- **Assuming leadership.** *American Ground* will present a situation in which legitimacy is earned even by those who do not occupy institutional leadership roles, and explore how moral leadership – the capacity for which belongs to everyone – translates into real and effective leadership.

NOTES

1   See for instance John Gardner, *On Leadership*, New York: Free Press, 1993, pp. 67–70, for a discussion of historical examples.
2   Robert Coles, *Lives of Moral Leadership*, New York: Random House, 2001, p. 193.
3   See Ronald Heifetz, *Leadership Without Easy Answers*, Cambridge, MA: Belknap Press, 2001, pp. 49–57.
4   Ibid.
5   See for example Michael Ledeen, *Machiavelli on Modern Leadership: Why Machiavelli's Iron Rules Are as Timely and Important Today as Five Centuries Ago*, New York: Truman Talley, 1999.
6   Gardner, op. cit., p. 23.
7   Ibid., p. 57.
8   For a summary of this scholarship, see "Current Thinking about Leadership: A Review and Critique" in Roger Gill, *Theory and Practice of Leadership*, London: Sage Publications, 2006.
9   Heifetz, op. cit., p. 57.
10 More recently, a good deal has been written on the subject of becoming secure in a new leadership role, especially from a management perspective. Much of this literature focuses on the process of translating a job title into an effective and influential position. Two examples are: Dan Ciampa and Michael Watkins, *Right from the Start: Taking Charge in a New Leadership Role*, Boston, MA: Harvard Business School Press, 1999, and John Gabarro, *The Dynamics of Taking Charge*, Boston, MA: Harvard Business School Press, 1987.

Chapter 14

The Prince

Exercising authority

IN THE ACTIONS OF ALL MEN, and especially of princes, where there is no court of appeal, one judges by the result.[1]

. . .

A prince, therefore, need not necessarily have all the good qualities I mentioned above, but he should certainly appear to have them. I would even go so far as to say that if he has these qualities and always behaves accordingly he will find them harmful; if he only appears to have them they will render him service. He should appear to be compassionate, faithful to his word, kind, guileless, and devout. And indeed he should be so. But his disposition should be such that, if he needs to be the opposite, he knows how.[2]

. . .

. . . it is far better to be feared than loved if you cannot be both . . . Men worry less about doing an injury to one who makes himself loved than to one who makes himself feared. For love is secured by a bond of gratitude which men, wretched creatures that they are, break when it is to their advantage to do so; but fear is strengthened by a dread of punishment which is always effective. The prince must nonetheless make himself feared in such a way that, if he is not loved, at least he escapes being hated. For fear is quite compatible with an absence of hatred; and the prince can always avoid hatred if he abstains from the property of his subjects and citizens and from their women[3] . . . So, on this question of being loved or feared, I conclude that since some men love as they please but fear when the prince pleases, a wise prince should rely on what he controls, not on what he cannot control. He must only endeavor, as I said, to escape being hated.[4]

. . .

Nonetheless, so as not to rule out our free will, I believe that it is probably true that fortune is the arbiter of half the things we do, leaving the other half or so to be controlled by ourselves.[5]

THE PRINCE: THEMES AND QUESTIONS

The requirements of leadership

Roughly half-way through *The Prince*, Machiavelli reminds readers of his purpose: "[s]ince my intention is to say something that will prove of practical use to the inquirer, I have thought it proper to represent things as they are in real truth, rather than as they are imagined."[6] Machiavelli prided himself on being willing to tell the "real truth" about leadership, and for the five hundred years since the publication of *The Prince* many readers have agreed, finding it one of the most clear-eyed and realistic descriptions of the requirements of leadership ever written. Our goal in analyzing this text, that is perhaps familiar to you, is to create a basis for understanding the nature of the leader's role and what it requires – a foundation you will build on to construct your view of what *moral leadership* consists in.

Exercising authority

Power is one of the defining attributes of leadership, and Machiavelli concerns himself with all aspects of a prince's power over a state – laying out in the first half of his treatise the different conditions under which this power is obtained, and then providing advice, some of it quite surprising, for how to maintain authority thereafter. Machiavelli's dispassionate approach will allow us to appreciate the context of leadership, the determination of ends and means that leaders must make, and to press the moral questions that come with a leader's exercise of power: What is permissible? What is required? What, if anything, is prohibited? You may also want to consider the goals of Machiavelli's prince and the kind of state that a prince, following Machiavelli's advice, would create.

We will also want to examine Machiavelli's advice on the relationship between leaders and their followers. Machiavelli describes the members of the state, and then lays out suggestions for what leaders can or should do to earn the support of those over whom they hold power. Machiavelli describes a prince with nearly absolute authority, so we will want to question why such support is even needed in Machiavelli's view.

Fundamental assumptions

Machiavelli asserts that *The Prince* is "a representation of things as they are." The world he describes is surprisingly contemporary; and, while his guidance and promises of success are based on historical examples, he extracts from these a set of assumptions that you will want to analyze, particularly his assumptions about "man" and human nature. And, since the purpose of *The Prince* is actionable instruction, you will want to ask how central are these assumptions to the successful adoption of his recommended strategies and tactics?

ASSIGNMENT

READING: *The Prince*, by Niccolò Machiavelli.

In Chapters I–XIV, the first half of *The Prince*, Machiavelli describes the various circumstances by which a Prince can obtain power over a state; he offers strategies tailored to each situation, as well as advice on how to manage the martial resources necessary to the task of securing power. In Chapters XV–XXVI, the book's second half, Machiavelli offers more general advice focused on the Prince's behavior toward his subjects and allies.

1   As you read *The Prince*, ask yourself what kind of leadership Machiavelli is depicting.

2   What lessons can be learned from the first half of the book? Are these useful to leaders today?

3   What are the most important lessons from the book's second half?

4   This book has variously been called a "handbook for thugs" and a "justification for public morality." What do you think?

5   What is the relevance of this book to the exercise of moral leadership?

THE PRINCE: BACKGROUND

The Prince has been read, studied, condemned, and admired for hundreds of years. The following background materials will provide context on the times Machiavelli lived in and on the nature of the political systems – and conflicts – that stimulated his handbook. Machiavelli was a player himself – not a fully disinterested observer – so a brief review of his life will offer additional insight into his motives and goals. The materials also examine the long and rich legacy and many applications that Machiavelli's ideas have been put to, since few texts have had as much influence on as wide a range of subjects as *The Prince*.

Culture and politics in Renaissance Europe

The Renaissance

What today is referred to as the Renaissance – a "revival" and "rediscovery" of Classical (Greek and Roman) learning in Europe during the fifteenth and sixteenth centuries – was not so characterized at the time. In fact, it was not even considered a revival as much as it was experienced as a period of invention and exploration into much that was new. This included, for instance, expeditions into the New World, experimentation in science and artistic expression (as in the burgeoning use of perspective in painting), and a "Europeanized" scholarly zeal engendered by the printing press, which allowed for a rapid dissemination of information. Alongside these developments came new intellectual movements that connected the educated urban elite across Europe. Humanism, for example, was aimed at reforming and rationalizing the Church, widening religious participation and, more broadly, ending the abuses of seemingly archaic medieval institutions.[7] Thomas More's *Utopia*, a scathing critique of contemporary society's rulers, was a model for weaving together these new intellectual strands.

City-states in Italy

Over the course of several centuries, the regions of northern Italy increasingly fractured into competing autonomous city-states such as Florence, Venice, Genoa, and Milan. A long-lasting rivalry over the region between the Holy Roman Empire (based in what is now Germany) and the papacy in Rome allowed local nobilities, as well as the increasingly enriched urban merchant classes that engaged in widespread and highly lucrative trade, to play one side against the other, and thus carve out autonomous spheres centered on wealthy commercial cities. Politically, these city-states were often republics (as Machiavelli defined them), although, with limited citizen participation even in the most "democratic" of times, political life was in practice commonly controlled by oligarchies, family rule, or single individuals (princes).

Politics and diplomacy were fraught with dangers both within city-states and between them. Not only were commercial interests constantly being challenged, but the very autonomy of these city-states often seemed precarious. Politics was consequently defined by diplomatic cunning, intrigue, unstable alliances, and mutual suspicion, as well as by covert assassinations and war. This period, then, one of great cultural and scientific advances, was also "a time of pillage, rapine and turmoil. Italy became a playground for petty tyrants and oligarchs, rulers with questionable titles to legitimacy."[8] In a world where power constantly shifted, Machiavelli's topic in *The Prince* was particularly appropriate to local politics.

Politics in Florence

Niccolò Machiavelli, born in 1469 in Florence, was raised in a city-state that encapsulated all these developments. Florence was an undisputed center of the new artistic currents, which were encouraged by the Medici family – the foremost political and financial elite of Florence throughout much of the fifteenth century. Florence was the first European city to have a public secular library; and, indeed, intellectuals schooled in classical learning were a part of the urban elite, and were closely associated with the local civic government.[9]

Florence was also a city in which the great tensions of the era were clearly manifested. Humanism and the new artistic developments, for example, did not go unchallenged, as the brief rule of Girolamo Savonarola (1494–1498), a Dominican priest known for public bonfires of "vanities" which included "pagan" books, clearly demonstrated.[10] The city-state also exhibited the geopolitical insecurities of the era, caught as it was between the emerging national powers of France and Spain and the armies of the Holy Roman Empire, and at the same time engaged in fierce competition with rival city-states. Internal instability was also endemic, with brief periods of "Republican" rule in which the Medici were temporarily forced out of power.

Niccolò Machiavelli: political and literary career

Political career

The intellectual, artistic, and political currents that affected Florence had a profound influence on Machiavelli's own life. In his career, Machiavelli was not exempt from the abiding power fluctuations that shook the city and Europe as a whole: A statesman and diplomat on behalf of the Republic after the exile of the Medici in 1494, the return of the Medici in 1512 spelled the end of his fourteen-year career in service to the state. Marked as a traitor for his service in the absence of the Medici, he was sent into virtual exile to his family's property outside Florence.

The Prince, written during this exile and dedicated to "The Magnificent Lorenzo de Medici," was, in fact, above all an attempt to regain favor with the Medici family. Courting the Medici ultimately paid dividends, especially after the death of Lorenzo in 1519. The Medici became Machiavelli's patrons, and while his employment in matters of state was limited (although not completely insignificant) he was granted access and favors, and given the funds with which to continue his literary career.

Political instability continued to plague Machiavelli, however. When the Medici were once again temporarily driven out in 1527 and the Republic restored, Machiavelli was denied any role in government owing to his connections to the Medici. He died soon after.

Literary career and conflicting roles

Besides *The Prince*, Machiavelli authored numerous other works, all influenced by – although not necessarily in accordance with – the intellectual currents of the time. These works included the important *Discourses on Livy*, written also in his period of exile. Vastly different from the straightforward-sounding advice of *The Prince*, the *Discourses* were a complex defense of Republican government and guidelines as to how best to safeguard it. Under the patronage of the Medici, Machiavelli composed the *Florentine Histories*, commissioned by the Pope (a Medici) and completed in 1525; even while he was a statesman for the Republic he had authored several poems, many on the subject of the history of Florence. He also penned three plays over the course of his lifetime.

With patronage from the Medici as well as from religious personalities including the Pope, Machiavelli, as a "freelancer," was often placed in contradictory roles.

His *Discourses*, for instance, contained enigmatic critiques of the Church, as well as of Christianity as a whole; not surprisingly, these critiques were toned down in his *Florentine Histories*, which were presented to the Pope. And yet, in a work commissioned by the Pope on the politics of Florence, Machiavelli criticized the Medici, and even went so far as to advocate the restoration of the Republic.[11]

The legacy of Machiavelli and "Machiavellianism"

Currents in political science and philosophy

Machiavelli's reputation spread rapidly after his death, and reactions – mostly denunciations – were quick in coming. A Catholic cardinal called *The Prince* a diabolical handbook for sinners, and the work was opposed by Protestant theologians as well. In Elizabethan England, allusions to Machiavelli were used to elicit images of cunning and cruelty. Indeed, even Shakespeare had a villain in *Henry VI, Part 3* describe himself as surpassing "murtherous Machevil."[12]

Political philosophers, on the other hand, have seen more in Machiavelli than just criminal advice, especially when his other works have been taken into account and applied to current contexts. In the eighteenth century, for instance, Jean-Jacques Rousseau, the great French political thinker and author of *The Social Contract*, argued that Machiavelli was a misunderstood Republican, a good citizen attempting to expose the dangers and duplicity of despotism. In the same century, by contrast, the German nationalist thinker Johann von Herder saw in Machiavelli a cunning diplomat devoted to Italian patriotism.[13] Subsequently, during the movement for Italian unity in the nineteenth century, Machiavelli was regarded as a home-grown Italian hero.

The twentieth century has seen even more variation in interpreting Machiavelli. Some consider him to have been the "Galileo of Politics"; others deem him to be the father of political science – the first author to study politics in a detached and "scientific" manner.[14] Machiavelli's passionate defense of Republican values has even acquired Marxist overtones. According to the Italian communist writer Antonio Gramsci, Machiavelli was an advocate of the creative use of politics for engendering change.[15] During the Cold War, Machiavelli was rediscovered less for his ideology and morality than for his strategic advice, elevated alongside other thinkers such as Carl von Clausewitz and Sun Tzu.[16]

This controversy over Machiavelli's political intentions, morality, and ethics has never truly abated. Indeed, the discussion has been intensified by thinkers such as Isaiah Berlin who have written extensively on the topic. For Berlin, Machiavelli's greatest achievement was his introduction of an alternative system of morality:

> By breaking the original unity [between "public" and "private" morality]
> he helped to cause men to become aware of the necessity of making
> agonizing choices between incompatible alternatives, incompatible in
> practice or, worse still, for logical reasons, in public and private life (for
> the two could not, it became obvious, be genuinely kept distinct). His

achievement is of the first order, if only because the dilemma has never given men peace since it came to light . . . Men had, no doubt, in practice, often enough experienced the conflict that Machiavelli made explicit. He converted its expression from a paradox into something approaching a commonplace.[17]

"Machiavellianism"

Although the multiplicity of conclusions political scientists have held about Machiavelli suggests we should be wary of oversimplifying him and his philosophy, a highly caricaturized view of Machiavelli, largely based on *The Prince*, continues to exist outside political science – not only in popular culture, but also in other academic disciplines.

In history and literature, for instance, characters, historical figures, and ideas are often labeled "Machiavellian" by dint of their seemingly remorseless pragmatism. In business settings, "Machiavellian" approaches to marketing, sales, and management are routinely explored.[18] Meanwhile, the field of psychology has virtually institutionalized "Machiavellian" approaches in its discipline through the use of the "Mach" – a unit of measurement used to quantify and compare the sociopolitical intelligence and coercive abilities inherent in personalities.[19] For example, one psychology article is entitled "The Relationship between Social Power and Machiavellianism, Need for Control, Gender, and Locus-of-Control."[20] In addition, of particular importance to overzealous students everywhere, is another psychology article entitled "On the Relationship between Machiavellianism and Anxiety among Italian Undergraduates."[21]

BACKGROUND BIBLIOGRAPHY AND FURTHER READING

Berlin, Isaiah, "The Question of Machiavelli," *The New York Review of Books*, 1971, vol. 17, no. 7, online: http://www.nybooks.com/articles/10391 (accessed December 8, 2006).
  Investigates the ethical concerns raised by *The Prince*, and presents an interpretation of Machiavelli's lasting legacy in the realm of ethics and morality.

Femia, Joseph. *Machiavelli Revisited*, Cardiff: University of Wales Press, 2004.
  Places Machiavelli in both an intellectual and a political context, examines specific elements of his thought and philosophy, and analyzes his legacy and subsequent interpretations.

Fiore, Silvia. *Niccolò Machiavelli: An Annotated Bibliography of Modern Criticism and Scholarship*, New York: Greenwood Press, 1990.
  Summarizes twentieth-century English and non-English scholarly works relevant to Machiavelli studies. Helpful for understanding the wide range of Machiavelli "uses."

Grafton, Anthony. "Introduction" in *The Prince*, New York/London: Penguin Books, 1999, pp. xiii–xxviii.
  Presents an overview of academic scholarship on *The Prince* and also locates Machiavelli and *The Prince* in historical context.

Kocis, Robert. *Machiavelli Redeemed: Retrieving His Humanist Perspectives on Equality, Power and Glory*, Bethlehem, PA: Lehigh University Press, 1998.

A thorough examination of Machiavelli's thought in an intellectual-historical context. Provides a useful timeline of events related to Machiavelli's political and literary career.

Paret, Peter (ed.), *The Making of Modern Strategy: From Machiavelli to the Nuclear Age*, Princeton, NJ: Princeton University Press, 1986.

A telling example of how Machiavelli's strategic concerns have proven timeless.

NICCOLÒ MACHIAVELLI: BIOGRAPHY

Niccolò Machiavelli was born in Florence in 1469 into an aristocratic, although not especially wealthy, family. Although little is known about the first half of his life, his writings indicate that he had been thoroughly educated in the classics, being especially well versed in classical works of history.

Much more is known about Machiavelli after the forced exile of the Medici, the ruling family of Florence, in 1494. In 1498 he was appointed chancellor and secretary of the second chancellery of the Florentine Republic: "His duties consisted chiefly of executing the policy decisions of others, carrying on diplomatic correspondence, digesting and composing reports, and compiling minutes; he also undertook some twenty-three missions to foreign states,"[22] on which he was able to observe some of the leading figures in Italian politics.[23] Additionally, he spearheaded the organization of a citizen militia in order to help protect Florence from the many threats to the city's security.

Machiavelli held that position until 1512, when the return of the Medici to power not only put a temporary end to his political career, but also cast him under suspicion as a conspirator against the Medici family; he was forced to endure imprisonment, torture, and exile to his family's villa outside Florence.

With his political career on hold, he turned to writing, composing the *Discourses on Livy*, a defense of Republican government with examples from Roman history. It is likely that he interrupted that project in order to author his best-known work, *The Prince*, which, dedicated to "The Magnificent Lorenzo de Medici," was an attempt to win favor with the reinstated Medici family.

The Medici eventually provided Machiavelli with patronage, allowing him to be involved in matters of state, including inspecting Florence's fortification and embarking on minor diplomatic missions. His literary endeavors during this period included his well-known work, *The Art of War*, three plays including the comedy *The Mandrake,* and a history of Florence, which was commissioned by the Pope (who was also a Medici). In the words of Sebastian de Grazia, author of a Pulitzer prize-winning biography of Machiavelli, "depending usually on [his] particular responsibilities or on the subject he is dealing with or on the genre he is writing in," Machiavelli could be viewed as "an author, as Florentine Secretary, citizen, envoy, poet, playwright, military theorist, sermonizer, jurist, counselor, historian, political and moral philosopher."[24]

In 1527, the last year of his life, the Medici were again deposed and the "Republic" restored, and Machiavelli once again fell out of favor with the rulers of Florence. He died only a short time later, reviled by many contemporaries as a promoter of immorality,[25] although, in time, he would be accepted into the pantheon of the greatest Western political thinkers.

AUTHOR BIBLIOGRAPHY

De Grazia, Sebastian. *Machiavelli in Hell*, New York: Vintage Books 1994.

Femia, Joseph. *Machiavelli Revisited*, Cardiff: University of Wales Press, 2004.

"Niccolò Machiavelli," *Encyclopedia of World Biography*, Vol. 10, Farmington Hills, Mich.: Gale Research, 1998, pp. 97–99.

Wilson, Norman J. (ed.), "Niccolò Machiavelli," *World Eras*, Vol. 1, *European Renaissance and Reformation (1350–1600)*, Farmington Hills, Mich.: Gale Group, 2001, pp. 258–259.

NOTES

1   Niccolò Machiavelli, *The Prince*, New York/London: Penguin Books, 1999, p. 58.
2   Ibid., p. 57.
3   Ibid., p. 54.
4   Ibid., pp. 55–56.
5   Ibid. p. 79.
6   Ibid., p. 49.
7   Joseph Femia, *Machiavelli Revisited*, Cardiff: University of Wales Press, 2004, p. 22.
8   Ibid., p. 21.
9   Anthony Grafton, "Introduction," in *The Prince*, New York/London: Penguin Books, 1999, p. xv.
10 For timeline of events, see Robert Kocis, *Machiavelli Redeemed*, Bethlehem, PA: Lehigh University Press, 1998, p. 226.
11 "Machiavelli, Niccolò." *Encyclopedia Britannica Online*, 2005, online: http://www.search. eb.com/eb/article-242864 (accessed October 27, 2005).
12 Femia, op. cit., p. 7.
13 Ibid., p. 7.
14 Ibid., p. 8.
15 Ibid., p. 9.
16 Peter Paret (ed.), *The Making of Modern Strategy: From Machiavelli to the Nuclear Age*, Princeton, NJ: Princeton University Press, 1986.
17 Isaiah Berlin, "The Question of Machiavelli," *The New York Review of Books*, 1971, vol. 17, no. 7, online: http://www.nybooks.com/articles/10391 (accessed December 8, 2006).
18 Silvia Fiore, *Niccolò Machiavelli: An Annotated Bibliography of Modern Criticism and Scholarship*, New York: Greenwood Press, 1990, pp. 616, 620, for example.
19 Ibid. pp. 268, 270, for example.
20 See Ibid., p. 626.
21 See Ibid., p. 616.
22 "Niccolò Machiavelli," *Encyclopedia of World Biography*, Vol. 10, Farmington Hills, MI: Gale Research, 1998, pp. 97–99.
23 Norman J. Wilson (ed.), "Niccolò Machiavelli." *World Eras*, Vol. 1, *European Renaissance and Reformation (1350–1600)*, Farmington Hills, MI: Gale Group, 2001, pp. 258–259.
24 Sebastian de Grazia, *Machiavelli in Hell*, New York: Vintage Books 1994, p. 365.
25 Joseph Femia, *Machiavelli Revisited*, Cardiff: University of Wales Press, 2004, p. 7.

Chapter 15

The Secret Sharer

Earning legitimacy

IT MUST BE SAID, too, that I knew very little of my officers . . . But what I felt most was my being a stranger to the ship; and if all the truth must be told, I was somewhat of a stranger to myself. The youngest man on board, (barring the second mate), and untried as yet by a position of the fullest responsibility, I was willing to take the adequacy of others for granted. They had simply to be equal to their tasks; but I wondered how far I should turn out faithful to that equal conception of one's own personality every man sets up for himself secretly.[1]

. . .

"There's a ship over there," he murmured.

"Yes, I know. The *Sephora*. Did you know of us?"

"Hadn't the slightest idea. I am the mate of her—" He paused and corrected himself. "I should say I *was*."

"Aha!"—Something wrong?"

"Yes, very wrong indeed. I've killed a man."

"What do you mean? Just now?"

"No, on the passage. Weeks ago. Thirty-nine south. When I say a man—"

"Fit of temper," I suggested, confidently.

The shadowy, dark head, like mine, seemed to nod imperceptibly above the ghostly gray of my sleeping suit. It was, in the night, as though I had been faced by my own reflection in the depths of a somber and immense mirror.

"A pretty thing to have to own up to for a Conway boy," murmured my double, distinctly.

"You're a Conway boy?"

"I am," he said, as if startled. Then, slowly . . . "Perhaps you too—"[2]

. . .

> I walked to the break of the poop. On the overshadowed deck all hands stood by the forebraces waiting for my order. The stars ahead seemed to be gliding from right to left. And all was so still in the world that I heard the quiet remark "She's round," passed in a tone of intense relief between two seamen.
>
> . . .
>
> The foreyards ran round with a great noise, amidst cheery cries. And now the frightful whiskers made themselves heard giving various orders. Already the ship was drawing ahead. And I was alone with her. Nothing! No one in the world should stand now between us, throwing a shadow on the way of silent knowledge and mute affection, the perfect communion of a seaman with his first command.[3]

THE SECRET SHARER: THEMES AND QUESTIONS

The novel responsibility of command

All of us wonder what it feels like to take on a first leadership role. Even people who have done so find themselves reflecting on their initial experiences. So much is learned, and yet so much seems left to learn about how to present oneself: How to move, how to act, what to do, and what to leave for others to do. These questions are all the more compelling for people intent on demonstrating *moral leadership*. Not only must they master the requirements of leadership; they must exhibit other qualities as well.

The Secret Sharer tells the story of a young captain facing the "novel responsibility of command." Joseph Conrad writes from the inside out, narrating, in the captain's own voice, that young man's concerns and fears. For those of us who are leaders or who are aspiring to be leaders, the story is **a roadmap of the step change to a "position of highest authority."**[4]

As you read this powerful tale, you will want to consider what this step change consists of. **What challenges do new leaders face?** What should be done with the inevitable insecurities and questions that accompany the rise to leadership? What risks do new leaders encounter? How should they make decisions?

The captain's test

Conrad's protagonist faces more than the usual difficulties of a captain who is brand new to his role. On his very first night of command he is presented with a staggering challenge: A naked swimmer comes to the side of the ship while the captain is alone on watch. The swimmer, Leggatt, claims to have escaped from the ship *Sephora*, where he served as first mate. He fled to avoid being turned over to civil authorities and tried for the murder of a fellow seaman. Leggatt does not deny the murder; he justifies his act as necessary, part of the successful effort he undertook to keep the *Sephora* from going under during a ferocious storm. The captain must decide how to respond to Leggatt's sudden and clearly unexpected arrival.

Earning legitimacy

Conrad's captain-narrator arrives on the scene appointed by his ship's owners, and cloaked in the extensive powers given to maritime "masters," or captains, by the laws of the sea. *The Secret Sharer* allows us to consider how the captain interacts with his new crew while burdened with the mysterious appearance of Leggatt, of which he, alone, is aware. We can use the story to ask and to answer vital questions: **How does any leader create a positive relationship with "followers" – those whom he or she leads? What factors contribute to the perceptions that others hold? What are the consequences of success or failure – what is at stake?** *The Secret Sharer* allows us to examine the many ways in which *legitimacy* can be understood. We will also consider how this new captain weighs his various duties and obligations, the actions he chooses to take, and whether, in his view and our own, the captain has earned the right to lead.

ASSIGNMENT

READING: *The Secret Sharer,* by Joseph Conrad.

1 What leadership challenges did the captain face *before* Leggatt arrived at the ship?

2 Why did the captain hide Leggatt? Do you agree with his decision to do so?

3 Think about the captain's relationship with his crew. Has he been able to establish legitimacy? Why or why not?

4 What lessons do you take from this story about the "novel responsibility of command"?

THE SECRET SHARER: BACKGROUND

Joseph Conrad knew more about his subject than many other authors who have written about the sea; he served as a captain himself, and took over his first command under harrowing conditions. The following background materials provide details on Conrad's life, as well as valuable information about life at sea, in general and at the time of the story. Ship captains represent a particular form of leadership –

an extreme example, perhaps, owing to the distance of the ship and its crew from other sources of authority, and the reliance that all of those on board have on each other. You will also find historical background on the maritime trade and its importance to the British Empire, context that will help you evaluate the importance of the mission that the captain and his crew were on.

The British Empire and maritime trade, c.1850–1900

When Queen Victoria celebrated her Golden Jubilee in 1887, marking her fiftieth year on the throne, an increasingly industrialized Great Britain commanded a worldwide colonial empire on which, proverbially and literally, "the sun never set." She did not go unchallenged, however. India, after rebelling against the authority of the chartered British East India Company, was now a crown territory, with Victoria as its Empress. Britain also controlled other major trading centers in East Asia such as Hong Kong and Singapore, and operated less formal spheres of influence in China through "Treaty Ports" including Shanghai. During this period, British authority rapidly expanded elsewhere, for example in Australia and, along with other colonial powers, in Africa. Between 1884 and 1899 alone, nearly 4 million square miles of territory were added to Britain's possessions[5] – more than the entire United States including Alaska and Hawaii.

The British economy, as well as the economic rationale of Empire, was predicated on trade between Britain's industrial cities like Birmingham and Manchester, able to produce and export cheap manufactured goods, and the colonies, which not only served as a ready market for these exports, but also provided the food and raw materials needed to sustain British industry. With its head-start over other European countries in industrialization, this network of trade became immense.[6]

Sustaining the British Empire and its trade was based on control of the seas during this period of intense rivalry among colonial powers, and on maintaining Britain's position as the world's principal maritime nation. This did not require only naval prowess – although the British were indeed leaders in that regard thanks to the Royal Navy; it also assumed the ability to provide merchant ships in extraordinary numbers in order to be the foremost carrier of goods to and from Great Britain and among other countries and colonies as well.

The Merchant Marine

A nation's "Merchant Marine" is, and was, the total number of merchant ships – both publicly and privately owned – flying a country's flag. In Britain in the late nineteenth century the Royal Navy and Merchant Marine were distinct institutionally and in terms of personnel and ships, although seamen in the Merchant Marine could still join the Royal Navy. In times of war, merchant ships could be appropriated by the Crown and converted into warships.[7]

Table 15.1 *Tonnage (in millions) of merchant fleets*

	British Empire's sailing fleet	British Empire's steam fleet	Other countries'[1] total sailing fleet	Other countries' total steam fleet
1870	5.9	1.2	6.3	0.6
1880	5.5	2.9	6.4	1.0
1890	4.3	5.4	4.9	2.3

Source: From Ronald Hope, *A New History of British Shipping*, London: John Murray, 1990, p. 309

1 Includes the United States (ships engaged in foreign trade only), France, Germany, Norway, Sweden, Denmark, Italy, and Austria-Hungary.

Scale of operations

In terms of the tonnage (cargo capacity, in tons) of its Merchant Marine, the British Empire was immense (see Table 15.1); on a par with, and even at times surpassing, the total combined tonnage of other chief maritime *countries*. In 1870, the number of seamen serving in the Merchant Marine was estimated to be more than 200,000.[8]

Although maritime trade was in most cases facilitated by competing profit-seeking shipping companies and ship owners, the Merchant Marine as a whole was valued and prided for its sheer scale, and for its importance to the functioning of the British economy and Empire. A British writer in 1900 expressed the feeling that:

> It is impossible to arrive at any other conclusion than that the British Mercantile Marine is not only the greatest British industry, but that, for its overwhelming importance and far-reaching effect upon mankind, it is the most stupendous monument of human energy and enterprise that the world has ever seen.[9]

Steam and sail

Britain's merchant fleet, comprised almost solely of sailing vessels before the steam engine was introduced to shipping in 1807, paved the way for important sailing innovations. Sailing vessels remained dominant until the last decades of the nineteenth century, when steam ships – which had an estimated three times the lifting power of sailing ships, and which also proved safer and more seaworthy[10] – began to gain ground, and eventually took over as the primary mode of maritime transport. Sailing ships nonetheless remained important, and continued to carry bulky commodities in expanding trades, such as iron, coal, rice, grain, and wool.[11]

Aboard the merchant ships

Sailors in the Merchant Marine commonly worked under hazardous conditions for extended periods – journeys were slow, and to the Far East could easily last longer than a year. Loading and unloading cargo in itself could take weeks, even months.

141

In addition to the thousands of sailors – 2,259 in 1865 alone – who died of diseases, including cholera, dysentery, and yellow fever, 3,000 seamen a year on average drowned or died in accidents between 1872 and 1884.[12] Indeed, in 1883 Joseph Conrad was shipwrecked when the merchant sailing ship on which he was serving, the *Palestine*, caught fire in the middle of the Indian Ocean and quickly became "nothing but a furnace."[13]

Especially on sailing ships, the risk to sailors was great, and became more so as competition forced ship owners to reduce the number of crew; although ship owners were amassing personal fortunes, very little was spent on the welfare or training of the sailors.[14] A crewman from the period described the experience on board a sailing ship as follows:

> The higher up one travels, the ladder narrows and becomes almost perpendicular. Envisage the conditions on a dark night, the wind blowing, the rain driving. And when one finally reaches the yard one finds a great sail thrashing and ballooning over the spar, threatening to knock you off.[15]

According to an official report that examined shipwrecks between 1856 and 1872, whereas 30 percent of shipwrecks in this period occurred owing to weather or other uncontrollable forces, 65 percent of ship losses were attributed to incompetence, ignorance, or drunkenness among the sailors.[16] Regarding the quality of the sailors, one ship owner testified that many firms "are compelled to send their ships into the river and lie at anchor for twenty-four hours to let the crews become sober."[17]

"Masters" of merchant ships

Typical career

Officially, the title of "captain" was reserved for commanders of Royal Navy vessels, and therefore commanders of merchant ships were referred to as "masters." A seaman could rise to the position of master either through nautical training colleges such as the HMS *Conway* or through an extended apprenticeship, both of which would allow him eventually to become licensed by the Board of Trade – the governmental agency with chief control over maritime affairs[18] – as an officer.

Once hired by a shipping firm or a ship owner, the officer would likely start as a second mate, the little-respected assistant of the chief mate and "everybody's dog."[19] Once he graduated to chief mate, his responsibilities on a sailing ship would include day-to-day management of the ship's operations, specifically its sails: "No loose ends, frayed seizings, or chafed running gear . . . must be neglected, since such neglect may be fatal, or in any case must be expensive."[20] Once in a position of chief mate – or even, in some instances, while still second mate – he could be promoted to a master after receiving another license from the Board of Trade based on references from his superiors that attested to his skill and experience.[21]

Qualified sailors who sought opportunities with shipping firms or ship owners as officers or masters were often hard-pressed to find positions, and were lucky if they did. Joseph Conrad, for example, after a year of unsuccessfully seeking a position as a master (he had previously been a chief mate, but was qualified as a master), was unexpectedly entrusted with the command of a ship in Singapore in 1888 after its captain had suddenly died.[22]

Once hired by shipping firms or ship owners, masters and officers frequently stayed with a ship for several long voyages.[23] Crews, meanwhile, tended to be far more transient.

Responsibilities and necessary qualities

The overarching duty of a master was safely and effectively to utilize his ship in trading on behalf of the shipping firm or ship owner. He represented not only the owners of the ship, but the owners of the cargo as well. Ultimate responsibility for the fate of the ship and its cargo fell to him, as did the responsibility for paying the crew and keeping accounts.

Except in perilous circumstances when his experience and skill were directly needed, the master generally did not manage the day-to-day operations of the ship, a responsibility which fell to the chief mate. Nonetheless, he was expected, above all else, to be concerned with the ship's and the crew's welfare. "The ideal relationship between master and [chief] mate is where the master, in consultation with the mate, keeps in touch with everything that is going on, never interfering in public with the everyday work of the ship."[24]

When Conrad took his first command, he was surprised to find that his predecessor had been a recluse in his cabin, indifferent to the crew, unwilling to keep accounts, and had not even kept the ship stocked with quinine – an especially taxing oversight that plagued Conrad when his crew began falling ill with fever. "The new captain must have been profoundly shocked by his predecessor's betrayal of the principles and long traditions of the community of ship captains into which he himself had just been initiated."[25]

Besides having the skills and responsibilities necessary to command a ship, the master of a sailing ship also needed to be an accomplished sailor, able to navigate precisely towards a destination while at the same time chasing even the slightest breezes that might propel the ship forward. Detailed and first-hand knowledge of winds, geography, nautical astronomy and sailing techniques was therefore essential, especially in maintaining the trust of the officers and crew.[26] The Board of Trade only allowed those masters who had first-class qualifications – the most advanced technical knowledge and abilities – to command ships that crossed the equator, which included voyages to the Far East.[27]

In addition, the master's perceived courage and poise were especially important in maintaining discipline, as suggested by the following statement about a disgruntled crew:

A more abject specimen of a coward I never saw. All hands noted [the master's] behaviour, and from that day forward he was treated with utter contempt. His authority was a thing of naught . . . At last the men refused

143

to obey a most necessary order, simply because it necessitated work in their watch below . . . When we arrived in Calcutta he had them up before the shipping-master for punishment, and that worthy fined them two days' pay, at which they laughed hugely.[28]

Discipline could not be easily maintained with force alone, since the law, to which officers and masters were bound, would not always be on the master's side; an 1873 law took away the power of a master to punish a sailor for anything less than outright mutiny.[29] In one instance, a London court in 1876 gave a light sentence to a sailor who had been put in irons for assaulting the ship's chief mate and refusing duty, while the ship's master was imprisoned for twenty-one days for having used the irons on the sailor.[30] "If the master or officers, worried beyond endurance, take the law into their own hands, their punishment and subsequent ruin is almost certain to ensue promptly."[31]

BACKGROUND BIBLIOGRAPHY AND FURTHER READING

Bullen, Frank. *The Men of the Merchant Marine,* New York: Frederick Stokes Company, 1900.

> Written by a former Merchant Marine officer, this is a vivid description of the ships, institutions and personnel of the Merchant Marine, as well as a first-hand recollection of life on board.

Burgess, C. F. *The Fellowship of the Craft: Conrad on Ships and Seaman and the Sea,* Port Washington, NY: National University Publications, 1976.

> A work of literary criticism incorporating all of Conrad's works. Important for understanding Conrad's view of the sea and how he incorporated his experiences into his literary works.

Course, A. G. *The Merchant Navy: A Social History,* London: Frederick Muller Ltd, 1963.

> Provides the history of the Merchant Marine. Especially useful for understanding the plight of common sailors, and the laws and regulations which were instituted in order to protect them. See in particular Chapters 7 and 8.

Hope, Ronald. *A New History of British Shipping,* London: John Murray, 1990.

> Provides historical context, as well as a useful depiction of the operations of the Merchant Marine during this period. See especially Chapter 17.

Jean-Aubry, Gerard. *The Sea Dreamer: A Definitive Biography of Joseph Conrad,* New York: Doubleday, 1957.

> An excellent biography of Joseph Conrad, with a special focus on his life at sea.

Moyse-Bartlett, H. *A History of the Merchant Navy,* London: George G. Harrap, 1937.

> Traces the British Merchant Marine through history. Especially useful for understanding the laws and regulations under which the Merchant Marine operated.

JOSEPH CONRAD: BIOGRAPHY

Józef Teodor Konrad Korzeniowski was born in 1857 into a Polish family in what was then considered to be part of Russian-occupied Poland. Both of Conrad's parents hailed from families that were active in the Polish resistance movement against Russian occupation, and his parents' continuing activities in the movement led to the family's forced exile into Russia and later into Ukraine. Conrad's mother died in exile when he was only five, and his father later died of illness, exacerbated by depression, not long after.[32]

When he was twelve, Conrad was placed in the care of his wealthy uncle, a lawyer, who sent Conrad to school in Cracow and later Switzerland. In search of adventure, however, Conrad joined the French merchant service in the southern French city of Marseilles in 1874 as an apprentice, and he sailed on several voyages. While in Marseilles, Conrad was injured, and his biographers have disagreed as to whether this was in a duel or, as he seems to indicate in a private letter, a failed suicide attempt.

In 1878 he landed in England, where he remained, despite speaking only a few words of English at first. He spent sixteen years in the British Merchant Marine, where his fellow sailors nicknamed him "Polish Joe." His journeys took him to, among other places, Australia, India, Singapore, Java, and Borneo.[33] He quickly attained the qualifications to be promoted to an officer, and became a naturalized British subject in 1886. In 1888 he unexpectedly received his first command of a ship in the Far East.[34]

In the following year Conrad set out to the Belgian-ruled Congo in command of a Belgian steam ship, a traumatic experience on which he based his most widely known work, *The Heart of Darkness*. He later wrote of colonialism in Africa that it was "the vilest scramble for loot that ever disfigured the history of human consciousness and geographical exploration."[35] His journey into the Congo wrecked his health, and ended his career as a sea-farer.

Conrad lived the remainder of his life in poor health in southeastern England, where he married, raised two sons, and dedicated himself to literary endeavors in the English language. His first novel, *Almayer's Folly: The Story of an Eastern River*, was published in 1895. Over the course of his career, Conrad would author more than a dozen novels, twenty-nine short stories, two collections of essays, two memoirs, and three plays.[36] The works he produced in the first half of his literary career, which included *The Heart of Darkness* (1899), were generally autobiographical in nature, and earned him a reputation as a teller of great sea stories. His later works capitalized on this reputation, and dealt with more political themes.

By the 1920s, Conrad had become a widely acclaimed author whose works continue to enthrall readers today. Indeed, "heart of darkness" has entered the language as a metaphor for all that he intended it to signify. Also, thanks to his American publisher, Conrad finally became financially secure. In 1923 he visited the United States to great acclaim. Despite such success, however, he reportedly said, "I'd rather dream a novel than write it, for the dream of the work is always much more lovely than the reality in print."[37] Conrad died in 1924.

AUTHOR BIBLIOGRAPHY

Jean-Aubry, Gerard. *The Sea Dreamer: A Definitive Biography of Joseph Conrad*, New York: Doubleday, 1957.

"Joseph Conrad," *Contemporary Authors Online*, Farmington Hills, MI: Thomson Gale, 2006.

"Joseph Conrad," *Encyclopedia of World Biography*, Vol. 4, Farmington Hills, MI: Gale Research, 1998, pp. 205–207.

NOTES

1   Joseph Conrad, *The Secret Sharer*, New York: Dover, 1993, p. 84.
2   Ibid., pp88–89.
3   Ibid., p. 113.
4   Ibid., p. 84.
5   Ronald Hope, *A New History of British Shipping*, London: John Murray, 1990, p. 309.
6   In the words of one historian: "Never before and never since has one country so dominated the world economy." See ibid., p. 306.
7   H. Moyse-Bartlett, *A History of the Merchant Navy*, London: George G. Harrap, 1937, pp. 271–273.
8   Hope, op. cit., p. 321.
9   Frank Bullen, *The Men of the Merchant Marine*, New York: Frederick Stokes Company, 1900, p. 1.
10 Hope, op. cit., pp. 307, 320.
11 Ibid., p. 310.
12 Ibid., p. 320.
13 Gerard Jean-Aubry, *The Sea Dreamer: A Definitive Biography of Joseph Conrad*, New York: Doubleday, 1957, p. 97.
14 Hope, op. cit., p. 325.
15 Ibid., p. 323.
16 Ibid., p. 320.
17 Ibid., p. 323.
18 Moyse-Bartlett, op. cit., p. 267.
19 Bullen, op. cit., p. 130.
20 Ibid., pp. 92–93.
21 Ibid., pp. 4–9.
22 Jean-Aubry, op. cit., p. 130.
23 Bullen, op. cit., p. 9.
24 Ibid., p. 93.
25 Jean-Aubry, op. cit., p. 132.
26 Bullen, op. cit., p. 27.
27 A. G. Course, *The Merchant Navy: A Social History*, London: Frederick Muller Ltd, 1963, p. 211.
28 Bullen, op. cit., p. 39.
29 Course, op. cit., p. 235. Also in the interest of sailors' safety, ship owners were bound by law never to overload ships or engage in similar practices which might endanger the ship and the crew.

30 Ibid., p. 236.
31 Bullen, op. cit., p. 48.
32 "Joseph Conrad," *Contemporary Authors Online*, Farmington Hills, MI: Thomson Gale, 2006.
33 "Joseph Conrad," *Encyclopedia of World Biography*, Vol. 4, Farmington Hills, MI: Gale Research, 1998, pp. 205–207.
34 Jean-Aubry, op. cit., p. 130.
35 Quoted in *Contemporary Authors Online*, op. cit.
36 Ibid.
37 Ibid.

Chapter 16

Truman and the Bomb

Balancing benefits and harms

THE MORAL REALITY OF WAR is divided into two parts. War is always judged twice, first, with reference to the reasons states have for fighting, second, with reference to the means they adopt.[1]

. . .

Mr. Tanimoto found about twenty men and women on the sandspit. He drove the boat onto the bank and urged them to get aboard. They did not move and he realized that they were too weak to lift themselves. He reached down and took a woman by the hands, but her skin slipped off in huge, glovelike pieces. He was so sickened that he had to sit down for a moment. Then he got out of the water and, though a small man, lifted several of the men and women, who were naked, into his boat . . . On the other side, at a higher spit, he lifted the slimy living bodies out and carried them up the slope away from the tide. He had to keep consciously repeating to himself, "These are human beings".[2]

. . .

Henry L. Stimson, Secretary of War
Memorandum for the President, July 2, 1945, on proposed program for Japan:
. . . A question then comes: Is there any alternative to such a forceful occupation of Japan which will secure for us the equivalent of an unconditional surrender of her forces and a permanent destruction of her power again to strike an aggressive blow at the "peace of the Pacific"? I am inclined to think that there is enough such chance to make it well worthwhile our giving them a warning of what is to come and a definite opportunity to capitulate. As above suggested, it should be tried before the actual forceful occupation of the homeland islands is begun and furthermore the warning should be given in ample time to permit a national reaction to set in.[3]

. . .

> *President Harry. S. Truman*
> The final decision of where and when to use the atomic bomb was up to me. Let there be no mistake about it. I regarded the bomb as a military weapon and never had any doubt that it should be used. The top military advisers to the President recommended its use, and when I talked to Churchill he unhesitatingly told me that he favored the use of the atomic bomb if it might aid to end the war.
>
> In deciding to use the bomb I wanted to make sure that it would be used as a weapon of war in the manner prescribed by the laws of war. That meant I wanted it dropped on a military target. I had told Stimson that the bomb should be dropped as nearly as possibly [sic] upon a war production center of prime military importance.[4]

TRUMAN AND THE BOMB: THEMES AND QUESTIONS

Balancing benefits and harms

Leaders make decisions that have consequences ranging from local effects on a small number of people directly involved, to major impacts on large numbers – hundreds or thousands or even millions of individuals, depending on the leader's role. These decisions can cover a nearly endless variety of topics, from stem cell research, to global warming and climate change, to workplace practices at home or in countries far away, to intervention on political or humanitarian grounds, to global pandemics, to environmental concerns, to international security.

The consequences can be positive or negative for the people affected; in fact, in many situations leaders have to determine which individuals or groups will receive benefits and which will be harmed. Benefits and harms are themselves multi-dimensional, so the decision is usually not *whether* harm or benefit will result, but *how much benefit* and *how much harm* the leader is willing to confer and inflict to accomplish the goals he or she pursues.

The readings for this class bring us into one of the most difficult moral leadership choices of the twentieth century: The decision of US President Harry S. Truman to use the atomic bomb in 1945 in the Allies' war against Japan. Most of us will probably never face a situation quite like Truman's, but we can certainly learn from our analysis of it. It will enable us to evaluate how well Truman balanced the benefits and harms that resulted from his decision, and force us to clarify our assumptions about what does, and does not, constitute an act of moral leadership.

The leader as process designer

The class features two very different kinds of readings. The first is a compilation of readings, *Truman and the Bomb*, which combines excerpts from John Hersey's book *Hiroshima,* an account of the impact of the atomic bomb on that city, with a selection of historical and autobiographical accounts of the decision-making process that led to the use of the weapon. The *Hiroshima* excerpts begin and end the compilation, and provide graphic details that illustrate the human costs of the bomb, as well as statistical data on its effect. The historical and autobiographical writings provide a chronological review of the advice given to President Truman, the arguments his advisors mounted, opposing points of view, as well as Truman's own account of his decision.

While by no means exhaustive, the readings will allow us to enter into an analysis and judgment not just of Truman's decision but of the process he used to come to it, and the quality of the advice he was given. **Most of us think of leaders as sole decision-makers, but this reading lays out a vital theme for moral leadership: The leader as designer of the *process* through which decisions with moral and ethical stakes are made.**

Leadership as a rule-governed activity

The second reading is a series of excerpts from political scientist Michael Walzer's 1977 classic, *Just and Unjust Wars.* Written in response to the Vietnam War, Walzer's aim was to study war as a "rule-governed activity,"[5] through contemporary and historical examples and with reference to medieval and modern "just war" theory. His premise, central to the study of moral leadership, is: "**. . . war is the hardest place: If comprehensive and consistent moral judgments are possible there, they are possible everywhere.**"[6] This is the rationale for reading about Truman and the bomb, and we can use Walzer's framework to inform our evaluation of his decision.

Walzer lays out the two primary categories by which wars are judged.[7] The first is *jus ad bellum,* or justice *of* war, which is concerned with questions of ends: "[*j*]*us ad bellum* requires us to make judgments about [what constitutes] aggression and self-defense."[8] The second category is *jus in bello,* or justice *in* war, which is concerned with questions of means: "*jus in bello* [is] about the observance or violation of the customary and positive rules of engagement."[9]

Walzer uses historical examples to exemplify and analyze these principles; we will find that he has made his own assessment of Truman's decision along with other, possibly related decisions made by leaders during World War II. You may also find Walzer's book useful as an illustration of what it looks like to reason morally – to work through the meaning and application of principles, such as the positive rules of war, to specific situations.

TRUMAN AND THE BOMB: BACKGROUND

You will want to examine Truman's decision in light of its broader context, which consists of several related strands, described in the background materials that follow. The first strand is military and political, and includes information on World War II leading up to the time of Truman's 1945 decision, evolving standards

ASSIGNMENT

READINGS: *Truman and the Bomb,* found in Appendix 2 (pp. 213–229); *Just and Unjust Wars,* by Michael Walzer.

Just and Unjust Wars Assignment	*Pages*
Preface to the third edition (topic: Humanitarian Interventions)	xi–xvi
Chapter 2: "The Crime of War" (whole chapter)	21–33
Chapter 3: "The Rules of War" (whole chapter)	34–47
In Chapter 4: "Law and Order in International Society" – "The Legalist Paradigm" (excerpt)	61–63
Chapter 5: "Anticipations" (whole chapter)	74–85
In Chapter 8: "War's Means and the Importance of Fighting Well" – Introduction and "Utility and Proportionality" (excerpt)	127–133
In Chapter 9: "Noncombatant Immunity and Military Necessity" – "Double Effect"	151–159
Chapter 14: "Winning and Fighting Well" (whole chapter)	225–232
Chapter 16: "Supreme Emergency" (whole chapter)	251–268

1   Did Harry Truman demonstrate moral leadership in his decisions about the atomic bomb? Why? Why not? Please note that this question involves thinking about the decision-making process and the analysis of options that led up to Truman's decisions.

2   In considering the Walzer reading, do you think it is reasonable to think about war as a rule-governed activity? Why or why not?

for the conduct of war, and the progress of the war in the Far East. A second strand is information about the "atomic race" and the particulars of the Manhattan Project to develop military applications of the fission process in the United States and elsewhere. Third is a sense of Harry Truman himself – a brief review of his life and career.

Two world wars

World War I (1914–1918) was the first true instance of mass mechanized combat, in which stalemated trench warfare, poison gas, and disease, among other things, took the lives of an estimated 8.5 million soldiers throughout Europe. An estimated 13 million civilians died a war-related death.[10] So traumatic were the casualties and the daily killing that the war could only be rationalized as "The war to end all wars."

And yet World War II (1939–1945) surpassed World War I in numbers of dead, geographical scope, physical destruction, and horror. Whereas casualties in World War I had been primarily concentrated in Europe, and destruction was generally limited to battlefield zones, World War II saw heavy fighting both in Europe and in the Far East, and in both theaters the purposeful targeting of civilians and the destruction of civilian structures became regular occurrences.

Aerial bombing of cities was originally used both by Japan and Germany, the former using brutal force against cities in China, and the latter damaging or destroying nearly 30 percent of all homes in Great Britain and decimating entire sections of London, among numerous other cities across Europe.[11] Allied forces ultimately used similar methods against Germany and Japan, laying waste entire cities in an effort to cripple industry and production by targeting ("de-housing") workers.

In addition, racial motivations led not only to unconscionable atrocities such as the industrial murder of the Holocaust in Europe, but also to fierce "total war" in which the distinctions between military and civilian broke down. This was evident along Germany's eastern front with Russia, where fighting was especially fierce, and where the native populations, seen by Nazi ideology as inferior, continued to resist occupation. The residents of the besieged Russian city of Leningrad (St. Petersburg) were starved to death, and Hitler's plans for a conquered Moscow included liquidating the city. The Soviet Union sustained losses of around 20 million soldiers and civilians – nearly 10 percent of its entire population.

Estimates for the total number of war-related deaths range widely, from 35 million to 60 million,[12] although actual losses were probably at the higher end of this spectrum.

The war in the Far East

War had come to the Far East earlier than 1939, with Japan's invasion of Manchuria in 1931 and full-fledged hostilities flaring up in 1937. Although the Emperor was the sacred symbol of Japanese sovereignty, the Japanese government held power in practice, and was controlled by militarists who saw continuing territorial expansion as the key to Japan's future. The Japanese invasion of Indochina, its pact concluded with Nazi Germany and Fascist Italy, and its war in China led to a US embargo of Japan, including oil sales. With negotiations unworkable, and faced with a perceived stranglehold on resources, the Japanese government opted for war, and attacked Pearl Harbor, Hawaii, on December 7, 1941.[13]

The resulting war against the Allies was mainly fought in the Pacific, often in dense jungles where disease was as grave a danger to troops as was the enemy. The Far East rivaled the European theater in its horror and lack of restraint; Japanese treatment of American prisoners of war, for instance, was often cruel, as were the depictions of Japanese in the American press and the government's policy of forced detention of Japanese-American citizens.

Japanese soldiers earned a reputation for fighting to the death, and the phenomenon of the Kamikaze pilot – pilots trained to crash into naval ships – reinforced the notion that Japan would not surrender. Although it was clear quite early on that the Japanese could not turn the tide of the war, Japanese troops continued to fight and fiercely to resist every American advance, even after the defeat of Germany in Europe. In the American invasion of Okinawa, a Japanese "home island" (although geographically removed from the rest of the Japanese home islands), over 100,000 Japanese troops fought to the death, taking with them 12,000 American soldiers (a total of 41,700 were confirmed killed, injured, or missing[14]), and sinking 34 ships.

The Manhattan Project

Research on the atom was not originally focused on military applications, but was rather part of a broad scientific research effort on atomic structures and atomic reactions, which was ascendant in physics during the 1930s. Throughout that decade, scientists in Europe and America had been discovering and experimenting with the process of fission, i.e., the "shooting" of neutrons at an atom in order to split its nucleus and release its energy.[15] Once scientists discovered that, besides energy, fission also released stray neutrons, they began to explore the possibility of a controlled, self-sustaining chain reaction able to release even greater amounts of energy.

The Manhattan Project was begun when scientists – many of whom, like Albert Einstein, had fled the growing Nazi menace – petitioned President Roosevelt, Truman's predecessor, to fund research on the military applications of the fission process. Not only was such an application possible, they claimed, but the United States needed to realize and harness the power of the atom before Germany could. The project began in 1940 with a $6,000 governmental grant.

Once the United States was at war in December 1941, the project rapidly expanded in budget and scope: Nearly $2 billion would ultimately be spent on research and production by the time the atomic bomb was dropped on Hiroshima in 1945, a huge sum for the time. For purposes of both research and production, vast resources and production facilities were required across the country, and the US Army Corp of Engineers was assigned to the project.

Fissionable uranium had to be separated from regular uranium in a large and complex process that required massive amounts of electricity; after the process was discovered, this was done on a large tract of land in Tennessee, later known as Oak Ridge. Meanwhile, fissionable plutonium was researched and produced at University of Chicago laboratories, and large-scale production reactors were built in the state of Washington. Ultimately, in 1943 a laboratory was constructed at Las Alamos in New Mexico for developing and producing the actual weapon, a process that required overcoming numerous scientific hurdles.

The United States, with its immense home-front war mobilization, was well placed to command the resources necessary to spearhead this nation-wide process.

Niels Bohr, a Danish physicist working on the project, originally expressed his skepticism in claiming that the US would need to become one large factory in order to produce the bomb;[16] he later was fascinated that the US did just that. The United Kingdom, which had its own nuclear program, could not command these resources, and ultimately virtually merged its program and personnel with the Manhattan Project in 1943.

By July 1945, enough fissionable material had been produced, and the research on the bomb's construction was far enough advanced, for a bomb to be finally tested – a huge process in itself. The bomb was tested in New Mexico on a night that those living within 100 miles remember as having had two sunrises. The desert surface fused into a radioactive glass for hundreds of yards around the blast area.

The atomic race

The "atomic race" was, from the point of view of the Americans and the British, seen primarily as being fought against Nazi Germany. Germany was suspected of having nuclear ambitions, technical knowhow (the Nobel Prize-winning physicist Werner Heisenberg, for example, remained loyal to the Nazi regime), and even the means of eventually producing a bomb. Whether or not these fears of Germany's nuclear ambitions were justified – a question that still remains hotly debated[17] – suspicion of Germany's nuclear advances and capabilities remained high throughout the war. In fact, during the D-Day landings in June 1944[18] certain Allied officers carried geiger counters (radiation detection devices).[19] The atomic bomb, therefore, was meant to be used in the European theater against Germany, and it would have been were it not for Germany's surrender. In the words of a top scientist on the project, "We were motivated to produce the bomb because we feared the Germans would get ahead of us, and the only way to prevent them from dropping bombs on us was to have bombs in readiness ourselves."[20]

Japan, for its part, also had a nuclear program, although historians disagree about how advanced it was or how much the United States knew of it. It is generally agreed, though, that Japan lacked the extensive resources necessary to produce the weapon, especially after the near-leveling of its major cities in Allied bombing runs. Nonetheless, by 1945 the fear that nuclear material from recently surrendered Germany could find its way to Japan appeared to be justified; a captured German submarine en route to Japan carrying precisely this cargo – one-fifth the nuclear material needed to make an atomic bomb – proved that the threat did indeed exist.[21]

HARRY TRUMAN: BIOGRAPHY

Born in 1884 in Missouri to a modest farming family, Harry Truman managed his family farm after his father's death in 1914. In 1917, when he was 33 years old, America entered World War I, and Truman volunteered for service. Upon returning from Europe, army friends introduced him to the local Democratic party "boss" (the man who pulled all the strings in the local party branch), who allowed Truman to begin his political career as a county judge in 1924, where he gained a reputation for honesty. In 1934 the party boss convinced Truman to run for the US Senate – an election he won. In the Senate, Truman achieved national recognition for leading an inquiry into corruption and waste in the military.

In 1944, President Franklin Delano Roosevelt chose Truman as his vice-presidential running-mate in his bid for reelection to a fourth term. The bid was successful, and Truman became Vice-President in January 1945. That April, President Roosevelt died of a sudden hemorrhage, and Truman, who had no previous foreign-policy experience, was catapulted into the role of Commander-in-Chief of US armed forces in the largest war the country had ever fought.

As President (he ran for and was elected President in 1948), Truman led US forces to victory in World War II, helped establish the United Nations, spearheaded the reconstruction of Europe and faced off against an increasingly belligerent Soviet Union. In 1950 he committed US forces to Korea in the first military conflict of the Cold War. Truman did not seek another election bid in 1952. He retired to Missouri, and died in 1972.[22]

TIMELINE OF EVENTS

1884   Harry Truman born in Missouri

1914   World War I begins in Europe

1917   US enters World War I
         Truman fights in Europe

1918   World War I ends

1931   Japan occupies Manchuria

1932   Discovery of neutrons by James Chadwick in England initiates research into fission

1933   Franklin D. Roosevelt inaugurated as President

1934   Truman makes successful bid for US Senate

1937   Japan begins all-out war in China

1939   World War II begins in Europe with Germany's invasion of Poland
         Scientists including Albert Einstein petition President Roosevelt to fund atomic research for military use

1940   Germany occupies France, Belgium, Luxembourg and the Netherlands
         Air war over Britain and German bombing of British cities
         Military applications of atomic research first receive US government funding

1941   Germany declares war on the Soviet Union
         December 7 – Japanese attack Pearl Harbor, Hawaii; US joins World War II

1942	Battle of Midway in the Pacific begins to turn tide of war to US advantage
1943	Germany's loss to the Soviet Union in the Battle of Stalingrad marks the first major German defeat
	British scientists join US effort towards atomic bomb development
	Laboratory at Las Alamos constructed for purposes of building atomic bomb
1944	June 6 – "D-Day" landings of Allied forces in Normandy
1945	Truman becomes Vice-President to Roosevelt
	April 12 – Roosevelt dies, Truman becomes President.
	Battle of Okinawa begins in April
	May 8 – Germany surrenders
	July 16 – Atomic bomb tested at Alamogordo, New Mexico
	August 6 – Atomic bomb dropped on Hiroshima
	August 9 – Atomic bomb dropped on Nagasaki
	September 2 – Formal surrender of Japan

BACKGROUND BIBLIOGRAPHY AND FURTHER READING

Benke, Richard. "New Evidence Tracks Japan's Efforts to Create Atomic Bomb." *Associated Press*, June 1, 1997.
  A short account of different theories on Japan's progress towards an atomic bomb.

Iriye, Akira. *Origins of World War II in Asia and the Pacific*, London: Longman, 1987.
  Explains the Japanese motivations in fighting the United States during World War II.

Karlsch, Rainer. "New Light on Hitler's Bomb," *Physics World*, June 2005, online: http://physicsweb.org/articles/world/18/6/3 (accessed December 7, 2006).
  Presents the historical debate concerning Nazi Germany's atomic bomb project.

McCullough, David. *Truman*, New York: Simon & Schuster, 1992.
  A comprehensive biography of Harry Truman. See especially Chapters 9 and 10.

Rhodes, Richard. *The Making of the Atomic Bomb*, New York: Touchstone, 1986.
  Detailed but accessible information on the science behind the atomic bomb, profiles of the major scientists associated with the Manhattan Project, and a thorough account of the Manhattan Project itself.

Takaki, Ronald. *Hiroshima: Why America Dropped the Atomic Bomb*, New York: Little, Brown & Co., 1995.
  Provides detailed background on the state of the war in the Pacific in 1945 as well as background on the atomic bomb and the Manhattan Project.

The British Broadcasting Corporation (BBC) has excellent information concerning all aspects of World War II, online: http://www.bbc.co.uk/history/worldwars/wwtwo/ (accessed December 7, 2006).

MICHAEL WALZER: BIOGRAPHY

Michael Walzer was born in 1935 in New York City, and graduated from Brandeis University in 1956. After a year studying at Cambridge University on a Fulbright Scholarship, he began studying towards his doctorate at Harvard, completing his dissertation in 1961. He taught at Harvard and Princeton in the government and politics faculties before being inducted in 1980 as a Permanent Faculty Member into Princeton's Institute of Advanced Study as a professor of social science.[23]

A political scientist who has, in writing, expressed his views on politics, society and international affairs (he was a fierce critic of the Vietnam War), Walzer has written over a dozen books on topics ranging from political science to moral philosophy, as well as numerous scholarly articles.

Referring to *Just and Unjust Wars*, published in 1977, Walzer noted that:

> I wrote that book in the late 70s after a number of years of working in the movement against the Vietnam War. I was listening to myself making speeches, using all the words that political figures use in such moments, like "terror bombing," "intervention," "aggression" . . . and I began to think afterwards, as a political theorist, what do these words really mean? And do they hold together?[24]

The problem, he noted, was especially acute, since he had grown up during World War II, a war which he considered to be a good and just war.[25]

Just and Unjust Wars is one of the most widely read modern scholarly books on the ethics of war, and has been translated into several languages, including Hebrew, Spanish, Italian, German, and French. Recently, Walzer has published another book on the subject, representing a collection of published essays, entitled *Arguing About War* (2004).

AUTHOR BIBLIOGRAPHY

"Michael Walzer," *Contemporary Authors Online,* Farmington Hills, MI: Thomson Gale, 2006.

Walzer, Michael, Video interview, "The Roots of Terror," online: http://www. thirteen.org/bigideas/walzer.html (accessed December 7, 2006).

Walzer, Michael. "The Triumph of Just War Theory (and the Dangers of Success)," lecture given to US Naval Academy, and accompanying biography, online: http://www.usna.edu/Ethics/Publications/WalzerPgs 1–20_Final.pdf (accessed December 7, 2006).

NOTES

1   Michael Walzer, *Just and Unjust Wars: A Moral Argument with Historical Illustrations*, New York: Basic Books, 1977, 2000, p. 21.

2   John Hersey, *Hiroshima*, New York: Alfred A. Knopf, 1998, pp. 60–61.

3   Henry L. Stimson (1867–1950), Secretary of War under President Roosevelt from July 1940 to April 1945 and under President Truman from April to September 1945, was in overall charge of the United States atomic development program. This selection by Stimson is excerpted in *On Active Service in Peace and War*, by Henry L. Stimson and McGeorge Bundy, New York: Harper & Brothers, 1947, p. 621.

4   Harry S. Truman, *Memoirs by Harry S. Truman*, Vol. I, *Year of Decisions*, Garden City, NY: Doubleday, 1955, quoted with permission in Truman and the Bomb, op. cit., pp. 419–420.

5   Walzer, op. cit., p. 36.

6   Ibid., p. xxiii.

7   In *Arguing About War*, New Haven, Conn.: Yale University Press, 2004, Walzer establishes a third and new category for moral judgment of the conduct of war: *jus post bellum*, or justice *after* war. See, for example, p. xiii and pp. 18–22. Written in response to more recent conflicts than those covered in the 1977 *Just and Unjust Wars*, including the 2003 US war in Iraq, Walzer takes up the issue of "war's endings" and the criteria that should be used to judge the situation following the conclusion of hostilities, including the condition of the state and efforts that are made to restore it to a functioning level.

8   Walzer, 2000, op. cit., p. 21.

9   Ibid., p. 21.

10   "World War II," *Encyclopedia Britannica Online*, 2005, online: http://www.search.eb.com/eb/article-53608 (accessed November 15, 2005).

11   Ibid.

12   Ibid.

13   See Akira Iriye, *Origins of the Second World War in Asia and the Pacific*, London: Longman, 1987.

14   Ronald Takaki, *Hiroshima: Why America Dropped the Atomic Bomb*, New York: Little, Brown, & Co., 1995, p. 23.

15   Energy was released according to Einstein's famous proportion, $E=MC^2$.

16   Richard Rhodes, *The Making of the Atomic Bomb*, New York: Touchstone, 1986, p. 294.

17   Rainer Karlsch, "New Light on Hitler's Bomb," *Physics World*, June 2005, online: http://physicsweb.org/articles/world/18/6/3 (accessed December 7, 2006).

18   On June 6, 1944, Allied troops landed in Normandy amidst heavy resistance, opening another major front in the war. The invasion would eventually bring Allied troops to Berlin within a year.

19   Takaki, op. cit., p. 19.

20   Quoted in Ibid., p. 19.

21   Richard Benke, "New Evidence Tracks Japan's Efforts to Create Atomic Bomb," *Associated Press*, June 1 1997.

22   See David McCullough, *Truman*, New York: Simon & Schuster, 1992.

23   "Michael Walzer," *Contemporary Authors Online*, Farmington Hills, Mich.: Thomson Gale, 2006.

24   Michael Walzer, video interview, "The Roots of Terror," online: http://www.thirteen.org/bigideas/walzer.html (accessed December 7, 2006).

25   Ibid.

Chapter 17

Katharine Graham: *Personal History*

Taking a stand

Katharine Graham

Fritz was on the other end of the [phone] line. He told me about the argument between the lawyers and the editors over whether to publish the next day, outlined the reasoning on both sides, and concluded by saying, "I'm afraid you are going to have to decide."

I asked Fritz for his own view; since he was so editorial-minded and so decent, I knew I could trust his response. I was astonished when he said "I guess I wouldn't." I then asked for time to think it over, saying, "Can't we talk about this? Why do we have to make up our minds in such haste when the *Times* took three months to decide?"

At this point, Ben and the editors got on various extensions at Ben's house. I asked them what the big rush was, suggesting we at least think about this for a day. No, Ben said, it was important to keep up the momentum for publication and not to let a day intervene after getting the story. He also stressed that by this time the grapevine knew we had the Papers. Journalists inside and outside were watching us.

I could tell from the passion of the editors' views that we were in for big trouble on the editorial floor if we didn't publish. I . . . remember Phil Geyelin's response when I said that deciding to publish could destroy the paper. "Yes," he agreed, "but there's more than one way to destroy a newspaper."

. . .

I was extremely torn by Fritz's saying that he wouldn't publish . . . [A]fter all, he was the lawyer, not I. But I also heard *how* he said it: he didn't hammer at me, he didn't stress the issues related to going public, and he didn't say the obvious thing – that I would be risking the whole company on this decision. He simply said he guessed he wouldn't. I felt that, despite his stated opinion, he had somehow left the door open for me to decide on a different course. Frightened and tense, I took a big gulp and said, "Go ahead, go ahead, go ahead. Let's go. Let's publish." And I hung up.[1]

. . .

Ben Bradlee
We did know that the Pentagon Papers experience had forged forever between the Grahams and the newsroom a sense of confidence within the *Post*, a sense of mission and agreement on new goals, and how to attain them. And that may have been the greatest result of the publication of the Pentagon Papers.

After the Pentagon Papers, there would be no decision too difficult for us to overcome together.[2]

. . .

Katharine Graham
I have often been credited with courage for backing our editors in Watergate. The truth is that I never felt there was much choice. Courage applies when one has a choice.[3]

KATHARINE GRAHAM: PERSONAL HISTORY: THEMES AND QUESTIONS

Taking a stand

We like to think we would be willing to defend a cherished principle – to take a stand in defense of something we believe in deeply. And we eagerly read stories about people who distinguish themselves in this way; these men and women serve as potential role models, proof that such behavior is possible, not just in theory, but in the lives of human beings like the rest of us. At the same time, we ask ourselves some practical questions: **What kind of principles would inspire us sufficiently to have the fortitude to take a stand, particularly in the face of heavy odds against us? How long would we be willing or even able to persist?** And (perhaps most important for leaders): **What impact would our decisions have on those we are leading?**

Defending "the truth"

For *Washington Post* publisher Katharine Graham, the principle in question was *defending the truth* – no abstract or theoretical matter for a newspaper. We will examine the actions of Graham, who took such a stand, not once, but many times, in back-to-back challenges that have come to be known by their shorthand titles as the "Pentagon Papers" and "Watergate."

We will read an excerpt from Graham's autobiography, *Personal History,* covering the Pentagon Papers incident and the Watergate investigation, as well as a chapter on the Pentagon Papers from the autobiography of Ben Bradlee, the *Post*'s executive editor under Graham. These accounts overlap and will allow us to examine in detail Graham's rationale for her actions, and the impact of those actions on people inside and outside her organization.

Graham had to make weighty decisions; analyzing them will allow us to consider the multiple obligations that leaders hold, and to debate the priority that should be given to moral principles that at the same time embody an organization's mission *and* put the organization at risk, perhaps for its very existence. We will also be able to explore broader issues raised by these leadership challenges: the importance of truth in a democracy, and the boundaries of investigation, truth telling, and disclosure in times of war.

The process of decision-making

The materials for this class provide an almost minute-by-minute depiction of actual decisions being made; and, since we are reading autobiographical accounts (famous for their candor), we will be able to look at these situations through the eyes of the principals involved. We will see the ways that organizations *pull* leaders into decisions, an inescapable feature of their authority and role, and have the opportunity to assess the *process* of decision-making that Graham follows in two different situations.

The Pentagon Papers incident focuses on a single, specific decision of whether to publish articles that analyze classified documents describing the origins of the Vietnam conflict in the face of powerful government opposition and a court injunction against similar articles drawn from the same source at a rival paper. The Watergate investigation, on the other hand, will allow us to examine decision-making in an ambiguous and uncertain situation that stretched over years. Begun as a simple crime story about a break-in and burglary at the national headquarters of the Democratic Party (in the Watergate Hotel complex), the news coverage evolved, slowly, into a journalistic search for the parties responsible, leading to the executive branch of the US government, and eventually to the White House.

Graham's decisions thus allow us to examine leadership in one situation in which taking a stand is pivotal, and a second, in which staying the course and moral consistency are required; we will be able to evaluate how well she *supports* direction as well as how she sets it.

KATHARINE GRAHAM'S *PERSONAL HISTORY,* AND BEN BRADLEE'S, *A GOOD LIFE:* BACKGROUND

Graham's decisions were made against a backdrop of political unrest in the United States, described below in a review of the Cold War and the Vietnam War, a description of the legal concept of "prior restraint" of the press and its use by the

ASSIGNMENT

READINGS: *Personal History,* by Katharine Graham, pp. 433–508; Chapter 13 from *A Good Life,* by Ben Bradlee, found in Appendix 3 (pp. 230–239)

1   The Graham reading presents us with two distinct episodes: The Pentagon Papers and Watergate. In what ways are the challenges in these situations similar? In what ways are they different?

2   What is your assessment of the choices Graham makes in response to these two situations?

3   At the conclusion of the assigned Bradlee chapter, Ben Bradlee recounts: "*After the Pentagon Papers, there would be no decision too difficult for us to overcome together.*" What does he mean by that?

Nixon administration, and a timeline of Watergate events. You will also be able to learn more about the business environment in which newspapers operated during this period and the particular challenges of managing a newspaper in America's capital, since Graham's decisions were inextricably entwined with the fate of her paper, *The Washington Post.* Kay Graham was a pioneer – the first businesswoman to achieve a leadership role of prominence in the United States; so, in addition to a biographical note about her, you will find a brief examination of the status of women leaders at the time. Ben Bradlee, the *Post's* executive editor during this period, was, and is, a colorful figure and a revered journalist; he is also described in a biographical note.

The Cold War and Vietnam

The Cold War began after World War II (1939–1945) when the two emergent superpowers, the United States and the Soviet Union, quarreled over the political and economic future of the planet based on a stark distinction between communism and capitalism. Thus began a worldwide ideological and geopolitical struggle between these two worldviews. While the superpowers never (formally) fought against each other, many battles of the Cold War were fought by proxy, with each supporting a side in a local conflict. These macro intentions often ignited local grievances.

Southeast Asia, Vietnam, once part of France's colony of Indochine, exemplified the battlefield and its repercussions. After France's catastrophic defeat at Dien Bien Phu in 1954, the conflict, by the early 1960s, offered possibilities for ideological supremacy between the superpowers but also fanned local flames. Elements in the northern parts of the country were supported by the Soviet Union while elements in the southern parts were eventually supported by the United States. Given the stakes of the Cold War (with the US and the Soviet Union pointing nuclear weapons at each other), Vietnam attained a significance for America far larger than any definable interests in the region itself. A stated commitment to the containment of communism – and the fear of a "domino effect" should communism gain ground – meant that US leaders, for credibility abroad and for political support at home, could not be seen as giving an inch to communism.

The Vietnam War was never a declared war[4] but was, rather, a continually escalating commitment by presidents of Democratic and Republican parties alike in the United States. In 1961, President John F. Kennedy began committing US "advisors" to aid the South Vietnamese forces; President Lyndon B. Johnson drastically escalated the American commitment, with over 500,000 American troops stationed in Vietnam by 1968. By the time President Richard M. Nixon succeeded in extricating US forces from the by then un-winnable conflict in 1973, 58,148 Americans had been killed and around 304,000 wounded out of more than 2.5 million who served in the war. Countless Vietnamese, of course, were killed and maimed as well.

Vietnam became an especially unpopular war as its years of fighting wore on. There was a large protest movement at home (and elsewhere), which was often seen as part of the larger so-called counterculture movement in the 1960s. However, one didn't need to be a "hippie" to be uncomfortable with the war effort, and even lawmakers were troubled by the increasingly elusive enemy and the undeclared war's lack of oversight and restraint. This was especially true in the Nixon administration, a presidency virtually defined by secrecy, distrust, and ultimately scandal. In 1973 Congress defied Nixon by passing the War Powers Act, which limited the President's ability to engage US troops in military conflicts without Congressional approval.

Newspapers in the 1960s and 1970s

Before the majority of America's large newspapers came to be controlled by publicly owned media entities, many operated as privately and, in many cases, family-owned enterprises dedicated solely to newspaper publishing. These companies were often motivated as much by responsibility – an attitude keenly felt by many reporters themselves – as by profit. The family-owned *New York Times*, for example, earned respectability and credibility from its practices during World War II: at a time when newsprint was rationed, the *Times* chose to print news instead of advertise-ments. Yet, until the early 1960s, the *Times*, which commanded great power and influence, was only marginally profitable, and sometimes even operated at a loss.[5] Nonetheless, business considerations certainly played a role in managing newspapers, and in some instances selling newspapers took priority even if that meant dishonest journalism. As an extreme example, the Hearst family newspapers, facing intense competition for readership, were especially bellicose in foreign affairs, and have been credited with virtually causing the Spanish-American War of 1898.

Even so, a common press culture united the publishing elite based on the ideal of independence from government and politics, which allowed the publishers a degree of comfort in taking risks, both politically and in business.[6] As Joseph Pulitzer, a major publisher at the turn of the century, noted, "A newspaper should have no friends."

Newspaper publishers often took care in determining what their paper "stood for," and if a publisher's politics or philosophy changed it was often reflected in editorial decisions.[7] Executive editors such as Ben Bradlee, who made the day-to-day editorial decisions for publication at the *Washington Post*, were still subordinate to the publisher.

Reporting in Washington

Especially in Washington, "in this power-obsessed city by the Potomac press lords dine with presidents and seek to buttress their influence by extending their reach into the throne room of governmental power."[8] Access was often taken for granted, since publishers and politicians were in many cases part of the same social class, a male-dominated network of elites who had commonly attended the same schools – very dissimilar to Katharine Graham's experience. Long before Katharine Graham's father, Eugene Meyer, had taken control of the *Post* in 1933, the paper's publishers were known for their deep involvement in Washington politics, specifically in several White House scandals.[9] Even Ben Bradlee's first wife was the daughter of a US Senator.

Freedom of the press, the law of prior restraint, and the Nixon administration

The freedom of the American press is predicated on the First Amendment to the Constitution, which affirms that:

> Congress will make no law respecting an establishment of religion, or prohibiting the free exercise thereof; or abridging the freedom of speech, or of the press; or the right of the people peaceably to assemble, and to petition the Government for a redress of grievances.

At the same time, there exists in the Anglo-American legal tradition a notion called *prior restraint*, which refers to a government's ability to prohibit material in advance of being published. Prior restraint differs from laws concerning libel, where someone has been "defamed" in a published work. To prove charges of libel, a plaintiff needs not only to establish that the publication is false and intended to harm, but also to specify the damages that were done. Additionally, charges of libel can be brought only *after* publication. Thus, even if someone is prosecuted for libel, the material has nonetheless already been published. In essence, whereas libel cases "chill" speech, prior restraint "freezes" it.[10]

In the Anglo-American judicial tradition, prior restraint has therefore been seen as the most oppressive form of censorship possible. In a 1931 case, the US Supreme Court noted that throughout American history there had been few attempts to impose prior restraint, reflecting "the deep-seated conviction that such restraints would violate constitutional right."[11] That case, however, left open the possibility that prior restraint could be used in exceptional circumstances, such as where national security was involved. The question of how this was defined, or how far the burden of proof rested with the government, remained – and remains – an open question. Indeed, in the matter of the Pentagon Papers, the Nixon administration invoked prior restraint as the basis of its national security argument and, more generally, routinely attacked the press, accusing it of having a "liberal bias." Nixon's vice-president, Spiro Agnew, even suggested that the press should no longer be allowed to "wield a free hand in selecting, presenting, and interpreting the great issues of the nation."[12]

Women in business in the 1970s

According to Katharine Graham, "If you were a woman in those days at the head of an organization . . . people were entirely unused to you and didn't know what to make of you."[13] As the CEO of a powerful enterprise, and ultimately a public one, Katharine Graham was indeed an anomaly. She records that, "Even at my own company there were no women managers and few women professionals – and probably no women within four levels of me."[14] She herself was originally ambivalent about the rapidly growing feminist movement of the 1960s and 1970s, perhaps given the age difference between her and it leaders and her own longstanding assumptions about gender roles.[15]

Women at the beginning of the 1970s were unrepresented not just as the heads of organizations, but in the business world generally: in 1972, women owned only 4 percent of all American businesses.[16] Women were also vastly underrepresented in the professions: in 1972 only 9 percent of professional degrees awarded in medicine went to women, and, similarly, in 1972 women constituted less than a quarter of full- or part-time university faculty.[17]

As much as Katharine Graham was an anomaly, she was also in some ways a herald of progress in women's inclusion. In 1972, the famous Title IX of the Education Amendments was passed, signaling an end to overt gender discrimination. And, by 2006, 40.2 percent of all firms were women-owned; these businesses were responsible for generating $1.9 trillion in sales, and employing 12.8 million workers.[18]

TIMELINE OF WATERGATE EVENTS[19]

January 21, 1969	Richard Nixon inaugurated president after one of the closest presidential races in US history.
June 13, 1971	*The New York Times* begins printing the Pentagon Papers; *The Washington Post* begins printing them later in the week.
June 17, 1972	Five men are arrested for a late-night break-in at the Democratic National Committee at the Watergate Hotel in Washington, DC.

August–October 1972	*The Washington Post* reports heavily on the emerging scandal, including that a $25,000 check earmarked for the Nixon campaign was cashed in one of the burglars' accounts, and that the Nixon campaign commanded a network of political spying and sabotage.
November 7, 1972	Nixon reelected, winning an overwhelming majority of the vote.
January 30, 1973	Nixon aides G. Gordon Liddy and James McCord plead guilty to conspiracy, and five others are convicted. Several top Nixon staffers are soon after forced to resign.
May–October 1973	Senate Watergate Committee begins nationally televised hearings. Evidence mounts against Nixon, and controversy builds over his refusal to release taped conversations from his office.
October 12, 1973	"Saturday Night Massacre" – Nixon fires the special prosecutor, and the Attorney General and Deputy Attorney General resign. Pressure mounts in Congress for impeachment.
April 30, 1974	Nixon releases transcripts of tapes, but House Judiciary Committee demands tapes themselves. Nixon had earlier been at a loss to explain an 18.5 minute gap on a subpoenaed tape.
July 24, 1974	Supreme Court reject's Nixon's argument of "Executive Privilege" and orders the tapes be turned over.
July 27, 1974	House Judiciary Committee passes first of three articles needed for an impeachment.
August 8, 1974	Nixon resigns, the first US president to do so. Vice-President Gerald Ford becomes President, and later pardons Nixon of all Watergate-related charges.

BACKGROUND BIBLIOGRAPHY AND FURTHER READING

Gerber, Robin. *Katharine Graham: The Leadership Journey of an American Icon,* New York: Portfolio, 2005.

A comprehensive biography of Katharine Graham. See especially Chapters 7 and 8 on the Watergate period.

Graham, Katharine. *Personal History,* New York: Vintage, 1997.

See especially Chapter 21 for her thoughts on women in business.

"Impact of Civil Rights Laws," US Department of Education, 1999, online: http://www.ed.gov/about/offices/list/ocr/docs/impact.html (accessed December 7, 2006).

Provides statistics on the differences in women's education between the 1970s and the 1990s.

Linard, Laura. "Enterprising Women: A History," *HBS Working Knowledge*, November 18, 2002.

> A short review article on the history of women in business. For up-to-date statistics, see also "Key Facts About Women in Business" (Center for Women's Business Research, 2003).

Squires, James. *Stop the Press! The Corporate Takeover of America's Newspapers*, New York: Random House, 1993.

> A valuable look at the ethos and history of newspapers in America, especially the manner in which they changed to accommodate corporate responsibilities.

Stone, Geoffrey. *Perilous Times: Free Speech in Wartime*, New York: Norton, 2004.

> Presents the legal history of free speech in America. See especially Chapter 7 on the Vietnam War and the Pentagon Papers.

Thomas, Dana. *The Media Moguls*, New York: Putnam, 1981.

> See Chapter 3 for a detailed history of the *Washington Post* through 1980.

KATHARINE MEYER GRAHAM: BIOGRAPHY

Katharine Meyer Graham was born in New York City in 1917. Her father, Eugene Meyer, was a banker, and her mother, Agnes Meyer, a journalist. Katharine was raised in New York and Washington, DC, and attended Madeira, in Virginia, where she edited the student magazine. She then studied at Vassar College as well as the University of Chicago, from which she graduated in 1938.

Meanwhile, in 1933, Graham's father purchased *The Washington Post* for $825,000 at a bankruptcy sale. The fourth of five children, Katharine was alone among her siblings to be interested in journalism, and after graduating college worked for $24 a week covering labor news in San Francisco. Her father subsequently invited her back to Washington to be an editor at the *Post*.

In 1940, Katharine Meyer married Philip Graham, a law-school graduate to whom her father offered the role of publisher at the *Post*. Graham remained a devoted mother and wife and while her husband led the company. The Graham household was a center of social activity in Washington; the couple formed close friendships with US presidents John F. Kennedy and Lyndon B. Johnson and their families, as well as with other politicians and journalists.

In 1963, after a long struggle with mental illness, Philip Graham committed suicide. Wanting to sustain her family's commitment to the *Post* and to the vital role of the media, Graham ultimately decided to assume an executive role, and was voted president of the company one month after her husband's death. "What I essentially did", she wrote, "was to put one foot in front of the other, shut my eyes, and step off the ledge. The surprise was that I landed on my feet."[20]

Among the many critical decisions Graham subsequently made, the hiring of Ben Bradlee, then at *Newsweek*, to serve as editor of the *Post* stands out. Indeed, she later claimed this was one of the best.[21] With Graham in charge and Bradlee at the helm, the *Post* achieved worldwide renown by publishing the Pentagon Papers and reporting on the burgeoning Watergate scandal, transforming Graham into a figure with a particularly high public profile. The Washington Post Company, the fifth-largest publishing company in the country, saw rapid growth under Graham's leadership, and profits grew more than 20 percent annually between 1975 and 1985.[22] When it went public in 1971, the company's stock traded at $26 a share; by the late 1980s, the price was as high as $300 a share.[23]

In 1979, Graham relinquished her role as publisher to her son, Donald, but remained active in the business. She advised the newspaper on editorial policy and worked to diversify its holdings, expanding into television stations and a paper company.[24] She remained a powerful presence in Washington. In 1997 she published her memoirs, *Personal History*, which won a Pulitzer Prize in 1998. Graham died in 2001.

BEN BRADLEE: BIOGRAPHY

Ben Bradlee was born in 1921 in Boston and attended Harvard University, graduating in 1942. After college, he worked with the Office of Naval Intelligence as a communications officer, and, at the end of World War II, joined the *New Hampshire Sunday News* as a reporter. He worked there for two years, and then signed on to the *Washington Post*. As a reporter with the *Post*, Bradlee became friendly with Philip Graham, who secured him a position as a press attaché with the American embassy in Paris.

After more than a year at the embassy, Bradlee joined *Newsweek* as its European bureau chief, remaining based in Paris. In 1957 he moved back to Washington as *Newsweek*'s Washington bureau chief, where he became close friends with his neighbors – John F. Kennedy, then a Senator from Massachusetts, and his family.

In 1965, Bradlee was once again hired by the *Washington Post*, this time as managing editor, and he became vice president and executive editor in 1968. In this role, he worked with Katharine Graham to improve the quality of the newspaper, and, in so doing, confronted the challenges posed by the Pentagon Papers and Watergate. (Until 2005, he was one of only four people who knew the identity of so-called Deep Throat, the celebrated but unnamed source for much of the *Post*'s information on the scandal.)

Although Bradlee retired as executive editor in 1991, he remained vice-president of the *Post*. In 1995 he published his memoirs, *A Good Life: Newspapering and Other Adventures*.[25]

AUTHOR BIBLIOGRAPHY

Bradlee, Ben. *A Good Life: Newspapering and Other Adventures*, New York: Touchstone Press, 1996.

Graham, Katharine. *Personal History*, New York: Vintage, 1997.

"Katharine Graham," *Newsmakers*, issue 3, Farmington Hills, Mich.: Gale Group, 2002. Reproduced in *Biography Resource Center*, Farmington Hills, MI: Thomson Gale, 2006, online: http://galenet.galegroup.com.ezp1. harvard.edu/servlet/BioRC (accessed December 12, 2006), Document number: K1618003523.

"Katharine Meyer Graham," *Contemporary Heroes and Heroines*, Book IV, Farmington Hills, MI: Gale Group, 2000. Reproduced in *Biography Resource Center*, Farmington Hills, MI: Thomson Gale, 2006, online: http://galenet.galegroup.com.ezp1.harvard.edu/servlet/BioRC (accessed December 12, 2006), Document number: K1607000334.

NOTES

1 Katharine Graham, *Personal History*, New York: Vintage Books, 1998, p. 450.
2 Ben Bradlee, *A Good Life: Newspapering and Other Adventures*, New York: Touchstone Books, 1996, p. 323.
3 Graham, op. cit., p. 505.
4 According to the US Constitution (Article 1, Section 8), only Congress may declare war.
5 James Squires, *Stop the Press! The Corporate Takeover of America's Newspapers*, New York: Random House, 1993, p. 7.
6 Ibid., p. 15.
7 Ibid., p. 11.
8 Dana Thomas, *The Media Moguls*, New York: Putnam, 1981, p. 53.
9 Ibid., pp. 55–58.
10 The Supreme Court would later make this distinction in the *Nebraska Press Association v. Stuart* (1976).
11 *Near v. Minnesota* (1931). See Geoffrey Stone, *Perilous Times: Free Speech in Wartime*, New York: Norton, 2004, p. 505.
12 Ibid., p. 504.
13 Robin Gerber, *Katharine Graham: The Leadership Journey of an American Icon*, New York: Portfolio, 2005, p. 137.
14 Graham, op. cit., p. 417.
15 Ibid., pp. 418–432.
16 Laura Linard, "Enterprising Women: A History," *HBS Working Knowledge*, November 18, 2002.
17 "Impact of Civil Rights Laws," US Department of Education, 1999, online: http://www.ed.gov/about/offices/list/ocr/docs/impact.html (accessed December 7, 2006). See also: "Women and the MBA: Gateway to Opportunity," University of Michigan, Ross School of Business, 2000, online: http://www.cew.umich.edu/PDFs/pubs/mbafacts.pdf (accessed December 8, 2006).

18 "2006 National Fact Sheet," Center for Women's Business Research, 2006, online: http://www.cfwbr.org/assets/344_2006nationalfactsheet.pdf (accessed December 8, 2006).

19 Adapted from "Watergate Chronology," *The Washington Post Company*, online: http://www.washingtonpostcom/wp-srv/onpolitics/watergate/chronology.htm#2002-Present (accessed December 7, 2006).

20 Katharine Graham, op. cit., p. 341.

21 "Katharine Graham," *Newsmakers*, issue 3, Farmington Hills, MI: Gale Group, 2002. Reproduced in *Biography Resource Center*, Farmington Hills, MI: Thomson Gale, 2006, online: http://galenet.galegroup.com.ezp1.harvard.edu/servlet/BioRC (accessed December 12, 2006), Document number: K1618003523.

22 "Katharine Meyer Graham," *Contemporary Heroes and Heroines*, Book IV, Farmington Hills, Mich.: Gale Group, 2000. Reproduced in *Biography Resource Center,* Farmington Hills, Mich.: Thomson Gale, 2006, online: http://galenet.galegroup.com.ezp1.harvard.edu/servlet/BioRC (accessed December 12, 2006), Document number: K1607000334.

23 Graham, op. cit., pp. 442, 619.

24 Ibid.

25 Bradlee, op. cit.

Chapter 18

American Ground: Unbuilding the World Trade Center

Assuming leadership

THE CITY GOVERNMENT ran the show. The agency charged with managing the physical work was an unlikely one. It was the Department of Design and Construction (DDC), an obscure bureaucracy 1,300 strong whose normal responsibility was to oversee municipal construction contracts – for sidewalk and street repairs, jails, and the like – and whose offices were not even in Manhattan but in Queens. The DDC was given the lead for the simple reason that its two top officials, a man named Kenneth Holden and his lieutenant, Michael Burton, had emerged from the chaos of September 11 as the most effective of the responders. Now they found themselves running a billion-dollar operation with the focus of the nation upon them.

Nearly everyone at the site was well paid. The money for the effort came from federal emergency funds, and it flowed freely. But despite some cases of corruption and greed, money was not the main motivation here – at least not until almost the end. Throughout the winter and into the spring the workers rarely forgot the original act of aggression, or the fact that nearly 3,000 people had died there, including the friends and relatives of some who were toiling in the debris ... Whether correctly or not, the workers believed that an important piece of history was playing out, and they wanted to participate in it – often fervently, and past the point of fatigue. There were some who could not stand the stress, and they had to leave. But among the thousands who stayed, almost all sought greater involvement rather than less.

. . .

The problems that had to be solved there were largely unprecedented. Actions and intervention were required on every level, often with no need or possibility of asking for permission. As a result, within the vital new culture that grew up at the Trade Center site even the lowliest laborers and firemen were given power. Many of them rose to it, and some of them sank. Among those who gained the greatest influence were people without previous rank who discovered balance and ability within themselves, and who in turn were discovered by others.[1]

AMERICAN GROUND: THEMES AND QUESTIONS

Emergent leadership: Earning the right to lead

American Ground chronicles the story of the "unbuilding" of New York City's World Trade Center, the enormous (and, until this account, relatively unknown) nine-month ordeal of stabilizing its 17-acre site following the terrorist attacks on September 11, 2001. The main elements of the task were clearing the site of 1.5 million tons of rubble – concrete, debris, and steel – which were all that remained of the twin towers and other Trade Center buildings, and doing this, moreover, within the context of a search for victims, first those who might still be alive, and then the nearly 3,000 dead.

The unlikely heroes of this unlikely tale are city bureaucrats and engineers, firemen, and demolition experts who combined to form a loose but highly effective leadership group. Individually and collectively they allow us to examine *emergent leadership,* **the kind of leadership that any of us might be expected to demonstrate long before we reach a position of highest responsibility, or, indeed, even if we never do so.**

Responsibility for the Trade Center site was supposed to flow to the New York City Mayor's Office of Emergency Management; in fact, **the leaders of the unbuilding project did not have procedural legitimacy: They were never fully authorized in their role.** The text allows us to consider: **How did this group of individuals earn the right to lead?**

Exercising authority

We will answer this question by examining the Trade Center leaders in light of the requirements of leadership. One essential requirement is the ability to *exercise authority,* and we will be able to analyze how the leaders of the unbuilding made decisions in the face of the enormous uncertainty – physical, social, organizational, emotional, moral – that was the defining context of the devastation at the World Trade Center site.

Technical legitimacy

We will also want to understand the sources of the largely unofficial leaders' authority, why the many institutions and individuals involved in the unbuilding were willing to trust them to make decisions. One possible source is **technical legitimacy, recognition by others** that the individual possesses **the ability to draw upon knowledge, experience, and skill to make judgments necessary to the structure and management of work.**

We will be able to analyze the degree to which the technical skills of the "unbuild-ing" leaders played a role in their standing at the Trade Center site, and, if it did, the kind of influence it gives. Most of us depend on the development of professional skills of various kinds to provide the basis for a satisfying and successful career, so an appreciation of the value of technical legitimacy is quite important to understanding the powers we may hold or want to cultivate.

Moral legitimacy

The unbuilders of *American Ground* were not just faced with a technical challenge of unprecedented complexity, uncertainty, and scale; they also confronted moral challenges of similar dimensions. The first attack on the World Trade Center in 1993 set a pattern that was expected to repeat: an hours-long evacuation of the gigantic complex from which thousands would emerge alive. And, indeed, some 15,000 workers did manage to escape from the September 11 wreckage. But, after that point, only 18 survivors were found in the entire unbuilding process, a devastating reality that set in slowly, and that turned the challenge from a search for survivors to a search for the remains of what turned out to be nearly 3,000 dead. Indeed, remains continue to be found years later.

How the unbuilders managed this challenge is at the heart of the story, and the **moral legitimacy of the WTC leaders depended on the ways in which they balanced the physical requirements of the unbuilding with two moral "ends": the safety of the workers on the site, and a respectful search for the remains of the victims.** We will be able to assess how well the unbuilders managed these two tasks, and to analyze the reactions that their actions stimulated in the wide swath of people connected in various ways to the events of September 11 at the Trade Center site.

Leaders' motives

American Ground will also allow us to examine **the role of motivation in moral leadership.** The individuals featured in the account are portrayed realistically, encumbered, as we all are, with goals for their future, and an awareness of the impact that their current actions may have on their prospects. *American Ground* will enable us to answer pressing questions: **How do leaders' motives influence the evaluation of their actions? Does moral leadership require a special type of person, or can it be demonstrated by people in the real world, in the course of living ordinary lives?**

Guide to the World Trade Center "Unbuilders"

There are many people and complicated, often confused, jurisdictions involved in *American Ground*. Table 18.1 helps order them.

AMERICAN GROUND: BACKGROUND

Examining the destruction and "unbuilding" of the World Trade Center inevitably sparks questions about its origins. The following background materials describe the design and construction and critical evaluation of the World Trade Center itself, which was opened in 1973. You will also find a brief review of the 1993 attack on the complex, useful in understanding the expectations that colored the reactions to the 2001 attacks. Many governmental agencies and organizations played a role in the unbuilding; the most frequently mentioned ones are described in the background materials as well as in Table 18.1.

Table 18.1 Guide to the World Trade Center "Unbuilders"

Name	Role at World Trade Center	Organization	Responsibility
Mike Burton	Trade Center "Czar"; oversees practical details of the cleanup[2]	Department of Design and Construction (DDC)	Second-in-command; "DDC's doer"[3]
Ken Holden	Burton's boss; behind-the-scenes leader; runs interference with Mayor Giuliani	DDC	Commissioner[4]
Peter Rinaldi	Supervises consultants brought in for specialized below ground engineering;[5] "the one man everyone turned to for an opinion"[6]	Port Authority of New York and New Jersey	Oversees engineering for all Port Authority tunnels and bridges[7]
Sam Melissi	"Saint Sam the Fireman"; mediator between warring factions[8]	New York Fire Department	Fireman; served on specialized collapsed-building team[9]

Source: From William Langewiesche, *American Ground: Unbuilding the World Trade Cener*, New York: North Point Press, 2002.

ASSIGNMENT

READING: *American Ground: Unbuilding the World Trade Center*, by William Langewiesche.

1   This is an astonishing story of emergent leadership. In your view, how did the leadership team acquire their status?

2   What moral dilemmas did this team face? How did the dilemmas evolve over time? How well do you think the leaders handled them?

3   What is the relevance of this story for you?

Building the World Trade Center

Design and construction

Planning for the redevelopment of Lower Manhattan – the city's financial district that was nonetheless perceived as being scarred with slums – began in earnest in the 1950s and 1960s. Proponents argued forcefully that "this great project constitutes the most important single source of continued vitality and progress for New York City and the entire bi-state port area."[10] Extensive political wrangling eventually brought the project under the aegis of the Port Authority of New York and New Jersey in 1961 (see below for an explanation of the Authority's jurisdiction), and the future World Trade Center site was selected to coincide with the terminus of a New York–New Jersey rail link operated by the Port Authority.[11]

The following year Minoru Yamasaki was hired as the architect in charge of the project; he had previously earned a reputation for building functional towers with a keen eye to diligent engineering.[12] He designed the towers with form, function, and safety in mind: the towers were meant specifically to withstand the force of a 747 jet shearing into them.[13] The two ("North" and "South") 110-story towers, the tallest in the world (only temporarily, as the Chicago Sears Tower would soon take the title, to be superseded by buildings elsewhere), required 4,000 workers and 7 years to build. They were dedicated in April 1973.

Reception

While many architects received the towers with enthusiasm, other voices were not as kind. One critic suggested that New York's skyline "will be rudely disrupted by Yamasaki's double intruders which are straight and stark and simply sawed off at the top." Lewis Mumford, the renowned writer and commentator on cities, architecture, and modern life, railed against the towers' "purposeless gigantism and technological exhibitionism."[14] Various advocacy groups blamed the towers for killing migrating birds, dumping raw sewage into the nearby Hudson River, and creating a dangerous wind vortex between the towers.[15]

Criticism and opposition to the towers were also based on the heavy-handed and seemingly secretive manner by which the World Trade Center site was acquired by the Port Authority. Residents and shopkeepers in Radio Row, the neighborhood (named for its small electronics stores) that was almost entirely torn down to make way for the site, opposed the process until the very end. They ultimately took their challenge to the US Supreme Court, which refused to hear their case, and held protest marches in which they carried a coffin bearing the mannequin of "Mr. Small Businessman."[16]

The towers also suffered in being slow to find tenants. Many offices remained vacant in the 1970s owing to an economic downturn that particularly affected New York City; those offices that were occupied were often inhabited by local government agencies. In 1976 the towers were operating at a $20-million-a-year deficit.[17] Only in the 1980s did the anticipated private (mostly financial) firms begin to move in.

Over the years, however, the World Trade Center complex and particularly its twin towers eventually were embraced as the defining architectural emblem of New York City, becoming a destination for tourists and even for daredevils. The latter group included the "human fly" who achieved celebrity status by scaling the South Tower, and the tightrope walker Philippe Petit, who performed what has perhaps been the world's most dangerous tightrope act between the North and South towers. Together with the instantly beloved observation-deck/restaurant, the Windows on the World, these daring acts "helped push along the fascinating but seemingly irrational process by which the cold, forbidding, and in many ways frightening towers were softened and humanized and finally loved by the ordinary citizens of New York City."[18]

The World Trade Center bombing, 1993

On February 26, 1993, a rental van packed with the equivalent of 1,500 pounds of dynamite exploded in the garage underneath the North Tower, with the intention of toppling the tower into its twin. While the explosion failed to achieve its goal, it nonetheless blew a crater five stories deep, disabled the electricity, emergency lighting, sprinkler systems, and elevators in the towers, sent smoke through the stairwells and triggered a panicked evacuation. Six people were killed and more than 1,000 injured. The effects were felt across New York City, cutting off telephone service for much of the area and causing the city's radio and television stations to lose their over-the-air broadcasting ability. The attack stunned the US public. New York State Governor Mario Cuomo emphasized the change wrought by the bombing in saying, "Until now we were invulnerable."

The attacks were planned by Ramzi Yousef, a relative of Khalid Sheikh Mohammed, one of the top leaders of al-Qaeda and later an alleged mastermind of the September 11 attacks. According to one prominent terrorism analyst, "In many ways it was the opening salvo of al-Qaeda's campaign against the West"[19] Before September 11, this campaign had consisted of the bombing of US embassies in Kenya and Tanzania in 1998, killing 224, and the bombing of the USS *Cole* off the coast of Yemen in 2000, which killed 17 sailors.[20]

Six men including Yousef were sentenced to life in prison for their involvement in the 1993 World Trade Center bombing. When arrested and brought back into the US, Yousef was shown that the towers were still standing. Reportedly, he said defiantly: "They wouldn't be if I had had enough money and explosives."[21]

Selected agencies and organizations mentioned in *American Ground*

Federal Emergency Management Agency (FEMA)

In 2001 FEMA was an independent agency charged with disaster relief, recovery, and mitigation programs.[22] After September 11, FEMA financed and authorized an investigation into the engineering and structural failures of the collapsed buildings.

FEMA spent only $100,000 on the investigation, and reportedly hampered the engineers' access to information. The investigation proved unsatisfactory, and Congress eventually authorized a new investigation for which it allocated $16 million.[23] FEMA has since become part of the Department of Homeland Security.

Port Authority of New York and New Jersey

A regional authority dating back to 1921 to manage the harbor interests of the states of New York and New Jersey, the Port Authority was the oldest public multi-state authority in the country, given jurisdiction over the "Port District" – approximately 1,500 square miles centered on the Statue of Liberty. Today, it "manages and maintains the bridges, tunnels, bus terminals, airports, PATH [trains between New York and New Jersey] and seaport that are critical to the bi-state region's trade and transportation capabilities."[24] The Port Authority even has its own police force. The Authority built, owned, and operated the World Trade Center, where it also had its headquarters.

New York City Office of Emergency Management (OEM)

Established in 1996, the OEM is charged with contingency planning, training and disaster-response exercises (including for the private sector), field response, recovery and relief, and public information. During major emergencies the OEM can activate the Emergency Operations Center (EOC), a center with room for over 100 representatives of city, state, federal, private, and non-profit entities, a "central clearinghouse for information coordination, resource requests, and decision making."[25] The EOC was located at the World Trade Center, and was destroyed on September 11. Following the tragedy, voters elected to elevate the OEM to departmental status within the city government.

Department of Design and Construction (DDC)

Created in 1995, the DDC is charged with performing "design and construction services related to streets and highways, sewers, water mains, correctional and court facilities; cultural institutions; libraries; schools; and other public buildings, facilities and structures. The Department coordinates a wide variety of construction projects with utilities, community representatives and private industry."[26] The DDC ultimately assumed much of the responsibility for "unbuilding" the World Trade Center.

New York City Fire Department (FDNY)

In 2005, the FDNY comprised 10,725 Uniformed Firefighters and Fire Officers, 2,740 EMTs (Emergency Medical Technicians) and Paramedics, 171 Fire Marshals, 247 Fire Inspectors, 174 Dispatchers, and 1,101 Administrative Support Personnel including mechanics/tradespeople, technologists, and civilian professional.[27] A total of 343 firefighters died on September 11th.

177

New York City Police Department (NYPD)

The NYPD is the largest police department in the United States, with around 40,000 uniformed officers and detectives in 2003 (a number which fluctuates with politics, funding, and crime rates) and thousands of support staff. The mission of the NYPD is to "enhance the quality of life in our City by working in partnership with the community and in accordance with constitutional rights to enforce the laws, preserve the peace, reduce fear, and provide for a safe environment."[28] A total of 23 NYPD officers were killed in the September 11 attacks.

BACKGROUND BIBLIOGRAPHY AND FURTHER READING

Darton, Eric. *Divided We Stand: A Biography of New York's World Trade Center*, New York: Basic Books, 1999.

> An examination of the politics, planning, design and construction of the World Trade Center, as well as its reception. Also discusses the World Trade Center within broader cultural phenomena.

Glanz, James and Eric Lipton. *City in the Sky: The Rise and Fall of the World Trade Center*, New York: Henry Holt, 2003.

> A comprehensive look at the planning, the building, and ultimately the destruction, of the World Trade Center.

"Lessons of the First WTC Bombing," *BBC News*, February 26, 2003, online: http://news.bbc.co.uk/2/hi/americas/2800297.stm (accessed December 8, 2006).

> Places the 1993 World Trade Center bombing in the context of September 11th and other terrorist attacks.

Reeves, Simon and Foden, Giles. "A New Breed of Terror," *The Guardian*, September 12, 2001, online: http://www.cew.umich.edu/PDFs/pubs/mbafacts.pdf (accessed December 8, 2006).

> Written just after September 11, the article provides a useful analysis of what has commonly been called the "New" terrorism.

For information on New York City departments and agencies, see online: http://www.nyc.gov (accessed December 7, 2006).

On the history of FEMA, see online: http://www.fema.gov/about/history.shtm (accessed December 7, 2006).

For information on the Port Authority of New York and New Jersey, see online: http://www.panynj.gov (accessed December 7, 2006).

WILLIAM LANGEWIESCHE: BIOGRAPHY

Born in the United States in 1950 the son of Wolfgang Langewiesche, a pilot and also an author, William Langeweische (pronounced "Lang-a-veesha") followed in his father's footsteps after graduating from Stanford University by becoming a "professional pilot-turned-award-winning-writer"[29] for the highly regarded literary and cultural magazine, the *Atlantic Monthly*. As a correspondent for the *Atlantic*, Langewiesche has written on an array of major events; in addition to the dismantling of the World Trade Center, for example, he covered the sinking of a Swedish ferry in 1994, which killed 852 people, and the crash of EgyptAir flight 990 in 1999.[30] The latter article used his knowledge of flying to posit that the crash was intentional, and the piece won a National Magazine Award in 2001.

Besides articles for the *Atlantic*, Langewiesche has also written several books, including *Cutting for Sign* (1993), an examination of life along the US–Mexican border, *Sahara Unveiled* (1996), a travelogue of his journey through North Africa, *Inside the Sky: A Meditation on Flight* (1998), and *The Outlaw Sea: A World of Freedom, Chaos, and Crime* (2004) detailing the potential for disorder on the high seas.

American Ground, published in 2002, Langewiesche's fourth book, was originally a three-part series commissioned by, and first published in, the *Atlantic*. At 60,000 words, it was, according to the magazine's editor, the longest work of non-fiction the magazine had ever commissioned. "We were looking for something that we could do that would make one large contribution to the story," he said, referring to the coverage of September 11, 2001.[31]

Flying to New York on September 12, 2001, Langewiesche put in a special request for total access to the recovery and removal site of the World Trade Center. Although reporters were typically allowed into the area for only several hours at a time, his request was granted by Ken Holden, a fan of both Langewiesche and the *Atlantic Monthly*, and the New York City administrator who became, in part, a major character in Langewiesche's book.

Shadowing the firefighters, police, and engineers throughout their daily routines, Langewiesche noted that his reporting style – which he used generally, and not just in this instance – was unconventional: "For one thing, I rarely interview people. I talk to them. I listen. I often don't take notes. I'm an immersion guy. It's a very unconventional way to go about reporting, I'm sure."[32]

Despite initially sparking controversy over its reports about the behavior of the firefighters and first responders, *American Ground* was nominated for several prestigious awards, including the National Book Critics Circle Award.

AUTHOR BIBLIOGRAPHY

"Reporter Digs Deep for WTC Recovery," *USA Today*, June 17, 2002, p. 3.

"William Langewiesche," *Contemporary Authors Online*, Farmington Hills, MI: Thomson Gale, 2006.

"How I Write: William Langewiesche," *The Writer*, 2004, vol. 117, no. 8, p. 66.

Zeitchik, Steven, "Author in NBCC Flap," *Publishers Weekly*, February 24, 2003, online: http://www.publishersweekly.com/article/CA278388.html (accessed December 8, 2006).

NOTES

1   William Langewiesche, *American Ground: Unbuilding the World Trade Center*, New York: North Point Press, 2002, pp. 9–10.
2   Ibid., p. 66.
3   Ibid., p. 93.
4   Ibid., p. 65.
5   Ibid., p. 26.
6   Ibid., p. 26.
7   Ibid., p. 25.
8   Ibid., p. 23.
9   Ibid., p. 97.
10 Eric Darton, *Divided We Stand: A Biography of New York's World Trade Center*, New York: Basic Books, 1999, p. 70.
11 Ibid., p. 95.
12 Ibid., p. 117.
13 Ibid., p. 117.
14 Quoted in ibid., pp. 127–128.
15 James Glanz and Eric Lipton, *City in the Sky: The Rise and Fall of the World Trade Center*, New York: Henry Holt, 2003, p. 217.
16 Ibid., pp. 85–87.
17 Ibid., p. 217.
18 Ibid., p. 218.
19 "Lessons of the First WTC Bombing," *BBC News*, February 26, 2003.
20 The period also saw the devastating act of domestic terrorism perpetrated by Timothy McVeigh in Oklahoma City in 1995, in which 168 people were killed.
21 Simon Reeves and Giles Foden "A New Breed of Terror," *The Guardian*, September 12, 2001, online: http://www.cew.umich.edu/PDFs/pubs/mbafacts.pdf (accessed December 8, 2006).
22 "FEMA History," FEMA, online: http://www.fema.gov/about/history.shtm (accessed December 7, 2006).
23 Glanz and Lipton, op. cit., pp. 330–331.
24 "About the Port Authority," The Port Authority of New York and New Jersey, online: http://www.panynj.gov/ (accessed December 7, 2006).
25 Briefing Document, New York City Office of Emergency Management, online: http://www.nyc.gov/html/oem/pdf/oem_briefing_document.pdf (accessed January 10, 2006).
26 "About DDC," New York City Department of Design and Construction, online: http://www.ci.nyc.ny.us/html/ddc/html/about.html (accessed December 7, 2006).
27 "Who We Are," New York City Fire Department, online: http://www.nyc.gov/html/fdny/html/general/mission.shtml (accessed December 7, 2006).
28 New York City Police Department, online: http://www.nyc.gov/html/nypd/home.html (accessed December 7, 2006).
29 "Reporter Digs Deep for WTC Recovery," *USA Today*, June 17, 2002, p. 3.
30 "How I Write: William Langewiesche," *The Writer*, 2004, vol. 117, no. 8, p. 66.
31 *USA Today*, op. cit.
32 Ibid.

Tom L. Beauchamp and James F. Childress "Moral Theories"[1]

UTILITARIANISM: CONSEQUENCE-BASED THEORY

Consequentialism is a label affixed to theories holding that actions are right or wrong according to the balance of their good and bad consequences. The right act in any circumstance is the one that produces the best overall result, as determined from an impersonal perspective that gives equal weight to the interests of each affected party. The most prominent consequence-based theory, utilitarianism, accepts one and only one basic principle of ethics: the principle of utility. This principle asserts that we ought always to produce the maximal balance of positive value over disvalue (or the least possible disvalue, if only undesirable results can be achieved). The classical origins of this theory are found in the writings of Jeremy Bentham (1748–1832) and John Stuart Mill (1806–1873).

At first sight, utilitarianism seems entirely compelling. Who would deny that agents should minimize evil and increase positive value? Moreover, utilitarians offer many examples from everyday life to show that the theory is practicable and that we all engage in a utilitarian method of calculating what should be done by balancing goals and resources and considering the needs of everyone affected. Examples include designing a family budget and creating a new public park in a wilderness region. Utilitarians maintain that their theory simply renders explicit and systematic what is already implicit in everyday deliberation and justification.

The concept of utility

Although utilitarians share the conviction that we should morally assess human actions in terms of their production of maximal value, they disagree concerning which values should be maximized. Many utilitarians maintain that we ought to produce *agent-neutral* or *intrinsic* goods – that is, goods such as happiness, freedom, and health that every rational person values.[2] These goods are valuable in themselves, without reference to their further consequences or to the particular values held by individuals.

Bentham and Mill are *hedonistic* utilitarians because they conceive utility entirely in terms of happiness or pleasure, two broad terms that they treat as synonymous.[3] They appreciate that many human actions do not appear to be performed for the sake of happiness. For example, when highly motivated professionals, such as research scientists, work themselves to the point of exhaustion in search of a new knowledge, they often do not appear to be seeking pleasure or personal happiness. Yet Mill proposes that such persons are initially motivated by success or money, both of which promise happiness. Along the way, either the pursuit of knowledge provides pleasure or such persons never stop associating their hard work with the success or money they hope to gain.

However, many recent utilitarian philosophers have argued that values other than happiness have intrinsic worth. Some list friendship, knowledge, health, and beauty among these intrinsic values, whereas others list personal autonomy, achievement and success, understanding, enjoyment, and deep personal relationships.[4] Even when their lists differ, these utilitarians concur that we should assess the greatest good in terms of the total intrinsic value produced by an action. Still other utilitarians hold that the concept of utility does not refer to intrinsic goods, but to an individual's preferences; that is, we are to maximize the overall satisfaction of the preferences of the greatest number of individuals.

A case of risk and truthfulness

To distinguish the major themes of each theory treated in this chapter, each section devoted to a theory explicates how its proponents might approach the same case, which centers on a five-year-old girl who has progressive renal failure and is not doing well on chronic renal dialysis. The medical staff is considering a renal transplant, but its effectiveness is "questionable" in her case. Nevertheless, a "clear possibility" exists that the transplanted kidney will not be affected by the disease process. The parents concur with the plan to try a transplant, but an additional obstacle emerges: The tissue typing indicates that it would be difficult to find a match for the girl. The staff excludes her two siblings, ages two and four, as too young to be donors. The mother is not histocompatible, but the father is compatible and has "anatomically favorable circulation for transplantation."

Meeting alone with the father, the nephrologist gives him the results and indicates that the prognosis for his daughter is "quite uncertain." After reflection, the father decides that he does not wish to donate a kidney to his daughter. His several reasons include his fear of the surgery, his lack of courage, the uncertain prognosis for his daughter even with a transplant, the slight prospect of a cadaver kidney, and the suffering his daughter has already sustained. The father then asks the physician "to tell everyone else in the family that he is not histocompatible." He is afraid that if family members know the truth, they will accuse him of intentionally allowing his daughter to die. He maintains that truth-telling would have the effect of "wrecking the family." The physician is uncomfortable with this request, but after further discussion he agrees to tell the man's wife that "for medical reasons, the father should not donate a kidney."[5]

Utilitarians evaluate this case in terms of the consequences of the different courses of action open to the father and the physician. The goal is to realize the greatest good by balancing the interests of all affected persons. This evaluation depends on judgments about probable outcomes. Whether the father ought to donate his kidney depends on the probability of successful transplantation as well as the risks and other costs to him (and indirectly to other dependent members of the family). The probability of success is not high. The effectiveness is questionable and the prognosis uncertain, although a possibility exists that a transplanted kidney would not undergo the same disease process, and there is a slight possibility that a cadaver kidney could be obtained.

The girl will probably die without a transplant from either a cadaveric or a living source, but the transplant also offers only a small chance of survival. The risk of death to the father from anesthesia in the kidney removal is 1 in 10,000 to 15,000; it is difficult to put an estimate on other possible long-term health effects. Nevertheless, because the chance of success is likely greater than the probability that the father will be harmed, many utilitarians would hold that the father or anyone else similarly situated is *obligated* to undertake what others would consider a heroic act that surpasses obligation. On a certain balance of probable benefits and risks, an uncompromising utilitarian would suggest tissue typing the patient's two siblings and then removing a kidney from one if there were a good match and parental approval. However, utilitarians differ among themselves in these various judgments because of their different theories of value and their different assessments of probable outcomes.

Probabilistic judgments would likewise play a role in the physician's utilitarian calculation of the right action in response to the father's request to camouflage why he will not donate a kidney. Primary questions include whether a full disclosure would wreck the family, whether lying to the family would have serious negative effects, and whether the father would subsequently experience serious guilt from his refusal to donate, thereby jeopardizing relations within the family. Studies indicate that families caring for chronically ill children break up at a higher rate than other families, and perhaps this family is already beyond repair. The utilitarian proposes that the physician is obligated to consider the whole range of facts and possible consequences in light of the best available information about their probability and magnitude.

So far we have taken primarily the perspective of a utilitarian who focuses on *particular acts.* Other utilitarians focus on the relevant *principles and rules* of parental obligation and professional practice that, over time, maximize overall welfare. We turn now to this distinction, which divides utilitarians in two major types.

Act and rule utilitarianism

The principle of utility is the ultimate standard of rightness and wrongness for all utilitarians. Controversy has arisen, however, over whether this principle pertains to particular acts in particular circumstances or instead to general rules that then determine which acts are right and wrong. Whereas the rule utilitarian considers the consequences of adopting certain rules, the act utilitarian skips the level of rules and justifies actions by appealing directly to the principle of utility, as the following chart indicates:

Rule Utilitarianism	Act Utilitarianism
Principle of Utility	Principle of Utility
↑	
Moral Rules	↑
↑	
Particular Judgments	Particular Judgments

The act utilitarian asks, "What good and bad consequences will result from *this action in this circumstance?*" For the act utilitarian, moral rules are useful in guiding human actions, but are also expendable if they do not promote utility in a particular context. For the rule utilitarian, by contrast, an act's conformity to a justified rule (that is, a rule justified by utility) makes the act right, and the rule is not expendable in a particular context, even if following the rule in that context does not maximize utility.[6]

Physician Worthington Hooker, a prominent nineteenth-century figure in academic medicine and medical ethics, was a rule utilitarian who attended to rules of truth-telling in medicine as follows:

> The good, which may be done by deception in a *few* cases, is almost as nothing, compared with the evil which it does in *many*, when the prospect of its doing good was just as promising as it was in those in which it succeeded. And when we add to this evil which would result from a *general* adoption of a system of deception, the importance of a strict adherence to the truth in our intercourse with the sick, even on the ground of expediency, becomes incalculably great.[7]

Hooker agreed that a physician can sometimes best advance a patient's health through deception, but he argued that widespread deception in medicine will have an increasingly negative effect over time and will eventually produce more harm than good. He therefore defended the rule-utilitarian prohibition of deception in medicine.

Act utilitarians, by contrast, argue that observing a rule such as truth-telling does not always maximize the general good, and that such rules are properly understood as rough guidelines. They regard rule utilitarians as unfaithful to the fundamental demand of the principle of utility: Maximize value. In some circumstances, they argue, abiding by a generally beneficial rule will not prove most beneficial to the persons affected by the action, even in the long run. According to one act utilitarian, J. J. C. Smart, a third possibility exists between never adopting any rules and always obeying rules – namely, *sometimes* obeying rules.[8] From this perspective, physicians do not and should not always tell the truth to their patients or their families. Sometimes physicians should even lie to give hope. They do so justifiably if it is better for the patients and for all concerned and if their acts do not undermine general conformity to moral rules. According to Smart, selective obedience does not erode either moral rules or general respect for morality.

Because of the benefits to society of the general observance of moral rules, the rule utilitarian does not abandon rules, even in difficult situations (although the rule utilitarian may accept rules only as statements of prima facie obligation). Abandonment threatens the integrity and existence of both the particular rules and the whole system of rules.[9] The act utilitarian's reply is that although promises usually should be kept in order to maintain trust, this consideration should be set aside in cases in which breaking the promise would produce overall good. The act utilitarian might also argue that making exceptions to accepted rules is consistent with ordinary moral beliefs, because we often make exceptions to rules without acting wrongly. The act utilitarian further contends that when breaking rules justifiably clashes with our traditional moral convictions, we need to revise our convictions rather than discard act utilitarianism.

An example of the act utilitarian's point appears in a comment by former Colorado Governor Richard Lamm, who once observed that, in light of increasing financial costs of medical care, the terminally ill have "a duty to die and get out of the way with all of our machines and artificial hearts and everything else." This statement clearly conflicts with ordinary morality and provoked an outcry of indignation and shock that a public official would brush aside considered moral rules that protect our rights. Lamm chose an unfortunate word when he stated that the terminally ill have a "duty" to die, but in context he provided an act-utilitarian answer to what he correctly referred to as an "ethical question." His point was that we cannot continue public funding for medical technology without assessing costs and trade-offs, even if we must subsequently revise our traditional views and let some people die because a technology is not funded. The act utilitarian likewise believes that traditional moral rules cannot handle many other questions posed by technological developments.

An absolute principle with derivative contingent rules

From the utilitarian's perspective, the principle of utility is the sole absolute principle. No derivative rule is absolute, and no rule is unrevisable. Even rules against killing in medicine may be overturned or substantially revised. For example, we had occasion ... to discuss current debates in biomedical ethics regarding whether seriously suffering patients should, at their request, be killed rather than "allowed to die," although such acts would revise traditional beliefs in medicine. The rule utilitarian argues that we should support rules permitting killing if and only if those rules would produce the most favorable consequences. Likewise, there should be rules against killing if and only if those rules would maximize good consequences. Utilitarians often point out that we do not presently permit physicians to kill patients because of the adverse social consequences that we believe would follow for those directly and indirectly affected. But if, under a different set of social conditions, legalization of mercy killing would maximize overall social welfare, the utilitarian would see no reason to prohibit such killing. Utilitarians thus regard their theory as responsive in constructive ways to changing social conditions.

A critical evaluation of utilitarianism

Several problems suggest that utilitarianism is not a fully adequate moral theory.

Problems with immoral preferences and actions

Problems arise for utilitarians who are concerned about the maximization of individual preferences when some of these individuals have what our considered judgments tell us are morally unacceptable preferences. For example, if a researcher derived supreme satisfaction from inflicting pain on animals or on human subjects in experiments, we would condemn this preference and would seek to prevent it from being actualized. Utilitarianism based on subjective preferences is thus a defensible theory only if we can formulate a range of *acceptable* preferences and determine "acceptability" independently of agents' preferences. This task seems inconsistent with a pure preference approach.[10]

There is an additional problem of immoral actions. Suppose the only way to achieve the maximal utilitarian outcome is to perform an immoral act (as judged by the standards of the common morality). For example, suppose a country can end a devastating war only by using extremely painful methods of torturing captured children whose soldier fathers instructed them not to reveal their fathers' location. Utilitarianism seems to say not only that torturing the children is permissible, but that it is morally obligatory. Yet this requirement seems immoral. If so, utilitarianism permits or requires apparently immoral actions without giving sufficient reason to abandon our reigning restraints on utilitarian thinking.

Does utilitarianism demand too much?

Some forms of utilitarianism seem to demand too much in the moral life, because the principle of utility requires *maximizing* value. Utilitarians have a difficult time maintaining a crucial distinction between (1) *morally obligatory actions*, and (2) *supererogatory actions* (those above the call of moral obligation and performed for the sake of personal ideals). Registering this objection, Alan Donagan describes situations in which utilitarian theory regards an action as obligatory against our firm moral conviction that the action is ideal and praiseworthy rather than obligatory.[11]

Donagan would regard the suicide of frail elderly and persons with severe disabilities who are no longer useful to society as an example of acts that could never rightly be considered obligatory, regardless of the consequences. Heroic donation of bodily parts such as kidneys and even hearts to save another person's life is another example. If utilitarianism makes such actions obligatory, then it is a defective theory. Donagan argues, and we agree, that all utilitarians face these problems, because none can rule out the ever-present possibility that what is today praiseworthy (but optional) will, through altered social circumstances, become obligatory by utilitarian standards. (At the same time, we should recognize that utilitarians are sometimes right in arguing that various moral conventions and beliefs are too weak or vague and need upgrading by more demanding requirements.)[12]

Bernard Williams and John Mackie offer extensions of the thesis that utilitarianism demands too much. Williams argues that utilitarianism abrades personal integrity by making persons as morally responsible for consequences that they *fail to prevent* and for those outcomes they *directly cause*, even when the consequences are not of their doing. Mackie similarly argues that a utilitarian "test of right actions" is so distant from our moral experience that it becomes "the ethics of fantasy," because it demands that people strip themselves of many goals and relationships they value in life in order to maximize outcomes for others. From this perspective, the utilitarian demands that we act like saints without personal interests and goals.[13] These criticisms also suggest that utilitarianism fails the test of *practicability* . . .

Problems of unjust distribution

A third problem is that utilitarianism, in principle, permits the interests of the majority to override the rights of minorities, and cannot adequately disavow unjust social distributions. The charge is that utilitarians assign no independent weight to justice and are indifferent to unjust distributions because they distribute value according to net aggregate satisfaction. If an already prosperous group of persons could have more value added to their lives than could be added to the lives of the indigent in society, the utilitarian must recommend that the added value go to the prosperous group.

An example of problematic (although not necessarily unjust) distribution appears in the following case. Two researchers wanted to determine the most cost-effective way to control hypertension in the American population. As they developed their research, they discovered that it is more cost-effective to target patients already being treated for hypertension than to identify new cases of hypertension among persons without regular access to medical care: younger men, older women, and patients with exceptionally high blood pressure. And they concluded that "a community with limited resources would probably do better to concentrate its efforts on improving adherence of known hypertensives (that is, those already identified as sufferers of hypertension), even at a sacrifice in terms of the numbers screened." If accepted by the government, this recommendation would exclude the poorest sector, which has the most pressing need for medical attention, from the benefits of high blood pressure education and management.

The investigators were concerned because of the apparent injustice in excluding the poor and minorities by a public health endeavor aimed at the economically advantaged sector of society. Yet their statistics were compelling. No matter how carefully planned the efforts, nothing worked efficiently (that is, nothing produced utilitarian results), except programs directed at known hypertensives already in contact with physicians. The investigators therefore recommended what they explicitly referred to as a utilitarian allocation.[14]

Medical research since this study has continued to support its findings. Nonadherence to treatment programs for hypertension is one of the most important antecedent conditions leading to serious hypertension-related medical problems. In poor sections of inner cities, nonadherence is much higher among patients who are screened and treated for hypertension in the emergency room than for those treated by their own primary-care physicians. This problem is significant because many poor people do not have primary-care physicians. Low economic status also correlates with fewer visits per year to physicians' offices. In addition, research indicates that the prevalence of hypertension is 50% higher among African Americans than among whites. Thus, the problems identified in the earlier study remain largely unchanged today: The society could probably achieve a greater net improvement in overall public health by targeting patients who have and who visit primary-care physicians, yet such a strategy is likely to underserve poor and minority populations who already suffer disproportionately from health problems.[15]

A constructive evaluation of utilitarianism

Despite these criticisms, utilitarianism has many strengths, two of which we have appropriated to other chapters. The first is the acceptance of a significant role from the principle of utility in formulating public policy. The utilitarian's requirements of an objective assessment of everyone's interests and of an impartial choice to maximize good outcomes for all affected parties are acceptable norms of public policy. Second, when we formulated principles of beneficence . . . utility played an important role. Although we have characterized utilitarianism as primarily a *consequence*-based theory, it is also *beneficence*-based. That is, the theory sees morality primarily in terms of the goal of promoting welfare.

A theory with a principle of beneficence that is balanced by other principles should eliminate all the problems with an unqualified use of the principle of utility that we encountered in the criticisms offered in the preceding section. This point holds even if beneficence is developed primarily in terms of producing good consequences. As political economist Amartya Sen notes, "Consequentialist reasoning may be fruitfully used even when consequentialism as such is not accepted. To ignore consequences is to leave an ethical story half told."[16]

A *strict* or *pure* utilitarianism also has strengths, as we can see by reconsidering the objection that utilitarianism is overdemanding. Utilitarianism often demands more than the rules of common morality do, but this apparent weakness can be a hidden strength. For example, morality generally demands that we not override individuals' rights to maximize social consequences. But if we can more effectively protect almost everyone's interests by overriding some property rights or autonomy rights, this course of action might not be wrong merely because it contravenes conventional morality and pursues the goal of social utility. In many circumstances, then, utilitarians make a compelling case in advising us to rely less on traditional convictions and more on judgments of overall social benefit.

KANTIANISM: OBLIGATION-BASED THEORY

A second type of theory denies much that utilitarian theories affirm. Often called *deontological* (i.e., a theory that some features of actions other than or in addition to consequences make actions right or wrong), this type of theory is now increasingly called *Kantian*, because the ethical thought of Immanuel Kant (1724–1804) has most deeply shaped its formulations.

Consider how a Kantian might approach the above-mentioned case of the five-year-old in need of a kidney. A Kantian would first insist that we should rest our moral judgments on reasons that also apply to others who are similarly situated. If the father has no generalizable moral obligation to his daughter, then no basis is available for morally criticizing him. The strict Kantian maintains that if the father chooses to donate out of affection, compassion, or concern for his dying daughter, his act would actually lack moral worth, because it would not be based on a generalizable obligation. Using one of the girl's younger siblings as a source of a kidney would be illegitimate because this recourse to children who are too young to consent to donation would involve using persons merely as means to others' ends. This principle would also exclude coercing the father to donate against his will.

Regarding the physician's options after the father requests deceiving the family, a strict Kantian views lying as an act that cannot without contradiction be universalized as a norm of conduct. The physician should not lie to the man's wife or to other members of the family, whether or not the lie would salvage the family (a consequentialist appeal). Even if the physician's statement was not, strictly speaking, a lie, he intentionally used this formulation to conceal relevant facts from the wife, an act Kantians typically view as morally unacceptable.

A Kantian will also consider whether the rule of confidentiality has independent moral weight, whether the tests the father underwent with the nephrologists established a relationship of confidentiality, and whether the rule of confidentiality protects information about the father's histocompatibility and his reasons for not donating. If confidentiality would prohibit the nephrologist from letting the family know that the father is histocompatible, then, even without considering possible effects on the family, the Kantian must face an apparent conflict of obligations: truthfulness in conflict with confidentiality. But before we can address such conflict, we need to understand Kantian theory.

Obligation from categorical rules

In an attempt to combat skeptical challenges to ethics, Kant argued that morality is grounded in reason, not in tradition, intuition, conscience, emotion, or attitudes such as sympathy. He saw human beings as creatures with rational powers to resist desire and with the freedom to do so.

One of Kant's most important claims is that the moral worth of an individual's action depends exclusively on the moral acceptability of the rule of obligation (or "maxim") on which the person acts. As Kant puts it, moral obligation depends on the rule that determines the individual's will, where the rule is understood as a morally valid reason that justifies the action.[17] For Kant, one must act not only *in accordance with* but *for the sake of* obligation. That is, to have moral worth, a person's motive for acting must come from a recognition that he or she intends what is morally required. For example, if an employer discloses a health hazard to an employee only because the employer fears a lawsuit, and not because of the importance of truth-telling, then the employer has performed the right action, but deserves no moral credit for the action. If agents do what is morally right simply because they are scared, because they derive pleasure from doing that kind of act, or because they are selfish, they lack the requisite good will that derives from acting for the sake of obligation.

To see how a Kantian would judge the moral worth of a proposed course of action, imagine a man who desperately needs money and knows that he will not be able to borrow it unless he promises repayment in a definite time, but who also knows that he will not be able to repay it within this period. He decides to make a promise that he knows he will break. Kant asks us to examine the man's reason, that is, his maxim: "When I think myself in want of money, I will borrow money and promise to pay it back, although I know that I cannot do so." This maxim, Kant says, cannot pass a test that he calls the *categorical imperative*. This imperative tells us what must be done irrespective of our desires. In its major formulation, Kant states the categorical imperative as follows: "I ought never to act except in such a way that I can also will that my maxim become a universal law." Kant says that this one principle justifies all particular imperatives of obligation (all "ought" statements that morally obligate).[18]

The categorical imperative is a canon of the acceptability of moral rules – that is, a criterion for judging the acceptability of the maxims that direct actions. This imperative adds nothing to a maxim's content. Rather, it determines which maxims are objective and valid. The categorical imperative functions by testing what Kant calls the "consistency of maxims": A maxim must be capable of being conceived and willed without contradiction. When we examine the maxim of the person who deceitfully promises, we discover, according to Kant, that this maxim is incapable of being conceived and willed universally without yielding a contradiction. It is inconsistent with what it presupposes. Lying works only if the person being lied to expects or presupposes that people are truthful, but in a world in which no one intended to keep promises, the maxim would make the purpose of promising impossible, because no one would believe the person who promises. Many examples from everyday life illustrate this thesis. For instance, maxims of lying are inconsistent with the practices of truth-telling they presuppose, and maxims permitting cheating on tests are inconsistent with the practices of honesty they presuppose.

Kant appears to have more than one categorical imperative, because his several formulations are very differently worded. His second formulation is at least as influential as the first: "One must act to treat every person as an end and never as a means only."[19] It has often been said that this principle categorically requires that we should never treat another as a means to our own ends, but this interpretation misrepresents Kant's views. He argues only that we must not treat another *merely* or *exclusively* as a means to our ends. When human research subjects volunteer to test new drugs, they are treated as a means to others' ends, but they have a choice in the matter and retain control over their lives. Kant does not prohibit those uses of consenting persons. He insists only that they be treated with the respect and moral dignity to which every person is entitled.

Autonomy and heteronomy

We saw in Chapter 3 that the word *autonomy* typically refers to what makes judgments and actions one's own. This conception of autonomy is emphatically not Kant's. Persons have "autonomy of will" for Kant if and only if they knowingly act in accordance with the universally valid moral principles that pass the requirements of the categorical imperatives. He contrasts this *moral* autonomy with "heteronomy," which refers to any controlling influence over the will other than motivation by moral principles.[20] If, for example, people act from passion, ambition, or self-interest, they act heteronomously, not from a rational will that chooses autonomously. Kant regards acting from desire, fear, impulse, personal projects, and habit as no less heteronomous than actions manipulated or coerced by others.

To say that an individual must "accept" a moral principle to be autonomous does not mean that the principle is subjective or that each individual must create (author or originate) his or her moral principles. Kant requires only that each individual *will the acceptance* of moral principles. If a person freely accepts objective moral principles, that person is a law-giver unto himself or herself. The importance of this account for Kant also extends beyond the *nature* of autonomy to its *value*. "The principle of autonomy," he contends, is "the sole principle of morals," and autonomy alone gives people respect, value, and proper motivation. A person's dignity – indeed, "sublimity" – comes from being morally autonomous.[21]

Contemporary Kantian ethics

Several writers in contemporary ethical theory have accepted and developed a Kantian account, broadly construed.

1. A straightforward example is *The Theory of Morality* by Alan Donagan. He seeks the "philosophical core" of the morality expressed in the Hebrew–Christian tradition (which he interprets in secular rather than religious terms). Donagan's philosophical elaboration of this point of view relies heavily on Kant's theory of persons as ends in themselves, especially the imperative that one must treat humanity as an end and never as a means only. Donagan expresses the fundamental principle of the Hebrew–Christian tradition as a Kantian principle grounded in rationality: "It is impossible not to respect every human being, oneself or any other, as a rational

creature."[22] He believes that all other moral rules rely upon this fundamental principle.

2. A second Kantian theory derives from the work of John Rawls. Rawls has challenged utilitarian theories while attempting to develop Kantian themes of reason, autonomy, and equality. For example, he argues that vital moral considerations, such as individual rights and the just distribution of goods among individuals, depend less on social factors, such as individual happiness and majority interests, than on Kantian conceptions of individual worth, self-respect, and autonomy.[23] For Rawls, any philosophy in which the right to individual autonomy legitimately outweighs the dictates of rational moral principles is unacceptable. Even courageous and conscientious actions do not merit respect unless they accord with moral principles derived from reason.[24]

In his recent writings, Rawls has stressed that his work presents a political conception of justice, rather than a comprehensive moral theory. That is, his account is "a moral conception worked out for a specific subject, namely, the basic structure of a constitutional democratic regime." As such, it does not presuppose a comprehensive moral doctrine such as Kant's, and Rawls maintains that his theory is Kantian by "analogy not identity."[25] The upshot seems to be that Rawls expresses Kantian themes without commitment to a general Kantian moral theory.

3. Several philosophers, including Robert Nozick, Bernard Williams, and Thomas Nagel, have developed a doctrine of "deontological constraints" based on Kant's injunction never to use another person merely as a means.[26] These philosophers argue that Kant was correct to maintain that certain actions are impermissible regardless of the consequences. To see how these constraints should operate, consider the following experiment with human subjects. From April 1945 to July 1947, a program of human subjects research was initiated to try to learn how to protect personnel from plutonium exposure. Researchers intentionally injected 17 patients with plutonium at three university hospitals in the United States, including The University of California at San Francisco (UCSF). The purpose of this research was to determine the excretion rate of plutonium in humans. Investigators at the time did not regard these plutonium experiments as highly risky. Based on experiences with radium, they did not expect immediate side effects or illness, but they also knew virtually nothing about long-term risk.

Work began with some studies on rats and cancer conducted by Dr. Joseph Hamilton. In January 1945, Hamilton decided "to undertake, on a limited scale, a series of metabolic studies with [plutonium] using human subjects." The purpose "was to evaluate the possible hazards ... to humans who might be exposed to them." Researchers did not expect the injections to have any therapeutic value for these three patients. It appears that the physicians did not obtain – and were not expected to obtain – consent in the first two cases. Even though the physicians obtained limited consent for experimentation from the third patient, it was not consent to *nontherapeutic* experimentation.[27]

In this case, the researchers thought that by experimenting on a few individuals they could help achieve several worthy social goals, such as protecting workers in the nuclear industry and developing an adequate system of military defense for Western nations during the Cold War. Even if achieving these goals would have good consequences for millions of people, deontologists maintain that the researchers treated their subjects unethically because they violated fundamental constraints on how we can permissibly treat persons. These "deontological constraints" limit our actions, even when we can bring about an overall good state of affairs.

Deontological constraints are essentially negative duties – that is, they specify what we cannot justifiably do to others, even in the pursuit of worthy goals; however, they do not specify any actions that we should perform for the sake of others. For example, while stealing a sibling's share of the family inheritance would violate deontological constraints, these constraints do not tell us how to divide the wealth among siblings.

This conception of deontological constraints highlights an obvious difference between deontologists and utilitarians. The latter require us to determine the best possible objective state of affairs, irrespective of the position of particular agents who act in those states of affairs. Utilitarians demand an external, impartial view of the situation in order to weigh each person's interests equally. From this perspective, a person's own position, role, and sense of integrity have no independent force. They are only important in so far as they are factors in the calculus of utilities. For the utilitarian, it is unimportant who brings about the best possible state of affairs; all that matters is that good outcomes occur.[28]

By contrast, many deontologists maintain that such factors as one's role or sense of integrity have moral weight independent of consequences. Imagine that a terminally ill patient in extreme pain asks his physician to kill him. The man's family agrees with his decision, and the doctor realizes that everyone will be better off if the man dies. Nonetheless, a deontologist might believe that her role as a physician, as well as her own sense of moral integrity, prevent her from taking this man's life. Similarly, in the plutonium case, a physician might feel constrained from engaging in nontherapeutic human experimentation, regardless of the good consequences that would follow from the experimental work.

In these examples, deontological constraints are *agent-relative*, because they make reference to the values and judgments of particular persons, such as physicians and scientists. Deontologists argue that each individual agent's perspective is important in moral deliberation, and that who performs an action and how a good state of affairs is to be brought about are significant, irrespective of consequences. As moral agents, we should not directly cause certain harms to others even if we cannot actually prevent those harms from occurring. For example, in the case of the doctor with a terminally ill patient, the doctor believes that she should not kill the patient, even though the patient will die soon anyway and the family agrees with the loved one's request.

A critical evaluation of Kantianism

Like utilitarianism, Kantian theory fails to provide a full and adequate theory of the moral life.

The problem of conflicting obligations

Kantianism has a severe problem with conflicting obligations. Suppose we have promised to take our children on a long-anticipated trip, but now find that if we do so, we cannot assist our sick mother in the hospital. A rule of promise-keeping and a rule of assistance or obligation of care generate this conflict. Conflict can also arise from a single moral rule rather than from two different rules – as, for example, when two promises come into conflict, although the promisor could not have anticipated the conflict when making the promises. To modify the previous example, consider a situation in which we have promised to take our children on a trip and promised to care for our mother when she is sick, and both promises come due at the same time.

Because moral rules are *categorical* for Kant, he seems to say that we are obligated to do the impossible and perform both actions. Although we cannot at the same time both take our children on a trip and help our mother in the hospital, Kant seems to require both. Any ethical theory that leads to this conclusion is incoherent, yet no clear way out exists for Kant or for any theory with truly categorical or absolutist rules. If even as many as two absolute rules exist, they will sometimes conflict. Either we must accept a system with only one absolute rule, or we must give up absolutes altogether (unless we can specify their meaning and scope in order to avoid conflict) . . .

Overemphasizing law, underemphasizing relationships

Kant's arguments concentrate on lawful obligations, and recent Kantian theories, such as Rawls's, feature a contractual basis for obligations. But whether freedom, choice, equality, contract, law, and other staples of Kantianism deserve to occupy such a central position in a moral theory is questionable. (They are, we can nonetheless agree, central ingredients in legal and political theories.) These visions of the moral life fail to capture much in personal relationships that generate moral responsibilities, and in relationships among friends and family, we rarely think or act in terms of law, contract, or absolute rules.[29]

This perspective suggests that Kant's theory (like utilitarianism) is better suited for relationships among strangers than for relationships among friends or other intimates. Parents, for example, do not see responsibilities to their children in terms of contracts, but in terms of care, needs, sustenance, and loving attachment. Only if all forms of moral relationship – and our moral sentiments, motivations, and virtues – could be reduced to a law-governed exchange would Kantian theory become a cogent general moral theory.

Abstractness without content

G. W. F. Hegel once criticized Kant's theory for lacking the power to develop specific duties, such as those needed in professional ethics.[30] We agree that the notions of "rationality" and "humanity" offer too thin a basis for a determinate set of moral norms. Kant's relatively empty formalisms have little power to identify or assign specific obligations in almost any context of everyday morality, thereby raising questions about the theory's practicability. Its abstractness and impractibility give us another reason why method in ethics should start with considered judgments and then specify principles and test moral claims in light of overall coherence.

A constructive evaluation of Kantianism

Kant argued that when good reasons support a moral judgment, those reasons are good for all relevantly similar circumstances. Simple as it may seem, this claim is far-reaching. For example, if we are required to obtain valid consent for all the subjects of biomedical research, we cannot make exceptions of certain persons merely because we could advance science by doing so. We cannot use institutionalized populations, for example, without consent any more than we can use people who are not in institutions without their consent. Kant and many Kantians have driven home the point that persons cannot act morally and privilege or exempt themselves or their favored group. If Kant had done nothing else than establish this point, he would have made a significant contribution to ethical theory.

LIBERAL INDIVIDUALISM: RIGHTS-BASED THEORY

Thus far, we have concentrated on terms such as the following from moral discourse: *obligation, permissible action, virtue,* and *justification.* The language of *rights* is no less important. Statements of rights provide vital protections of life, liberty, expression, and property. They protect against oppression, unequal treatment, intolerance, arbitrary invasion of privacy, and the like. Some philosophers and framers of political declarations even regard rights as the basic language for expressing the moral point of view.

An ethical analysis of the case of the five-year-old needing a transplant would, from this perspective, focus on the rights of all the parties, in an effort to determine their meaning and scope, as well as their weight and strength. The father could be considered to have rights of autonomy, privacy, and confidentiality that protect his bodily integrity and sphere of decision-making from interference by others. In addition, he has a right to information, which he apparently received, about the risks, benefits, and alternatives of living kidney donation. The father's decision not to donate is within his rights, as long as it does not violate another's rights. No apparent grounds support a general right to assistance that could permit anyone, including his own daughter, to demand a kidney. However, there are some special rights to assistance, and it might be argued that the daughter has a right to receive a kidney from her family, on the basis of either parental obligations or medical need. But even if such a right exists, which is doubtful, it would be sharply circumscribed. For example, it is implausible to suppose that such a right could be enforced against the girl's two siblings. Their right to noninterference, when the procedure is not for their direct benefit and carries risks, precludes their use as sources of a kidney.

Comprehensive analysis of this case in terms of rights would note that the father has exercised his rights of autonomy and privacy in allowing the physician to run some tests. He then seeks protection behind his right of confidentiality which he believes allows him to control access to any information generated in his relationship with the physician. However, the scope and limits of these alleged rights and competing rights need careful attention. For example, does the mother herself have a right to the information generated in the relationship between the father and the nephrologist, particularly information bearing on the fate of the daughter?

An analysis using rights would also consider whether the physician has a right of conscientious refusal. For example, the physician might resist becoming an instrument of the father's desire to keep others from knowing why he is not donating a kidney. But even if the physician does have a right to protect his integrity, does this right outstrip or trump the rights of others? Can a physician justifiably say "I have a right of conscience" and use this trump to escape the clutches of a moral dilemma?

The nature of liberal individualism

We analyze rights theory in this chapter as liberal individualism, the conception that a democratic society must carve out a certain space within which the individual may pursue personal projects. Liberal individualism has, in recent years, challenged the reigning utilitarian and Kantian moral theories. H. L. A. Hart has described this challenge as a switch from an "old faith that some form of utilitarianism . . . *must* capture the essence of political morality" to a new faith in "a doctrine of basic human rights, protecting specific basic liberties and interests of individuals."[31]

The faith may be new, but liberal individualism is not a new development in moral and political theory. At least since Thomas Hobbes, liberal individualists have employed the language of rights to buttress moral and political arguments, and the Anglo-American legal tradition has heavily relied upon this language. The language of rights has served, on occasion, as a means to oppose the status quo, to assert claims that demand recognition and respect, and to promote social reforms that aim to secure legal protections for individuals. Historically, this language was instrumental in wresting certain freedoms from established orders of religion, society, and state, such as freedom of the press and freedom of religious expression.

The legitimate role of civil, political, and legal rights in protecting the individual from societal intrusions is now beyond serious dispute, but the idea that individual rights provide the fountainhead for moral and political theory has been strongly resisted – for example, by many utilitarians and Marxists. They note that individual interests are often at odds with communal and institutional interests. In discussions of health care delivery, for example, proponents of a broad extension of medical services often appeal to the "right to health care," whereas opponents sometimes appeal to the "rights of the medical profession." Many participants in these moral, political, and legal debates seem to presuppose that arguments cannot be made persuasive unless they can be stated in the language of rights, although other participants prefer to avoid this language because it seems confrontational and adversarial.

The nature and status of rights

Rights are *justified claims* that individuals and groups can make upon other individuals or upon society; to have a right is to be in a position to determine, by one's choices, what others should do or need not do.[32] Claiming a right is a rule-governed activity. The rules may be legal rules, moral rules, institutional rules, or rules of games, but all rights exist or fail to exist because the relevant rules either allow or disallow the claim in question. As such, *legal* rights are claims that are justified by legal principles and rules, and *moral* rights are claims that are justified by moral principles and rules. A moral right, then, is a justified claim or entitlement, warranted by moral principles and rules.[33]

Absolute and prima facie rights

Some rights may be absolute (e.g., the right to choose one's religion or to reject all religion) but, typically, rights are not absolute. Like principles of obligation, rights assert prima facie claims . . .

Some writers seem to insist that rights are absolute, at least in restricted contexts. Ronald Dworkin has argued the well-known thesis that some rights are so basic that ordinary justifications for interference with rights by the state, such as reducing inconvenience or promoting utility, are insufficient. The stakes must be far more significant to justify such invasions, he argues, because rights are "trumps" held by an individual against general plans and background justifications in a political state.[34] Democratic governments typically frame their policies to promote the general welfare and to conform to majority decisions. In response, rights function to guarantee that individuals cannot be sacrificed to these government or majority interests. Rights are above the state's utilitarian goals for Dworkin, much in the way deontologists maintain that we cannot trade off rights secured by justice through political bargaining or a utilitarian calculus of social interests.

However, as Dworkin recognizes, if the claims of public utility are highly significant, the individual may not justifiably play a trump card.[35] Rights are not so strong that they may never be overridden. Dworkin has argued that if the state needs to protect the rights of others (e.g., the state needs to prevent the spread of a catastrophic disease), then it may legitimately override individual rights. What we cannot do, Dworkin insists, is to act as if the right did not exist and so make decisions based entirely on net social utility. Mere benefit to the community is not of itself sufficient to override rights – that is the whole point of rights guarantees. Dworkin's qualifications make "trumps" rather tamer than they first appear to be, and many utilitarians would not protest his milder formulation. He seems to advance a sound theory about the *purpose* of having rights, rather than a theory of their stringency or absoluteness.

We believe that all rights, like all obligations, are prima facie – that is, presumptively valid – claims that sometimes must yield to other claims. Even the right to life is not absolute, irrespective of competing claims or social conditions, as evidenced by common moral judgments about killing in war and killing in self-defense. In light of this need to balance claims, we should distinguish a *violation* of a right from an *infringement* of a right.[36] Violation refers to an unjustified action against a right, whereas infringement refers to a justified action overriding a right.

Positive and negative rights

A positive right is a right to receive a particular good or service from others, whereas a negative right is a right to be free from some action by others. A person's positive right entails another's obligation to do something for that person; a negative right entails another's obligation to refrain from doing something.[37] Examples of both sorts of rights appear in biomedical practice, research and policy. If a right to health care exists, for example, it is a positive right to goods and services grounded in a claim of justice . . . The right to forgo a recommended surgical procedure, by contrast, is a negative right grounded in the principle of respect for autonomy. The liberal individualist tradition has generally found it easier to justify negative rights, but the recognition of welfare rights in modern societies has led to an extension of the scope of positive rights.

Confusion about public policies governing biomedicine often reflects a failure to distinguish positive and negative rights. One example involves the U.S. Supreme Court decisions on abortion. The Court first ruled that a woman's right to privacy gives her a right to pursue an abortion prior to fetal viability (and after fetal viability if her life or health is threatened). The constitutionally protected right of privacy is here construed exclusively as a negative right that limits state interference. Many people thought that the Court had concomitantly recognized a positive right in its early decisions, namely a right to receive aid and assistance. They were surprised when the Court later ruled that the federal and state governments do not have obligations to provide funds for nontherapeutic abortions.[38] They contended that various abortion decisions are inconsistent, but they failed to see that the Court first recognized a negative right and later refused to recognize a positive right. The Court's reasoning is consistent. It affirms a negative right but denies a positive right.

The correlativity of rights and obligations

How are rights connected to obligations? To answer this question, consider the meaning of "X has a right to do or have Y." X's right entails that some party has an obligation either not to interfere if X does Y or to provide X with Y. Suppose a physician agrees to take John Doe as a patient and commences treatment. The physician incurs an obligation to Doe, and Doe gains correlative rights. If a state has an obligation to provide goods, such as food or health care to needy citizens, then any citizen who meets the relevant criteria of need can claim an entitlement to food or health care.

This analysis suggests a firm but untidy *correlativity* between obligations and rights.[39] This correlatively is untidy because at least one use of the words *requirement, obligation,* and *duty* indicates that not all obligations imply corresponding rights. For example, although we sometimes refer to requirements or obligations of charity, no person can claim another person's charity as a matter of right. If such norms of charity express what we "ought to do," they do so not from obligation but from personal ideals that exceed obligation. We can best construe these commitments as self-imposed "oughts" that are not required by morality and that do not generate rights-claims for other persons.

We conclude that rights language is correlative to obligation language, but in an untidy way that requires careful attention to particular contexts and often entails further specification of both rights and their correlative obligations.

Waivers and releases of rights

If one person holds a right against another, the first person is entitled to, but not required to, press the claim against the second party. The first party can release the second of the obligation owed, because the claimant of a right has discretion over its exercise. With legal rights, for example, an agent has the option to sue over another's failure to discharge a legal obligation. Any rights holder may, under any circumstances, *waive* his or her right. In doing so, the party who waives the right releases the other party from his or her obligation. For example, if a person has a right to a yearly contract from a university, the university is obligated to supply the person with the appropriate signed agreement. However, if the person waives his or her right to the contract, the university is no longer obligated to provide it.

The primacy of rights

The correlativity thesis does not determine whether rights or obligations, if either, is the more fundamental or primary category. The proposal made by some philosophers that ethical theory should be "rights-based"[40] springs from a particular conception of the function and justification of morality. If the function of morality is to protect individuals' interests (rather than communal interests), and if rights (rather than obligations) are our primary instruments to this end, then moral action-guides are rights-based. Rights, on this account, precede obligations.

A theory we encountered . . . illustrates this position: the libertarian theory of justice. One representative, Robert Nozick, maintains that "Individuals have rights, and there are things no person or group may do to them [without violating their rights]."[41] He takes the following rule to be basic in the moral life: All persons have a right to be left free to do as they choose. The obligation not to interfere with this right follows from the right itself. That it "follows" indicates the priority of a rule of right over a rule of obligation. That is, an obligation is derived from a right.

Alan Gewirth has proposed another rights-based argument that recognizes *positive* or *benefit* rights:

> Rights are to obligations as benefits are to burdens. For rights are justified claims to certain benefits, the support of certain interests of the subject or right-holder. Obligations, on the other hand, are justified burdens on the part of the respondent or duty-bearer; they restrict his freedom by requiring that he conduct himself in ways that directly benefit not himself but rather the right-holder. But burdens are for the sake of benefits, and not vice versa. Hence obligations, which are burdens, are for the sake of rights, whose objects are benefits. Rights, then, are prior to obligations in the order of justifying purpose . . . in that respondents have correlative obligations *because* subjects have certain rights.[42]

These rights-based accounts do not reject the *correlativity* thesis. Rather, they accept a *priority* thesis that obligations follow from rights, not the converse. Rights form the justificatory basis of obligations, they maintain, because they best capture the purpose of morality, which is to secure liberties or other benefits for a rights-holder.

A critical evaluation of liberal individualism

Problems with rights-based theories

One problem with basing ethics on rights is that rights are only a piece of a more general account that identifies what makes a claim valid. Justification of the system of rules within which valid claiming occurs is not itself rights-based. Pure rights-based accounts also run the risk of truncating or impoverishing our understanding of morality, because rights cannot account for the moral significance of motives, supererogatory actions, virtues, and the like. Such a limited theory would fare poorly under the criteria of comprehensiveness and explanatory and justificatory power. Accordingly, we should not understand a rights-based account as a comprehensive or complete moral theory, but rather as a statement of certain minimal and enforceable rules that communities and individuals must observe in their treatment of all persons.

Normative questions about the exercise of rights

Often the question is not whether someone has a right, but whether rights-holders should or should not exercise their rights. If a person says, "I know you have the right to do X, but you should not do it," this moral claim goes beyond a statement of a right. One's obligation or character, not one's right, is in question. Even if we had a full and complete theory of rights, we would still need a theory of obligation and character, and it does not appear possible to develop a satisfactory account by attending only to rights and their limits.

The neglect of communal goods

Liberal individualists sometimes write as if social morality's major concern is to protect individual interests against government intrusion. This vision is too limited, because it excludes not only bona fide communal demands and group interests, but also communal goods and forms of life, such as public health, biomedical research, and the protection of animals. The better perspective is that social ideals and principles of obligation are as critical to social morality as rights and that neither is dispensable.

The adversarial character of rights

Finally, the language of *claims* and *entitlements* is often unnecessarily adversarial. For example, the current interest in children's rights gives children many vital protections against abuse (for instance, when parents refuse to authorize life-saving therapies for children for inappropriate reasons), but the notion that children have claims against their parents provides an inadequate framework to express the moral character of the parent–child relationship. The attempt to understand this relationship and others, such as health care relationships, strictly in terms of rights, neglects and may even undermine the affection, sympathy, and trust at the core of the relationships. This is not to suggest either that rights are inherently adversarial or that they are dispensable, but rather to note that a rights-theory is a partial framework.

A constructive evaluation of liberal individualism

In recent ethical theory, some writers have sought to eliminate the language of rights. They suggest either that rights language can be replaced by another vocabulary (e.g., obligations and virtues) or that the assertion of valid individual claims against society has risky implications. We reject such views, and we accept both the correlativity thesis and the moral and social purposes served by traditional interpretations of basic human rights, in their positive as well as their negative forms.[43]

No part of the moral vocabulary has done more to protect the legitimate interests of citizens in political states than the language of rights. Predictably, injustice and inhumane treatment occur most frequently in states that fail to recognize human rights in their political rhetoric and documents. As much as any part of moral discourse, rights language crosses international boundaries and enters into treaties, international law, and statements by international agencies and associations. Rights thereby become acknowledged as international standards for the treatment of persons.

Being a rights-bearer in a society that enforces rights is both a source of personal protection and a source of dignity and self-respect. By contrast, to maintain that someone has an *obligation* to protect another's interest may leave the recipient in a passive position, dependent upon the other's good will in fulfilling the obligation. When persons possess enforceable rights correlative to obligations, they are enabled to be independent agents, pursuing their projects and making claims. What we often cherish most is not that someone is obligated to us, but that we have a right that secures for us the opportunity to pursue and claim as ours the benefit or liberty that we value.

COMMUNITARIANISM: COMMUNITY-BASED THEORY

Several approaches in contemporary philosophy and political theory have little sympathy with liberal individualism. In these theories, everything fundamental in ethics derives from communal values, the common good, social goals, traditional practices, and cooperative virtues. Communitarianism is such a theory. Conventions, traditions, loyalties, and the social nature of life and institutions figure more prominently in communitarianism than in the types of theory discussed to this point.

In the case of potential kidney transplantation discussed previously in this chapter, communitarians would not ask which rights are at stake, but which communal values and relationships are involved. They would focus on the family as a small community intermediate between the individual and the state. They would likely ask which acts, rules, and policies of organ donation, privacy, and confidentiality best reinforce and promote communal values, including family values.

Communitarian critics of the father's behavior, which reduces his daughter's chances of survival, would maintain that he is insufficiently committed to the goods of the family and that he asserts the values of liberal individualism in standing on his rights, without adequately attending to his responsibilities. The father contends that if the physician tells other members of the family the true reasons for his decision not to donate, it would wreck the family. The father's prediction about this negative impact may or may not be correct, but what his actions express about his own lack of commitment to the family's welfare is notable.

Communitarians might also view the physician as focused unduly on protecting rights, such as autonomy and privacy. From the communitarian perspective, the physician would be expected to consider whether his actions conform to traditions of medicine, with its communal goods, codes, and virtues. These traditions have often justified deception in treating patients, but the father asks the physician to deceive others, a relatively rare request and one with less clear historical precedent in medical practice . . . By contrast, nondisclosure to others because of confidentiality does have clear historical precedent in medicine, although rules of confidentiality are not absolute and have often been overridden by a larger social interest.

The repudiation of liberalism

Unfortunately, no systematic account of communitarianism exists that rivals the systematic theories of Mill, Kant, and other liberal philosophers. Contemporary communitarianism is usually analyzed in terms of a few key themes that emerge from a few leading writers. The most prominent themes are the influence of society on individuals (by contrast to the alleged emphasis in theories like Kant's and Mill's on free individual choice) and the roots of values in communal history, tradition, and practices.

Contemporary communitarians repudiate central tenets in what is often called *liberalism*, a term that is defined through cardinal premises in the types of theory discussed in the three previous sections: utilitarian, Kantian, and liberal individualist theories. What makes them jointly "liberal" is theory commitment to what Mill defended as *individuality*, what Kant called *autonomy*, and what liberal individualists protect as personal rights. Each type of theory protects the individual against the state, and – on the communitarian interpretation – each also asserts that the state should neither reward nor penalize different conceptions of the good life held by individuals. Postulates of individual autonomy, rights against the state, and community neutrality toward conflicting values, then, are the central liberal tenets that communitarians oppose.

Contemporary communitarians repudiate liberal *theory* and challenge *current societies* established on liberal premises, including many contemporary Western political states.[44] According to communitarians, these societies lack a commitment to the general welfare, to common purposes, and to education in citizenship, while expecting and even encouraging social and geographic mobility, distanced personal relations, welfare dependence, breakdowns in family life and marital fidelity, political fragmentation, and the like. The number of abandoned children and elderly parents, social and familial disintegration, the disappearance of meaningful democracy, and the lack of effective communal programs are, according to communitarians, the disastrous products of liberalism.

The meaning of *community* and its synonyms varies in these theories. Some communitarians refer almost exclusively to the political state as the community, whereas others refer to smaller communities and institutions with defined goals and role obligations. Some include the family as a basic communal unit, within which being a parent and being a child involve specific roles and responsibilities. Much of what a person ought to do in communitarian theories is determined by the social roles assigned to or acquired by this person as a member of the community. Understanding a particular system of moral rules, then, requires understanding the community's history, sense of cooperative life, and conception of social welfare.

With regard to theory, communitarian critics have regularly attacked Mill and Kant, but often they have aimed their criticisms at Rawls, particularly his liberal principle of justice that the rights of individuals cannot legitimately be sacrificed for the good of the community.[45] Communitarian criticisms of liberal theories seem to come to the following: Liberalism (1) fails to appreciate the constructive role of the cooperative virtues and the political state in promoting values and creating the conditions of the good life, (2) fails to acknowledge shared goals and obligations that come not from freely made contracts among individuals, but from communal ideals and responsibilities, and (3) fails to understand the human person as historically constituted by and embedded in communal life and social roles.[46]

Every major communitarian thinker has contested the thesis of the priority of individual rights over the common good. Charles Taylor's challenge is perhaps the most straightforward. He argues that all conceptions of the rights of individuals already contain within their fabric some conception of the individual and social good, at least in the form of the good of moral agency and the good of human associations, such as friendship. The liberal's claim of the priority of right is itself, from this perspective, premised on a conception of the human good (the good of autonomous moral agency, in particular). Furthermore, Taylor argues, the type of autonomy valued by liberals cannot be developed in the absence of family and other community structures. However, liberalism's emphasis on individual rights makes no provision for the development and maintenance of the necessary communities, and instead views individuals as isolated atoms existing independently of one another.[47]

Communitarians thus believe that liberals miss the essence of morality by unduly emphasizing abstract principles and abstract agents, while failing to see that both principles and agents are products of communal life.

Militant and moderate forms of communitarianism

We can distinguish communitarianism into *militant* and *moderate* forms. Militants firmly support community control and reject liberal theories. Several influential contemporary moral, social, and political thinkers, including Alasdair MacIntyre, Charles Taylor, and Michael Sandel, have supported this approach. By contrast, moderates emphasize the importance of various forms of community – including family and the political state – while attempting to accommodate strands in liberal theories. This kind of communitarianism includes figures as diverse as Aristotle, Hugo Grotius, David Hume, G. W. F. Hegel, John Mackie, and Michael Walzer. For them, social order and morality rest on historically developed norms, and moral rules derive their acceptability and correctness from these shared conventions. Although the term *communitarianism* was recently coined and typically applies to the militant form, we will use it for both forms. We will criticize militant theories, while relying on the moderate theories for our constructive evaluation.

Militant communitarianism sees liberalism as antagonistic to all tradition, and as opposed to rights and rights language. These communitarians aim to perpetuate and even impose on individuals conceptions of virtue and the good life that limit the rights conferred by liberal societies. Militant communitarians see persons as intrinsically *constituted* by communal values and as best suited to achieve personal goods through communal life.[48] In addition, MacIntyre argues that we have inherited many incoherent fragments of once-coherent schemes of thought and action, and only if we understand our peculiar historical and cultural situation can we recognize the problematic dimensions of moral evaluation and moral theory.[49]

The moderate communitarian takes a stance far less opposed to autonomy and individual rights. A typical example is J. L. Mackie's appeal to "intersubjective standards," meaning that community-wide agreements form the basis of acceptable moral rules and that these intersubjective agreements cannot be further validated or invalidated by appeals to rationality. Mackie understands morality entirely in terms of social practices that express what the community demands, allows, enforces, and condemns. Nonetheless, he insists that we need not view moral judgments as unchanging conventional rules beyond possibility of reform: "Of course there have been and are moral heretics and moral reformers ... But this can usually be understood as the extension, in ways which, though new and unconventional, seemed to them to be required for consistency of rules to which they already adhered as arising out of an existing way of life."[50]

The primacy of social practices

MacIntyre and other communitarians have traced to Aristotle the thesis that local community practices and their corresponding virtues should have priority over ethical theory in normative descisionmaking. MacIntyre uses "practice" to designate a cooperative arrangement in pursuit of goods that are internal to a structured communal life. Social roles of parenting, teaching, governing, healing, and the like involve practices. "Goods internal to a practice" are achievable, according to MacIntyre, only by engaging in the practice and conforming to its constraints and standards of excellence. In the practice of medicine, for example, goods internal to the profession exist, and these determine what it means to be a good physician. The virtues of physicians flow from communal and institutional practices of care, practical wisdom, and education. Medicine, like other professions and political institutions, has a history that sustains a tradition requiring participants in the practice to cultivate certain virtues.[51]

The importance of traditional practices and the need for communal intervention to correct socially disruptive outcomes are standard themes in communitarian thought. For example, Sandel proposes that we disallow plant closings that devastate local communities and that we ban pornography when it deeply offends a community's ways of life.[52]

As an example of communitarians' promotion of the common good in biomedical ethics, consider their debate with liberal individualists over policies of obtaining cadaveric organs for transplantation. Based on principles of liberal individualism, all states in the United States adopted the Uniform Anatomical Gift Act in the late 1960s and early 1970s. This act gives individuals the right to donate their organs after death and to express their decisions through a donor card or other documents of gift. If the individual has not made a decision prior to death, the law authorizes the family to decide whether to donate the decedent's organs. Opinion polls suggested that many individuals would sign donor cards and provide a sufficient supply of organs, thereby avoiding the need to search for living donors of kidneys.

In practice, however, few individuals sign donor cards, the cards are rarely available at the time of death, and procurement teams virtually always check with the family, even if the decedent left a valid donor card. As a result, a communitarian focus has emerged. The family has become the primary donor (that is, the decision-maker about donation) rather than the individual, and because the supply of organs has remained limited, various policies have been considered and some adopted that aim to promote the common good more vigorously. Even approaches that protect individual rights attempt to educate people about the need for organs, and some writers in ethics propose *requiring* people to make a decision about donation, for instance, when obtaining a driver's license. Recent laws and regulations require hospitals to ask families whether they know the wishes of the decedent and want to donate the decedent's organs.

Some communitarians now recommend still stronger laws and policies to make organ procurement a well-defined community project rather than a matter of individual or even family decisions. They defend *presumed consent* laws, which would parallel laws in several states for corneas (when bodies are under the auspices of the medical examiner's office) and laws in several countries for solid organs. These laws presume that individuals or families have decided to donate unless they have registered a dissent. A more straightforward rationale is the *routine salvaging* of organs unless objections are registered: Some communitarians defend such a policy of organ retrieval on grounds that members of a community should be willing to provide others objects of lifesaving value when they can do so at no cost to themselves.[53] A few commentators even recommend stricter policies of routine collection to reflect communal ownership of cadaveric body parts. The last approach conflicts so deeply with liberal individualist values that it has, as yet, not received serious consideration.[54]

An emphasis on the community and the common good also appears in debates about the allocation of health care ... According to Daniel Callahan's communitarian account, we should enact public policy from a shared consensus about the good society, not on the basis of individual rights. We should scrap liberal assumptions about government neutrality, and society should be free to implement a substantive concept of the good. Biomedical ethics should use communitarian values to implement or revise social laws and regulations governing the promotion of health, the use of genetic knowledge, the use of advances in medical technology, responsibilities to future generations, and the limits of heath care for the elderly. In each case, Callahan would ask "What is most conducive to a good society?," not "Is it harmful or does it violate autonomy?"[55]

Although many communitarians critique and propose specific acts, practices, and policies, such as procuring organs or allocating health care, few systematic communitarian proposals have emerged for biomedical ethics. One exception is Ezekiel Emanuel's vision of medical ethics, which rests on the following claims: Public laws and public values have shaped the ends of medicine, as affirmed by the profession. These ends are understood through a framework of shared political convictions, conceptions of justice, and ideas of the good life. In place of the liberalism that has undergirded much of medical ethics, Emanuel proposes a communitarianism closely connected to political theory. This communitarianism is moderate by virtue of its acceptance of pluralistic conceptions of the good life and its recognition of some individual rights. Yet it remains communitarian because democratic initiatives are necessary to fashion a community's conceptions of the good life into policies and laws. Emanuel envisions thousands of community health plans in which citizen-members deliberate about conceptions of the good life and debate policies, such as those for termination of life-sustaining treatment for incompetent patients and for the allocation of medical resources.[56]

A critical evaluation of communitarian ethics

Several claims made by more militant communitarians rely on questionable accusations and arguments. We concentrate on these problems in our criticisms. Many themes in moderate communitarianism we believe to be unproblematic and even acceptable to advocates of liberal theories. We will focus on these unproblematic themes in our constructive comments.

An unfair account of liberal theories

Militant communitarians suggest that liberal theorists defend atomistic, isolated individuals and have a corrupting skepticism about communal goods. This characterization is inaccurate. Mill and Rawls, the figures most frequently attacked by communitarians, never depict either individuals or the communal good in these terms, and both philosophers develop a theory of the common good, as well as an account of social traditions and political community.[57] Mill thought he had captured how historical traditions converge to the principle of utility, which he construed as a principle of communal welfare. Even in *On Liberty* (Mill's treatise on individual liberty rights), Mill argued that a community should take steps to ensure adequate public discussion of what constitutes the good of the community. Liberty functions in his arguments to protect individuals against mistakes in planning communal pursuits of the good, and he defends individuality *because* it conduces to a constantly readjusted and improved community. Similarly, Rawls defends rights and liberties, in part, because an open society can correct and revise social ends better than a society controlled by tradition.[58]

A false dichotomy: Community or autonomy

Communitarians present us with two false dichotomies: (1) either liberal accounts of rights and justice have priority or the communal good has priority,[59] and (2) either we protect radical autonomy in decision-making or we protect communal determination of social goals against the individual. A more accurate picture is that we inherit social roles and goals. We then critique, adjust, and attempt to improve our beliefs over time through free discussion and collective arrangements. Individuals and groups alike progressively interpret, revise, and sometimes even replace traditions with new conceptions that adjust and foster community values. This liberal outlook is, as Joe Feinberg notes, entirely compatible with communal interests: "It is impossible to think of human beings except as part of ongoing communities, defined by reciprocal bounds of obligation, common traditions, and institutions . . . The ideal [in liberal accounts] of the autonomous person is that of an authentic individual whose self-determination is as complete as it is consistent with the requirement that he is, of course, a member of a community."[60]

A failed challenge to rights

Communitarians sometimes argue against rights (especially natural rights) on grounds that they do not exist.[61] At other times, they argue against rights on grounds that rights function to give individuals too much power and that rights thereby stall communal organization and activities and dull our sense of social union. Both claims miss the valuable consequences that rights have for communities. We value rights because, when enforced, they provide protections against unscrupulous behavior, promote orderly change and cohesiveness in communities, and allow diverse communities to coexist peacefully within a single political state.[62] Rights are necessary both to enable individuals to live safely and to protect them from oppressive communities.

Even if we grant communitarian arguments that the best life is communal life, it would not follow that communities should determine the individual's goals or truncate individual rights. The major reason for the prominence of rights in moral and political theory is that they stand as a shield against communal intrusion.

A constructive evaluation of communitarianism

By emphasizing historical traditions and institutional practices, communitarian theories have redirected ethical theory in recent years and have helped us rediscover the importance of community, even if we accept liberal values. Communitarians rightly emphasized the need to foster neighborhood association, create communal ties, promote public health, and develop national goals. Also to be welcomed is the return in some communitarian theories to such landmarks in ethical theory as the writings of Aristotle, Hume, and Hegel. These more community-minded philosophers deserve status as great classical theorists, alongside Mill and Kant.

NOTES

1 "Chapter 8, Moral Theories" from *Principles of Biomedical Ethics* by Tom L. Beauchamp and James F. Childress, copyright © 1979, 1983, 1989, 1994, 2001 by Oxford University Press, Inc. Used by permission of Oxford University Press, Inc.
2 For analysis of this utilitarian thesis, see Samuel Scheffler, *Consequentialism and Its Critics*, Oxford: Clarendon Press, 1988.
3 Jeremy Bentham, *An Introduction to the Principles of Morals and Legislation*, J.H. Burns and H. L. A. Hart (eds), Oxford: Clarendon Press, 1970, pp. 11–14, 31, 34. John Stuart Mill, *Utilitarianism*, in vol. 10 of the *Collected Works of John Stuart Mill*, Toronto: University of Toronto Press, 1969, Chapter 1, p. 207; Chapter. 2, pp. 210, 214; Chapter 4, pp. 234–235.

4 A representative of the first list is G. E. Moore, *Principia Ethica*, Cambridge: Cambridge University Press, 1903, p. 90ff; a representative of the latter list is James Griffin, *Well-Being: Its Meaning, Measurement and Moral Importance*, Oxford: Clarendon Press, 1986, p. 67.

5 This case is based on Melvin D. Levine, Lee Scott, and William J. Curran, "Ethic Rounds in a Children's Medical Center: Evaluation of a Hospital-based Program for Continuing Education in Medical Ethics," *Pediatrics*, 1977, vol. 60, 205.

6 Among writers in bioethics, Joseph Fletcher and Peter Singer are good examples of act utilitarians, while R. M. Hare is a good example of rule utilitarianism. See, for example, Joseph Fletcher, *Humanhood: Essays in Biomedical Ethics*, Buffalo, NY: Prometheus Books, 1979; Peter Singer, *Practical Ethics*, 2nd edn, Cambridge: Cambridge University Press, 1993; and R. M. Hare, *Essays in Bioethics*, Oxford: Oxford University Press, 1993; and Hare, "A Utilitarian Approach to Ethics," in *A Companion to Bioethics*, Helga Kuhse and Peter Singer (eds), Oxford: Blackwell, 1998, pp. 80–85.

7 Worthington Hooker, *Physician and Patient*, New York: Baker and Scribner, 1849, pp. 357ff, 375–381.

8 J. J. C. Smart, *An Outline of a System of Utilitarian Ethics*, Melbourne: University Press, 1961; and "Extreme and Restricted Utilitarianism," in *Contemporary Utilitarianism*, Michale Bayles (ed.), Garden City, NY: Doubleday and Co., 1968, esp. pp. 104–107, 113–115

9 Richard B. Brandt, "Toward a Credible Form of Utilitarianism," in *Contemporary Utilitarianism* pp. 143–186 and in Brandt's *Morality, Utilitarianism, and Rights*, Cambridge: Cambridge University Press, 1992.

10 This question is discussed in Madison Powers, "Repugnant Desires and the Two-tier Conception of Utility," *Utilitas*, vol. 6, 1994, pp. 171–176.

11 Alan Donagan, "Is There a Credible Form of Utilitarianism?" in *Contemporary Utilitarianism*, pp. 187–202.

12 A subtle argument to this conclusion is found in Kagan, *The Limits of Morality, passim*.

13 Williams, "A Critique of Utilitarianism," in J. J. C. Smart and Bernard Williams, *Utilitarianism: For and Against*, Cambridge: Cambridge University Press, 1973, pp. 116–117; and J. L. Mackie, *Ethics: Inventing Right and Wrong*, New York: Penguin Books, 1977, pp. 129, 133. For an extension, see Edward Harcourt, "Integrity, Practical Deliberation and Utilitarianism," *Philosophical Quarterly*, 1998, vol. 48, 189–198; for critical commentary, see Alastair Norcross, "Consequentialism and Commitment," *Pacifica Philosophical Quarterly*, 1997, vol. 78, 380–403.

14 Milton Weinstein and William B. Statson, *Hypertension*, Cambridge, MA: Harvard University Press, 1977; and "Public Health Rounds at the Harvard School of Public Health: Allocating of Resources to Manage Hypertension," *New England Journal of Medicine*, 1977, vol. 296, 732–739; and "Allocation Resources: The Case of Hypertension," *Hastings Center Report*, 1977, vol. 7, pp. 24–29.

15 Jane Morely, *et al.*, "Hypertension Control and Access to Medical Care in the Inner City," *American Journal of Public Health*, 1998, vol. 88, 1696–1699; Steven Shea, *et al.*, "Correlates of Nonadherence to Hypertension Treatment in an Inner-city Minority Population," *American Journal of Public Health*, 1992, vol. 82, 1607–1612.

16 Amartya Sen, *On Ethics and Economics*, Oxford: Basil Blackwell, 1987, p. 75.

17 Kant sought to show that unaided reason can be and should be a proper motive to action. What we should do morally is determined by what we would do "if reason completely determined the will." *The Critique of Practical Reason* translated by Lewis White Beck, New York: Macmillan, 1985, pp. 18–19; Ak. 20. "Ak." designates the page-reference system of the 22-volume Preussische Akademie edition conveniently cited in Kant scholarship.

18 Kant, *Foundations of the Metaphysics of Morals*, translated by Lewis White Beck, Indianapolis, IN: Bobbs-Merrill Company, 1959, pp. 37–42; Ak. 421–424.

19 *Foundations,* p. 47; Ak. 429.

20 *Foundations,* pp. 51, 57–63; Ak. 432, 439–444.

21 *Foundations,* pp. 58; Ak. 439–440; and *Critique of Practical Reason,* p. 33; Ak. 33.

22 Alan Donagan, *The Theory of Morality,* Chicago: University of Chicago Press, 1977, pp. 63–66.

23 See *A Theory of Justice,* Cambridge, MA: Harvard University Press, 1971; revised edition, 1999, pp. 3–4, 27–31 (1999: pp. 3–4, 24–28). For Rawls's more technical interests in and development of Kant, see his "Themes in Kant's Moral Philosophy," in *Kant's Transcendental Deductions,* Eckart Förster (ed.), Stanford, CA: Stanford University Press, 1989, pp. 81–113.

24 Rawls, *A Theory of Justice,* pp. 252, 256, 515–520, (1999: pp. 221–222, 226–227, 452–456). See also Rawls, "A Kantian Conception of Equality," *Cambridge Review,* February 1975, 97ff.

25 Rawls, "The Priority of Right and Ideas of the Good," *Philosophy & Public Affairs,* 1988, vol. 17, 252; and "Justice as Fairness: Political not Metaphysical," *Philosophy & Public Affairs,* 1985, vol. 14, 223–251, esp. 224–225.

26 See, for example, Thomas Nagel, "Personal Rights and Public Space," *Philosophy & Public Affairs,* 1995, vol. 24, 83–107; and his *The View from Nowhere,* New York: Oxford University Press, 1986; and Bernard Williams, *Ethics and the Limits of Philosophy,* Cambridge, MA: Harvard University Press, 1985; and his *Moral Luck: Philosophical Papers, 1973–1980,* Cambridge: Cambridge University Press, 1981.

27 See Advisory Committee on Human Radiation Experiments, *Final Report of the Advisory Committee on Human Radiation Experiments,* New York: Oxford University Press, 1996; Keay Davidson, "Questions Linger on 1940s UCSF Plutonium Shots," *The San Francisco Examiner,* 23 February 1995, p. A6; and University of California at San Francisco (UCSF), *Report of the UCSF Ad Hoc Fact Finding Committee on World War II Human Radiation Experiments,* February 1995, unpublished but released to the public.

28 For an example of such a utilitarian approach to moral rules, see Richard B. Brandt, *Morality, Utilitarianism, and Rights.*

29 Annette Baier, "The Need for More than Justice," *Canadian Journal of Philosophy,* 1997, vol. 13, supp. vol. on *Science, Ethics and Feminism,* Marsha Hanen and Kai Nielsen (eds), 41–56. Reprinted in Baier, *Moral Prejudices,* Cambridge, MA: Harvard University Press, 1994.

30 G. W. F. Hegel, *Philosophy of Right,* translated by T. M. Knox, Oxford: Clarendon Press, 1942, pp. 89–90, 106–107.

31 H. L. A. Hart, "Between Utility and Rights," in *Jurisprudence and Philosophy,* Oxford: Clarendon Press, 1983, p. 198. For debates about liberalism, see Nancy L. Rosenblum (ed.), *Liberalism and the Moral Life,* Cambridge, MA: Harvard University Press, 1989.

32 Compare H. L. A. Hart, "Bentham on Legal Rights," in *Oxford Essays in Jurisprudence,* 2nd series, A. W. B. Simpson (ed.), Oxford: Oxford University Press, 1973, pp. 171–198.

33 See Joel Feinberg, *Social Philosophy,* Englewood Cliffs, NJ: Prentice-Hall, 1973, p. 67.

34 Ronald Dworkin, *Taking Rights Seriously,* Cambridge, MA: Harvard University Press, 1977, pp. xi; and *Law's Empire,* Cambridge, MA: Harvard University Press, 1986, p. 223.

35 Dworkin, *Taking Rights Seriously,* pp. xi, 92, 191, and "Is There a Right to Pornography?" *Oxford Journal of Legal Studies,* 1981, vol. 1, 171–212.

36 See Judith Jarvis Thomson, *The Realm of Rights,* Cambridge, MA: Harvard University Press, 1990, pp. 122ff.

37 See Feinberg, *Social Philosophy,* p. 59 and Eric Mack (ed.), *Positive and Negative Duties,* New Orleans: Tulane University Press, 1985.

38 The first decade of decisions began with *Roe v. Wade* 410 U.S. 113 (1973) and ran through *City of Akron v. Akron Center for Reproductive Health* (June 1983). Decisions of major importance pertaining to indigency and funding were *Maher v. Roe,* 432 U.S. 464 (1977) and *Harris v. McRae,* 448 U.S. 297 (1980). In *Planned Parenthood v. Casey*

(June 28, 1992), the U.S. Supreme Court further upheld the pregnant woman's right to terminate her pregnancy within limits, while abolishing the trimester framework. It recognized the state's interest in fetal life from the beginning of the pregnancy and allowed states to institute requirements that do not impose an undue burden on the pregnant woman's decisions and actions.

39 See David Braybrooke, "The Firm but Untidy Correlativity of Rights and Obligations," *Canadian Journal of Philosophy*, 1972, vol. 1, 351–363; and Carl P. Wellman, *Real Rights*, New York: Oxford University Press, 1995.

40 Ronald Dworkin argues that political morality is rights-based in *Taking Rights Seriously*, pp. 169–177, esp. 171. John Mackie has applied this thesis to morality generally in "Can There Be a Right-based Moral Theory?" *Midwest Studies in Philosophy* 1978, vol. 3, esp. p. 350. For a view that the ancients had a theory of rights in place, but not a theory of the primacy of rights, see Myles Burnyeat, "Did the Ancient Greeks Have the Concept of Human Rights?" *Polis*, 1994, vol. 13, 1–11.

41 Robert Nozick, *Anarchy, State, and Utopia*, New York: Basic Books, 1974, pp. ix, 149–182. See also Jan Narveson, *The Libertarian Idea*, Philadelphia, PA: Temple University Press, 1988.

42 Alan Gewirth, "Why Rights Are Indispensable," *Mind*, 1986, vol. 95, 333. See Gewirth's later book, *The Community of Rights*, Chicago, University of Chicago Press, 1996; and a partial challenge to his thesis that connects the theory to positive and negative rights in Jan Narveson, "Alan Gewirth's Foundationalism and the Well-being State," *Journal of Value Inquiry*, 1997, vol. 31, pp. 485–502.

43 For discussions of bioethical issues in the framework of human rights, see Lawrence O. Gaston and Zita Lazzarini, *Human Rights and Public Health in the AIDS Pandemic*, New York: Oxford University Press, 1997.

44 See Michael Sandel, "The Political Theory of the Procedural Republic," *Revue de métaphysique et de morale*, 1988, vol. 93, 57–68, esp. 64–67; Sandel, "Democrats and Community," *The New Republic*, February 22, 1988, 20–23; Sandel, *Democracy's Discontent: America in Search of a Public Philosophy*, Cambridge, MA: Harvard University Press, 1996; Alasdair MacIntyre, *After Virtue*, pp. 235–237; Michael Walzer, "The Communitarian Critique of Liberalism," *Political Theory*, 1990, vol. 18, 6–23.

45 See Michael Sandel, *Liberalism and the Limits of Justice*, Cambridge: Cambridge University Press, 1982, pp. 15–17.

46 Sandel, "Introduction," in *Liberalism and Its Critics*, Sandel (ed.), New York: New York University Press, 1984, p. 6; and "Morality and the Liberal Ideal," *The New Republic*, 7 May 1984, 15–17; MacIntyre, *After Virtue*, Chapter 1. For a balanced assessment of these theses, see Alisa L. Carse, "The Liberal Individual: A Metaphysical or Moral Embarrassment?" *Nous*, 1994, vol. 28, 184–209.

47 Charles Taylor, "Atomism," in *Powers, Possessions, and Freedom*, Alkis Kontos (ed.), Toronto: University of Toronto Press, 1979, pp. 39–62.

48 Sandel, *Liberalism and the Limits of Justice*, pp. 15–23, 84–87, 92–94, 139–151; Alasdair MacIntyre, *Who's Justice? Which Rationality?*, Notre Dame, IN: University of Notre Dame Press, 1988, p. 10 and *After Virtue*, p. 206.

49 MacIntyre, *After Virtue*, p. 53.

50 Mackie, *Ethics*, pp. 30, 36–37; see also 106–110, 120–124. See also Michael Walzer's argument in *Interpretation and Social Criticism*, Cambridge, MA: Harvard University Press, 1987.

51 MacIntyre, *After Virtue*, pp. 17, 187, 190–194.

52 Sandel, "Morality and the Liberal Ideal," p. 17.

53 See James L. Nelson, "The Rights and Responsibilities of Potential Organ Donors: A Communitarian Approach," *Communitarian Position Paper*, Washington, DC: The Communitarian Network, 1992; and James Muyskens, "Procurement and Allocation Policies," *Mount Sinai Journal of Medicine*, 1989, vol. 56, 202–206.

54 For the wide range of issues in organ procurement, see James F. Childress, *Practical Reasoning in Bioethics*, Bloomington, IN: Indiana University Press, 1997, Chapters 14–16.

55 Callahan, *What Kind of Life*, New York: Simon & Schuster, 1990, Chapter 4, esp. pp. 105–113, and *Setting Limits*, New York: Simon & Schuster, 1987, esp. pp. 104–114.

56 Ezekiel J. Emanuel, *The Ends of Human Life: Medical Ethics in a Liberal Polity*, Cambridge, MA: Harvard University Press, 1991. See also Troyen Brennan, *Just Doctoring: Medical Ethics in the Liberal State*, Berkeley, CA: University of California Press, 1991.

57 See arguments to this conclusion in Will Kymlicka, "Communitarianism, Liberalism, and Superliberalism," *Critical Review*, 1994, vol. 8, 263–284; "Liberalism and Communitarianism," *Canadian Journal of Philosophy*, 1988, vol. 18, 181–204; and "Liberal Individualism and Liberal Neutrality," *Ethics*, 1989, vol. 99, 883–905. Even John Locke and Thomas Hobbes – the communitarians' arch-enemies (see MacIntyre, *After Virtue*, pp. 233–234) – have a considerable emphasis on promoting the commonwealth. Locke, for example, gives an elegant statement in *Two Treatises of Civil Government, Works*, London: C. and J. Rivington, 1824, 12th edn, bk. 2, note 8, p. 357.

58 See Amy Gutmann, "Communitarian Critics of Liberalism," *Philosophy & Public Affairs*, 1985, vol. 14, 308–322; and Andrew Jason Cohen, "A Defense of Strong Voluntarism," *American Philosophical Quarterly*, 1998, vol. 35, 251–265.

59 Sandel interprets Rawls as creating this dilemma by his account of the alleged priority of the right over the good. See *Liberalism and the Limits of Justice*, pp. 1–10, 17–24, 168–172, and "Morality and the Liberal Ideal," pp. 16–17.

60 Joel Feinberg, *Harm to Self*, vol. 3, in *The Moral Limits of the Criminal Law*, New York: Oxford University Press, 1986, p. 47.

61 See MacIntyre, *After Virtue*, pp. 68.

62 See William R. Lund, "Politics, Virtue, and the Right To Do Wrong: Assessing the Communitarian Critique of Rights," *Journal of Social Philosophy*, 1997, vol. 28, 101–122; Allen Buchanan, "Assessing the Communitarian Critique of Liberalism," *Ethics*, 1989, vol. 99, 852–882, esp. 862–865; and William A. Galston, *Liberal Purposes*, Cambridge: Cambridge University Press, 1991.

Truman and the Bomb

The presidency of the United States carries with it a responsibility so personal as to be without parallel.

Very few are ever authorized to speak for the President. No one can make decisions for him. No one can know all the processes and stages of his thinking in making important decisions. Even those closest to him, even members of his immediate family, never know all the reasons why he does certain things and why he comes to certain conclusions. To be President of the United States is to be lonely, very lonely at times of great decisions.

Harry S. Truman[1]

HIROSHIMA[2]

The Reverend Mr. Tanimoto got up at five o'clock that morning. He was alone in the parsonage, because for some time his wife had been commuting with their year-old baby to spend nights with a friend in . . . a suburb to the north. Of all the important cities of Japan, only two, Kyoto and Hiroshima, had not been visited in strength by B-san, or Mr. B, as the Japanese . . . called the B-29; and Mr. Tanimoto, like all his neighbors and friends, was almost sick with anxiety . . . Mr. Tanimoto had been carrying all the portable things from his church, in the close-packed residential district . . . to a house . . . two miles from the center of town . . . That is why he had risen so early.

Mr. Tanimoto had studied theology at Emory College, in Atlanta, Georgia; he had graduated in 1940; he spoke excellent English; he dressed in American clothes; he had corresponded with many American friends right up to the time the war began . . . In compensation, to show himself publicly a good Japanese, Mr. Tanimoto had taken on the chairmanship of his local tonarigumi, or Neighborhood Association, and to his other duties and concerns this position had added the business of organizing air-raid defense for about twenty families . . .

Before six o'clock that morning, Mr. Tanimoto started for [the] house . . . A few minutes after [he] started, the air-raid siren went off – a minute-long blast that warned of approaching planes but indicated to the people of Hiroshima only a slight degree of danger, since it sounded every morning at this time, when an American weather plane came over . . . Hiroshima was a fan-shaped city . . . its main commercial and residential districts, covering about four square miles in the center of the city, contained three-quarters of its population, which had been reduced by several evacuation programs from a wartime peak of 380,000 to about 245,000. Factories and other residential districts, or suburbs, lay compactly around the edges of the city . . . A rim of mountains runs around the other three sides of the delta.

As [he] started up a valley away from the tight-ranked houses, the all-clear sounded. (The Japanese radar operators, detecting only three planes, supposed that they comprised a reconnaissance.) . . . Then a tremendous flash of light cut across the sky . . . it travelled from east to west, from the city toward the hills. It seemed a sheet of sun. [He] reacted in terror – and [he] had time to react (for [he was] 3,500 yards, or two miles, from the center of the explosion) . . . Mr. Tanimoto took four or five steps and threw himself between two big rocks in the garden . . . He felt a sudden pressure, and then splinters and pieces of board and fragments of tile fell on him. He heard no roar.

When he dared, Mr. Tanimoto raised his head and saw that the . . . house had collapsed. He thought a bomb had fallen directly on it. Such clouds of dust had risen that there was a sort of twilight around. In panic . . . he dashed out into the street . . . In the street, the first thing he saw was a squad of soldiers who had been burrowing into the hillside opposite, making one of the thousands of dugouts in which the Japanese apparently intended to resist invasion, hill by hill, life for life; the soldiers were coming out of the hole, where they should have been safe, and blood was running from their heads, chests, and backs. They were silent and dazed.

Under what seemed to be a local dust cloud, the day grew darker and darker . . . He reflected that, although the all-clear had sounded and he had heard no planes, several bombs must have been dropped. He thought of a hillock in the . . . garden from which he could get a view of . . . the whole of Hiroshima . . . and he ran back up to the estate.

From the mound, Mr. Tanimoto saw an astonishing panorama. Not just a patch of [the neighborhood], as he had expected, but as much of Hiroshima as he could see through the clouded air was giving off a thick, dreadful miasma. Clumps of smoke, near and far, had begun to push up through the general dust. He wondered how such extensive damage could have been dealt out of a silent sky; even a few planes, far up, would have been audible. Houses nearby were burning, and when huge drops of water the size of marbles began to fall, he half thought they must be coming from the hoses of firemen fighting the blazes. (They were actually drops of condensed moisture falling from the turbulent tower of dust, heat, and fission fragments that had already risen miles into the sky above Hiroshima . . .)

He had thought of his wife and baby, his church, his home, his parishioners, all of them down in that awful murk. Once more he began to run in fear – toward the city . . . He was the only person making his way into the city; he met hundreds and hundreds who were fleeing, and every one of them seemed to be hurt in some way. The eyebrows of some were burned off and skin hung from their faces and hands. Others, because of pain, held their arms up as if carrying something in both hands. Some were vomiting as they walked. Many were naked or in shreds of clothing. On some undressed bodies, the burns had made patterns – of undershirt straps and suspenders and, on the skin of some women (since white repelled the heat from the bomb and dark clothes absorbed it and conducted it to the skin), the shapes of flowers they had had on their kimonos. Many, although injured themselves, supported relatives who were worse off. Almost all had their heads bowed, looked straight ahead, were silent, and showed no expression whatever.

. . . Mr. Tanimoto saw, as he approached the center, that all the houses had been crushed and many were afire. Here the trees were bare and their trunks were charred. He tried at several points to penetrate the ruins, but the flames always stopped him. Under many houses, people screamed for help, but no one helped, in general, survivors that day assisted only their relatives or immediate neighbors, for they could not comprehend or tolerate a wider circle of misery. The wounded limped past the screams, and Mr. Tanimoto ran past them. As a Christian he was filled with compassion for those who were trapped, and as a Japanese he was overwhelmed by the shame of being unhurt . . .

Mr. Tanimoto's way around the fire took him across the East Parade Ground, which, being an evacuation area, was now the scene of a gruesome review: rank on rank of the burned and bleeding. Those who were burned moaned, "Mizu, mizu! Water, water!" Mr. Tanimoto found a basin in a nearby street and . . . he began carrying water to the suffering strangers. When he had given drink to about thirty of them, he realized he was taking too much time . . . He went to the river again, the basin in his hand, and jumped down onto a sandspit. There he saw hundreds of people so badly wounded that they could not get up to go further from the burning city . . . Two or three small boats were ferrying hurt people across the river from Asano Park, and when one touched the spit, Mr. Tanimoto . . . jumped into the boat. It took him across to the park. There, in the underbrush, he found some of his charges of the Neighborhood Association.

When Mr. Tanimoto . . . reached the park, it was very crowded, and to distinguish the living from the dead was not easy, for most of the people lay still, with their eyes open . . . he decided to try to get back to his church . . . but he did not get far; the fire along the streets was so fierce that he had to turn back. He walked to the riverbank and began to look for a boat in which he might carry some of the most severely injured across the river from Asano Park and away from the spreading fire. Soon he found a good-sized pleasure punt drawn up on the bank . . . He worked the boat upstream to the most crowded part of the park and began to ferry the wounded . . . He worked several hours that way . . .

Mr. Tanimoto found about twenty men and women on the sandspit. He drove the boat onto the bank and urged them to get aboard. They did not move and he realized that they were too weak to lift themselves. He reached down and took a woman by the hands, but her skin slipped off in huge, glovelike pieces. He was so sickened by this that he had to sit down for a moment. Then he got out into the water and, though a small man, lifted several of the men and women, who were naked, into his boat. Their backs and breasts were clammy, and he remembered uneasily what the great burns he had seen during the day had been like: yellow at first, then red and swollen, with the skin sloughed off, and finally, in the evening, suppurated and smelly . . . On the other side, at a higher spit, he lifted the slimy living bodies out and carried them up the slope away from the tide. He had to keep consciously repeating to himself, "These are human beings."

HENRY L. STIMSON[3]

The policy adopted and steadily pursued by President Roosevelt and his advisers was a simple one. It was to spare no effort in securing the earliest possible successful development of an atomic weapon. The reasons for this policy were equally simple. The original experimental achievement of atomic fission had occurred in Germany in 1938, and it was known that the Germans had continued their experiments. In 1941 and 1942 they were believed to be ahead of us, and it was vital that they should not be the first to bring atomic weapons into the field of battle. Furthermore, if we should be the first to develop the weapon, we should have a great new instrument for shortening the war and minimizing destruction. At no time from 1941 to 1945 did I ever hear it suggested by the President, or by any other responsible member of the government, that atomic energy should not be used in the war. All of us of course understood the terrible responsibility involved in our attempt to unlock the doors to such a devastating weapon; President Roosevelt particularly spoke to me many times of his own awareness of the catastrophic potentialities of our work. But we were at war, and the work must be done. I therefore emphasize that it was our common objective throughout the war to be the first to produce an atomic weapon and use it. The possible atomic weapon was considered to be a new and tremendously powerful explosive, as legitimate as any other of the deadly explosive weapons of modern war. The entire purpose was the production of a military weapon; on no other ground could the wartime expenditure of so much time and money have been justified.

 . . . As time went on it became clear that the weapon would not be available in time for use in the European theater, and the war against Germany was successfully ended by the use of what are now called conventional means. But in the spring of 1945 it became evident that the climax of our prolonged atomic effort was at hand. By the nature of atomic chain reactions, it was impossible to state with certainty that we had succeeded until a bomb had actually exploded in a full-scale experiment; nevertheless it was considered exceedingly probable that we should by midsummer have successfully detonated the first atomic bomb. This was to be done at the Alamogordo Reservation in New Mexico. It was thus time for detailed consideration of our future plans . . .

MARTIN J. SHERWIN[4]

... Stimson, for one, began to ponder seriously the revolutionary aspects of the atomic bomb during the winter of 1944–45. By March he was convinced that its development raised issues that "went right down to the bottom facts of human nature, morals and government." And yet this awareness of its profound implications apparently did not lead him to raise the sort of questions that might naturally seem to follow from such awareness. He never suggested to Roosevelt or Truman that its military use might incur a moral liability (an issue the Secretary did raise with regard to the manner in which conventional weapons were used), or that chances of securing Soviet postwar cooperation might be diminished if Stalin did not receive a commitment to international control prior to an atomic attack on Japan ... Yet it must be pointed out that Bush and Conant[5] never seriously questioned the assumption of the bomb's use either. Like Niels Bohr,[6] they made a clear distinction between, on the one hand, its military application, which they took to be a wartime strategic decision, and, on the other, its moral and diplomatic implications, which bore on the longer-range issues of world peace and security and relations among nations ...

The preoccupation with winning the war obviously helped to foster this dichotomy in the minds of these men. But a closer look at how Bohr and Stimson respectively defined the nature of the diplomatic problem created by the bomb suggests that for the Secretary of War and his advisers (and ultimately for the President they advised) the dichotomy was, after all, more apparent than real. As a scientist, Bohr apprehended the significance of the new weapon even before it was developed, and he had no doubt that scientists in the Soviet Union would also understand its profound implications for the postwar world. He also was certain that they would convey the meaning of the development to Stalin, just as scientists in the United States and Great Britain had explained it to Roosevelt and Churchill. Thus the diplomatic problem, as Bohr analyzed it, was not the need to convince Stalin that the atomic bomb was an unprecedented weapon that threatened the life of the world, but the need to assure the Soviet leader that he had nothing to fear from the circumstances of its development. It was by informing Stalin during the war that the United States intended to cooperate with him in neutralizing the bomb through international control, Bohr reasoned, that it then became possible to consider its wartime use apart from its postwar role.

Stimson approached the issue differently. Without Bohr's training and without his faith in science and in scientists, atomic energy in its *un*developed state had a different meaning for him. Memoranda and interviews could not instill in a non-scientist with policymaking responsibilities the intuitive understanding of a nuclear physicist whose work had led directly to the Manhattan Project.[7] The very aspect of the atomic bomb upon which Bohr placed so much hope for achieving a new departure in international affairs – its uniqueness – made it unlikely that non-scientists would grasp its full implications and therefore act upon his proposals ...

It was only after Bohr's proposal[8] was rejected ... in September 1944 that events forced Stimson to think deeply about the weapon under his charge. Beginning with the fixed assumption that the bomb would be used in the war, he developed a view of the relationship between it and American diplomacy that reinforced that assumption, or at least gave him no cause to question it. For he could not consider an untried weapon an effective diplomatic bargaining counter; on the contrary, its diplomatic value was related to, if not primarily dependent upon, its demonstrated worth as a military force . . .

The need for assurance that the bomb would work raises the central question: Did Stimson's understanding that the bomb would play an important diplomatic role after the war actually prevent him from questioning the assumption that the bomb ought to be used during the war? It must be stressed, in considering this question, that Stimson harbored no crude hatred or racial antagonism for the Japanese people. Nor was he blind to moral consideration that might affect world public opinion . . .

STIMSON

On March 15, 1945, I had my last talk with President Roosevelt. My diary record of this conversation gives a fairly clear picture of the state of our thinking at that time . . .

I went over with him the two schools of thought that exist in respect to the future control after the war of this project, in case it is successful, one of them being the secret close-in attempted control of the project by those who control it now, and the other being the international control based upon freedom both of science and of access. I told him that those things must be settled before the first projectile is used and that he must be ready with a statement to come out to the people on it just as soon as that is done. He agreed to that . . .

This conversation covered the three aspects of the question which were then uppermost in our minds. First, it was always necessary to suppress a lingering doubt that any such titanic undertaking could be successful. Second, we must consider the implications of success in terms of its long-range postwar effect. Third, we must face the problem that would be presented at the time of our first use of the weapon, for with that first use there must be some public statement.

I did not see Franklin Roosevelt again.[9] The next time I went to the White House to discuss atomic energy was April 25, 1945, and I went to explain the nature of the problem to a man whose only previous knowledge of our activities was that of a senator who had loyally accepted our assurance that the matter must be kept a secret from him. Now he was President and Commander-in-Chief, and the final responsibility in this as in so many other matters must be his . . .

Memorandum discussed with President Truman April 25, 1945:

1   Within four months we will in all probability have completed the most terrible weapon ever known in human history, one bomb of which could destroy a whole city.

2   Although we have shared its development with the U.K., physically the United States is at present in the position of controlling the resources with which to construct and use it and no other nation could reach this position for some years.

3   Nevertheless it is practically certain that we could not remain in this position indefinitely.

    a. Various segments of its discovery and production are widely known among many scientists in many countries, although few scientists are now acquainted with the whole process which we have developed.

    b. Although its construction under present methods requires great scientific and industrial effort and raw materials, which are temporarily mainly within the possession and knowledge of the United States and the U.K., it is extremely probable that much easier and cheaper methods of production will be discovered by scientists in the future, together with the use of materials of much wider distribution. As a result, it is extremely probable that the future will make it possible for atomic bombs to be constructed by smaller nations or even groups, or at least by a larger nation in a much shorter time.

4   As a result, it is indicated that the future may see a time when such a weapon may be constructed in secret and used suddenly and effectively with devastating power by a willful nation or group against an unsuspecting nation or group of much greater size and material power. With its aid even a very powerful unsuspecting nation might be conquered within a very few days by a very much smaller one . . .

5   The world in its present state of moral advancement compared with its technical development would be eventually at the mercy of such a weapon. In other words, modern civilization might be completely destroyed.

6   To approach any world peace organization of any pattern now likely to be considered, without an appreciation by the leaders of our country of the power of this new weapon, would seem to be unrealistic. No system of control heretofore considered would be adequate to control this menace. Both inside any particular country and between the nations of the world, the control of this weapon will undoubtedly be a matter of the greatest difficulty and would involve such thoroughgoing rights of inspection and internal controls as we have never heretofore contemplated.

7   Furthermore, in the light of our present position with reference to this weapon, the question of sharing it with other nations and, if so shared, upon what terms, becomes a primary question of our foreign relations. Also our leadership in the war and in the development of this weapon has placed a certain moral responsibility upon us which we cannot shirk without very serious responsibility for any disaster to civilization which it would further.

8   On the other hand, if the problem of the proper use of this weapon can be solved, we would have the opportunity to bring the world into a pattern in which the peace of the world and our civilization can be saved . . .

The next step in our preparations was the appointment of . . . the Interim Committee[10] [which] was charged with the function of advising the President on the various questions raised by our apparently imminent success in developing the atomic weapon. I was its chairman.

SHERWIN

. . . On May 16 [Stimson] reported to Truman that he was anxious to hold the Air Force to "precision bombing" in Japan because "the reputation of the United States for fair play and humanitarianism is the world's biggest asset for peace in the coming decades."[11] But his concern here, it is evident, was not with the use as such of weapons of mass destruction, but simply with the manner in which they were used. "The same rule of sparing the civilian population should be applied as far as possible to the use of any new weapon," he wrote in reference to the bomb. The possibility that its extraordinary and indiscriminate destructiveness represented a profound qualitative difference, and so cried out for its governance by a higher morality than guided the use of conventional weapons, simply did not occur to him. On the contrary, the problem of the bomb as he perceived it was how to effectively subsume its management under the existing canons of international behavior.

. . . Stimson consciously considered two diplomatic effects of a combat demonstration of the atomic bomb: first, the impact of the attack on Japan's leaders, who might be persuaded thereby to end the war; and second, the impact of that attack on the Soviet Union's leaders, who might then prove to be more cooperative. It is likely that the contemplation together of the anticipated effects upon both Japanese and Soviet leaders was what turned aside any inclination to question the use of the bomb.

In addition, however, to the diplomatic advantages policymakers anticipated, there were domestic political reactions they feared, and these, too, discouraged any policy other than the most devastating and rapid use of the bomb. Everyone involved in administering the atomic energy program lived with the thought that a congressional inquiry was the penalty he might pay for his labors . . .

Beyond reasons directly related to the war, to postwar diplomacy, or to domestic policies, there was another, more subtle consideration moving some advisers to favor a combat demonstration of the bomb. Stimson informed [a] news commentator . . . in February 1974:

President Conant has written me that one of the principal reasons he had for advising me that the bomb *must be used* was that that was the only way to awaken the world to the necessity of abolishing war altogether. No technological demonstration, even if it had been possible under the conditions of war – which it was not – could take the place of the actual use with its horrible results . . . I think he was right and I think that was one of the main things which differentiated the eminent scientists who concurred with President Conant from the less realistic ones who didn't.

On May 31, 1945 . . . the Interim Committee submitted a formal recommendation that the atomic bomb be used without warning against Japan. The Committee had met officially on three previous occasions . . . [y]et the question of whether the bomb should be used at all had never actually been discussed. The minutes of the Interim Committee suggest why. The committee members had come together as advocates, the responsible advisers of a new force in world affairs, convinced of the weapon's diplomatic and military potential, aware of its fantastic cost, and awed by their responsibilities. They were also constrained in their choices by several shared but unstated assumptions reinforced for scientists and policymakers alike by the entire history of the Manhattan Project: First, that the bomb was a legitimate weapon that would have been used against the Allies if Germany had won the race to develop it. Second, that its use would have a profound impact upon Japan's leaders as they debated whether or not to surrender. Third, that the American public would want it used under the circumstances. And fourth . . . that its use ultimately would have a salutary effect on relations with the Soviet Union. These assumptions suggested, at least obliquely, that there were neither military, diplomatic, nor domestic reasons to oppose the use of the weapon. On the contrary, four years of war and the pressures to end it, four years of secrecy and the prospect of more; $2 billion and the question "For what?", Japan's tenacious resistance and America's commitment to unconditional surrender; Soviet behavior and the need for international control – all these factors served to bolster the accepted point of view.

. . . There is no suggestion . . . in the questions the Secretary placed before the assembled group, that his memory was serving him well when he wrote in his autobiography: "The first and greatest problem [for the Interim Committee] was the decision on the use of the bomb – should it be used against the Japanese, and if so, in what manner?" The fact is that a discussion of this question was placed on the agenda only after it was raised casually in the course of conversation during lunch.

. . . Compton recalls that he asked Stimson whether it might not be possible to arrange something less than a surprise atomic attack that would so impress the Japanese that they would see the uselessness of continuing the war . . . Various possibilities were brought forward, but were discarded one after the other . . .

After considerable discussion of types of targets and the desired effect, Stimson expressed the conclusion, on which there was general agreement, that the Japanese would not be given any warning; and that the bombing would not concentrate on a civilian area, but that an attempt would be made to make a profound psychological impression on as many Japanese as possible. Stimson accepted Conant's suggestion that the most desirable target would be a vital war plant employing a large number of workers and closely surrounded by workers' homes. No member of the Committee spoke to the contradiction between this conclusion and their earlier decision not to concentrate on a civilian area.

This critical discussion on the use of the bomb was over. It had not only confirmed the assumption that the new weapon was to be used, but that the *two* bombs that would be available early in August should be used.

STIMSON

The Interim Committee and the Scientific Panel also served as a channel through which suggestions from other scientists working on the atomic project were forwarded to me and to the President. Among the suggestions thus forwarded was one memorandum which questioned using the bomb at all against the enemy. On June 16, 1945, after consideration of that memorandum, the Scientific Panel made a report, from which I quote the following paragraphs:

The opinions of our scientific colleagues on the initial use of these weapons are not unanimous: they range from the proposal of a purely technical demonstration to that of the military application best designed to induce surrender. Those who advocate a purely technical demonstration would wish to outlaw the use of atomic weapons, and have feared that if we use the weapons now our position in future negotiations will be prejudiced. Others emphasize the opportunity of saving American lives by immediate military use, and believe that such use will improve the international prospects, in that they are more concerned with the prevention of war than with the elimination of this special weapon. We find ourselves closer to these latter views: we can propose no technical demonstration likely to bring an end to the war; we see no acceptable alternative to direct military use.

... The ultimate responsibility for the recommendation to the President rested upon me, and I have no desire to veil it. The conclusions of the committee were similar to my own, although I reached mine independently. I felt that to extract a genuine surrender from the Emperor and his military advisers, they must be administered a tremendous shock which would carry convincing proof of our power to destroy the Empire. Such an effective shock would save many times the number of lives, both American and Japanese, that it would cost.

The facts upon which my reasoning was based and steps taken to carry it out now follow.

The principal political, social, and military objective of the United States in the summer of 1945 was the prompt and complete surrender of Japan. Only the complete destruction of her military power could open the way to lasting peace.

Japan, in July 1945, had been seriously weakened by our increasingly violent attacks. It was known to us that she had gone so far as to make tentative proposals to the Soviet government, hoping to use the Russians as mediators in a negotiated peace. These vague proposals contemplated the retention by Japan of important conquered areas and were therefore not considered seriously. There was as yet no indication of any weakening in the Japanese determination to fight rather than accept unconditional surrender. If she should persist in her fight to the end, she had still a great military force.

In the middle of July 1945 ... [t]he total strength of the Japanese Army was estimated at about five million men ... The Japanese Army was in much better condition than the Japanese Navy and Air Force. The Navy had practically ceased to exist except as a harrying force against an invasion fleet. The Air Force had been reduced mainly to reliance upon Kamikaze, or suicide, attacks. These latter, however, had already inflicted serious damage on our seagoing forces, and their possible effectiveness in a last ditch fight was a matter of real concern to our naval leaders.

As we understood it in July, there was a very strong possibility that the Japanese government might determine upon resistance to the end, in all the areas of the Far East under its control. In such an event the Allies would be faced with the enormous task of destroying an armed force of five million men and five thousand suicide aircraft, belonging to a race which had already demonstrated its ability to fight literally to the death.

The strategic plans of our armed forces for the defeat of Japan as they stood in July had been prepared without reliance on the atomic bomb, which had not yet been tested in New Mexico. We were planning an intensified sea and air blockade and greatly intensified strategic air bombing through the summer and early fall, to be followed on November 1 by an invasion of the southern island of Kyushu. This would be followed in turn by an invasion of the main island of Honshu in the spring of 1946. The total US military and naval force involved in this grand design was of the order of five million men; if all those indirectly concerned are included, it was larger still.

We estimated that if we should be forced to carry this plan to its conclusion, the major fighting force would not end until the latter part of 1946, at the earliest. I was informed that such operations might be expected to cost over a million casualties, to American forces alone. Additional large losses might be expected among our allies, and, of course, if our campaign were successful and if we could judge by previous experience, enemy casualties would be much larger than our own.

It was already clear in July that even before the invasion, we should be able to inflict enormously severe damage on the Japanese homeland by the combined application of "conventional" sea and air power. The critical question was whether this kind of action would induce surrender. It therefore became necessary to consider very carefully the probable state of mind of the enemy, and to assess with accuracy the line of conduct which might end his will to resist.

With these considerations in mind, I wrote a memorandum for the President, on July 2, which I believe fairly represents the thinking of the American government as it finally took shape in action . . .

Memorandum for the President, July 2, 1945, on proposed program for Japan:

> . . . A question then comes: Is there any alternative to such a forceful occupation of Japan which will secure for us the equivalent of an unconditional surrender of her forces and a permanent destruction of her power again to strike an aggressive blow at the 'peace of the Pacific'? I am inclined to think that there is enough such chance to make it well worthwhile our giving them a warning of what is to come and a definite opportunity to capitulate. As above suggested, it should be tried before the actual forceful occupation of the homeland islands is begun and furthermore the warning should be given in ample time to permit a national reaction to set in.
>
> We have the following enormously favorable factors on our side – factors much weightier than those we had against Germany:

Japan has no allies.

Her navy is nearly destroyed and she is vulnerable to a surface and underwater blockade which can deprive her of sufficient food and supplies for her population.

She is terribly vulnerable to our concentrated air attack upon her crowded cities, industrial and food resources.

She has against her not only the Anglo-American forces but the rising forces of China and the ominous threat of Russia.[12]

We have inexhaustible and untouched industrial resources to bring to bear against her diminishing potential.

We have great moral superiority through being the victim of her first sneak attack.

The problem is to translate these advantages into prompt and economical achievement of our objectives ... It is therefore my conclusion that a carefully timed warning be given to Japan by the chief representatives of the United States, Great Britain, China, and, if then a belligerent, Russia by calling upon Japan to surrender and permit the occupation of her country in order to insure its complete demilitarization for the sake of the future peace.

This warning should contain the following elements:

The varied and overwhelming character of the force we are about to bring to bear on the islands.

The inevitability and completeness of the destruction which the full application of this force will entail.

The determination of the Allies to destroy permanently all authority and influence of those who have deceived and misled the country into embarking on world conquest.

The determination of the Allies to limit Japanese sovereignty to her main islands and to render them powerless to mount and support another war.

The disavowal of any attempt to extirpate the Japanese as a race or to destroy them as a nation.

A statement of our readiness, once her economy is purged of its militaristic influence, to permit the Japanese to maintain such industries, particularly of a light consumer character, as offer no threat of aggression against her neighbors, but which can produce a sustaining economy, and provide a reasonable standard of living ...

The withdrawal from their country as soon as the above objectives of the Allies are accomplished, and as soon as there has been established a peacefully inclined government, of a character representative of the masses of the Japanese people. I personally think that if in saying this we should add that we do not exclude a constitutional monarchy under her present dynasty, it would substantially add to the chances of acceptance.

... Success of course will depend on the potency of the warning which we give her. She has an extremely sensitive national pride and, as we are now seeing every day, when actually locked with the enemy will fight to the very death. For that reason the warning must be tendered before the actual invasion has occurred and while the impending destruction, though clear beyond peradventure, has not yet reduced her to fanatical despair. If Russia is part of the threat, the Russian attack, if actual, must not have progressed too far. Our own bombing should be confined to military objectives as far as possible.

. . . It will be noted that the atomic bomb is not mentioned in this memorandum. On grounds of secrecy the bomb was never mentioned except when absolutely necessary, and furthermore, it had not yet been tested. It was of course well forward in our minds as the memorandum was written and discussed that the bomb would be the best possible sanction if our warning were rejected.

TRUMAN

The historic message of the first explosion of an atomic bomb was flashed to me in a message from Secretary of War Stimson on the morning of July 16. The most secret and the most daring enterprise of the war had succeeded. We were now in possession of a weapon that would not only revolutionize war but could alter the course of history and civilization. This news reached me at Potsdam the day after I had arrived for the conference of the Big Three.[13]

Preparations were being rushed for the test atomic explosion at Alamogordo, New Mexico, at the time I had to leave for Europe, and on the voyage over I had been anxiously awaiting word on the results. I had been told of many predictions by the scientists, but no one was certain of the outcome of this full-scale atomic explosion. As I read the message from Stimson, I realized that the test not only met the most optimistic expectation of the scientists but that the United States had in its possession an explosive force of unparalleled power . . .

We reviewed our military strategy in the light of this revolutionary development.[14] We were not ready to make use of this weapon against the Japanese, although we did not know as yet what effect the new weapon might have, physically or psychologically, when used against the enemy. For that reason the military advised that we go ahead with the existing military plans for the invasion of the Japanese home islands . . .

On July 24 I casually mentioned to Stalin that we had a new weapon of unusual destructive force. The Russian Premier showed no special interest. All he said was that he was glad to hear it and hoped we would make "good use of it against the Japanese" . . .

The final decision of where and when to use the atomic bomb was up to me. Let there be no mistake about it. I regarded the bomb as a military weapon and never had any doubt that it should be used. The top military advisers to the President recommended its use, and when I talked to Churchill he unhesitatingly told me that he favored the use of the atomic bomb if it might aid to end the war.

In deciding to use this bomb I wanted to make sure that it would be used as a weapon of war in the manner prescribed by the laws of war. That meant that I wanted it dropped on a military target. I had told Stimson that the bomb should be dropped as nearly as possibly [*sic*] upon a war production center of prime military importance.

Stimson's staff had prepared a list of cities in Japan that might serve as targets. Kyoto, though favored ... as a center of military activity, was eliminated when Secretary Stimson pointed out that it was a cultural and religious shrine of the Japanese.

Four cities were finally recommended as targets: Hiroshima, Kokura, Niigata, and Nagasaki. They were listed in that order as targets for the first attack. The order of selection was in accordance with the military importance of these cities, but allowance would be given for weather conditions at the time of the bombing. Before the selected targets were approved as proper for military purposes, I personally went over them in detail with Stimson, Marshall, and Arnold, and we discussed the matter of timing and the final choice of the first target.

General Spaatz, who commanded the Strategic Air Forces, which would deliver the bomb on the target, was given some latitude as to when and on which of the four targets the bomb would be dropped . . . The War Department was given orders to instruct General Spaatz that the first bomb would be dropped as soon after August 3 as weather would permit.

With this order the wheels were set in motion for the first use of an atomic weapon against a military target. I had made the decision. I also instructed Stimson that the order would stand unless I notified him that the Japanese reply to our ultimatum was acceptable.

STIMSON

... There [had been] much discussion in Washington about the timing of the warning to Japan. The controlling factor in the end was the date already set for the Potsdam meeting of the Big Three. It was President Truman's decision that such a warning should be solemnly issued by the United States and the U.K. from this meeting, with the concurrence of the head of the Chinese government, so that it would be plain that **all** of Japan's principal enemies were in entire unity. This was done, in the Potsdam ultimatum of July 26, which very closely followed the above memorandum of July 2, with the exception that it made no mention of the Japanese Emperor.

On July 28 the Premier of Japan, Suzuki, rejected the Potsdam ultimatum by announcing that it was "unworthy of public notice." In the face of this rejection we could only proceed to demonstrate that the ultimatum had meant exactly what it said when it stated that if the Japanese continued the war, "the full application of our military power, backed by our resolve, will mean the inevitable and complete destruction of the Japanese armed forces and just as inevitably the utter devastation of the Japanese homeland."

For such a purpose the atomic bomb was an entirely suitable weapon . . .

Hiroshima was bombed on August 6, and Nagasaki on August 9. These two cities were active working parts of the Japanese war effort. One was an army center; the other was naval and industrial. Hiroshima was the headquarters of the Japanese Army defending southern Japan and was a major military storage and assembly point. Nagasaki was a major seaport and it contained several large industrial plants of great wartime importance. We believed that our attacks had struck cities which must certainly be important to the Japanese military leaders, both Army and Navy, and we waited for a result. We waited one day.

. . . After a prolonged Japanese cabinet session in which the deadlock was broken by the Emperor himself, the offer to surrender was made on August 10. It was based on the Potsdam terms, with a reservation concerning the sovereignty of the Emperor. While the Allied reply made no promises other than those already given, it implicitly recognized the Emperor's position by prescribing that his power must be subject to the orders of the Allied Supreme Commander . . . Our great objective was thus achieved, and all the evidence I have seen indicates that the controlling factor in the final Japanese decision to accept our terms of surrender was the atomic bomb.

The two atomic bombs which we had dropped were the only ones we had ready, and our rate of production at the time was very small. Had the war continued until the projected invasion on November 1, additional fire raids of B-29s would have been more destructive of life and property than the very limited number of atomic raids which we could have executed in the same period. But the atomic bomb was more than a weapon of terrible destruction; it was a psychological weapon . . . On August 6 one B-29 dropped a single atomic weapon on Hiroshima. Three days later a second bomb was dropped on Nagasaki and the war was over. So far as the Japanese could know, our ability to execute atomic attacks, if necessary by many planes at a time, was unlimited. As Dr. Karl Compton has said, "It was not one atomic bomb, or two, which brought surrender; it was the experience of what an atomic bomb will actually do to a community, plus the *dread of many more*, that was effective."

HIROSHIMA

Mr. Tanimoto, after his long run and his many hours of rescue work, dozed uneasily. When he awoke, in the first light of dawn, he looked across the river and saw that he had not carried the festered, limp bodies high enough on the sandspit the night before. The tide had risen above where he had put them; they had not had the strength to move; they must have drowned. He saw a number of bodies floating in the river.

[Later,] [s]tatistical workers gathered what figures they could on the effects of the bomb. They reported that 78,150 people had been killed, 13,983 were missing, and 37,425 had been injured . . . As the months went by and more and more hundreds of corpses were dug up from the ruins . . . the statisticians began to say that at least a hundred thousand people had lost their lives in the bombing. Since many people died of a combination of causes, it was impossible to figure exactly how many were killed by each cause, but the statisticians calculated that about twenty-five per cent had died of direct burns from the bomb, about fifty per cent from other injuries, and about twenty per cent as a result of radiation effects. The statisticians' figures on property damage were more reliable: sixty-two thousand out of ninety thousand buildings destroyed, and six thousand more damaged beyond repair. In the heart of the city, they found only five modern buildings that could be used again without major repairs.

Scientists swarmed into the city. Some of them measured the force that had been necessary to shift marble gravestones in the cemeteries, to knock over twenty-two of the forty-seven railroad cars at Hiroshima station, to lift and move the concrete roadway on one of the bridges, and to perform other noteworthy acts of strength, and concluded that the pressure exerted by the explosion varied from 5.3 to 8.0 tons per square yard. Others found that mica, of which the melting point is 900° C., had fused on granite gravestones three hundred and eighty yards from the center; that telephone poles of Cryptomeria japonica, whose carbonization temperature is 240° C., had been charred at forty-four hundred yards from the center; and that the surface of gray clay tiles of the type used in Hiroshima, whose melting point is 1,300° C., had dissolved at six hundred yards; and, after examining other significant ashes and melted bits, they concluded that the bomb's heat on the ground at the center must have been 6,000° C.

NOTES

1   Selections by Truman are excerpted from Harry S. Truman, *Memoirs of Harry S. Truman, Vol. I: Year of Decisions*, Garden City, NY: Doubleday & Company, 1955, p. ix, 415–416, 419–421. Used by permission of Margaret Truman Daniel.

2   From *Hiroshima*, by John Hersey, copyright © 1946 and renewed 1974 by John Hersey, pp. 2–6, 17–18, 29–31, 36–37, 45, 49, 80–82. Used by permission of Alfred A. Knopf, a division of Random House, Inc. and reproduced by permission of Penguin Books Ltd. (UK)

3   Henry L. Stimson (1867–1950), Secretary of War under President Roosevelt from July 1940 to April 1945 and under President Truman from April to September 1945, was in overall charge of the United States atomic development program. Selections by Stimson are excerpted from *On Active Service in Peace and War*, by Henry L. Stimson and McGeorge Bundy, 1948, pp. 613, 615–626, 630, 635–636. Copyright 1948 by Henry L. Stimson and McGeorge Bundy. Copyright renewed 1974 by McGeorge Bundy. Reprinted by permission of Harper Collins Publishers, and Random House Group Ltd. (UK)

4   Selections from Sherwin are excerpted from Martin J. Sherwin, *A World Destroyed: The Atomic Bomb and the Grand Alliance*, New York: Alfred A. Knopf, 1975, pp. 195–200, 202–204, 207–209. Used by permission of Martin J. Sherwin, Walter S. Dickson Professor of History at Tufts University.

5   Dr. Vannevar Bush, director of the Office of Scientific Research and Development and president of the Carnegie Institution of Washington, and Dr. James B. Conant, chairman of the National Defense Research Committee and president of Harvard University.

6 Danish physicist who escaped to England from Nazi-occupied Denmark in September 1943 and was greatly concerned with the development of an atomic arms race after the war.

7 The code name for the US effort to develop an atomic bomb.

8 In the summer of 1944, Bohr tried to convince Roosevelt and Churchill that an agreement for international control could be accomplished only by inviting Soviet participation in postwar atomic energy planning, **before** the bomb was a certainty and **before** the war was over.

9 President Franklin D. Roosevelt died on April 12, 1945 and Vice President Harry S. Truman succeeded him.

10 Members of the Interim Committee included James F. Byrnes (then a private citizen) as personal representative of the president; Ralph A. Byrd, under secretary of the Navy; William L. Clayton, assistant secretary of State; Dr. Vannevar Bush; Dr. Karl Compton, chief of the Office of Field Service in the Office of Scientific Research and Development and president of the Massachusetts Institute of Technology; and Dr. James B. Conant. The committee was assisted by a Scientific Panel whose members included Dr. A. H. Compton, director of the atomic energy project at the University of Chicago; Dr. J. R. Oppenheimer, director of the atomic energy project at Los Alamos; Dr. E. O. Lawrence, director of the atomic energy project at the University of California, Berkeley; and Dr. Enrico Fermi.

11 On March 9–10, 1945, the Air Force launched its first incendiary raids on the Tokyo area. Hundreds of bombers took part and hundreds of tons of incendiaries were dropped. A quarter of the city of Tokyo was destroyed, 83,000 persons were killed and 40,000 were injured. Similar successive raids burned out a great part of the urban area of Japan. Stimson, with a long-standing aversion to urban-area bombing, was the one senior official who questioned the fire raids.

12 Joseph Stalin had given his word at Yalta in February 1945 that the Soviet Union would enter the war against Japan two or three months after the end of war in Europe.

13 The alliance of the United States, the United Kingdom, and the Soviet Union.

14 When General Dwight D. Eisenhower, as the victorious Allied commander in Europe, learned about Alamogordo from Henry Stimson at Potsdam – he hoped that "we would never have to use such a thing."

Ben Bradlee

"Pentagon Papers"[1]

Sometime in the early spring of 1971 we had begun hearing rumors that the *New York Times* was working with a "blockbuster," an exclusive that would blow us out of the water. News like this produces a very uncomfortable feeling inside an editor's stomach. Getting beaten on a story is bad enough, but waiting to get beaten on a story is unbearable.

We heard the *Times* had a special task force at work on its blockbuster. We heard the task force was working in special offices away from the newspaper's 43rd Street offices. But we never found out who was part of the task force, much less what they were task-forcing about.

And there was so much news in Washington, we were having trouble keeping up with it all. On May Day the city hosted yet another in a growing number of anti-Vietnam demonstrations. *Post* reporters described Day One in West Potomac Park this way: " . . . at dawn's light . . . about 45,000 people were dancing, nodding their heads to music, making love, drinking wine and smoking pot." More than twelve thousand demonstrators were arrested – a record seven thousand on a single day. Downtown reeked of tear gas. Helicopters chop-chop-chopped across the city at tree-level day and night, a strange new addition to the capital scene.

At the beginning of June, we paused for a few days to focus on Tricia Nixon's wedding to Edward Cox. The Nixons had refused to accredit *Post* reporter Judith Martin to cover the White House on the wedding day. They didn't like *Post* reporters in general, but they particularly did not like stories she had written about the family. Any other reporter, but not Judy, we were told. And because we weren't about to let the White House – much less the Nixon White House – tell us who could or could not cover any story, we insisted on assigning Ms. Martin. We covered it from the TV tubes – and nobody but us gave a damn.

On Sunday, June 13, 1971, the top half of the *Post*'s page one was devoted to the White House wedding, but the top half of the *New York Times* revealed at last what their long-awaited blockbuster was all about: Six full pages of news stories and top-secret documents, based on a 47-volume, 7,000-page study, "History of U.S. Decision-Making Process on Vietnam Policy, 1945–1967." The *Times* had obtained a copy of the study, and had assigned more than a dozen top reporters and editors to digest it for three months, and write dozens of articles.

The *Post* did *not* have a copy, and we found ourselves in the humiliating position of having to rewrite the competition. Every other paragraph of the *Post* story had to include some form of the words "according to the *New York Times*," blood – visible only to us – on every word.

On Monday, June 14, the next installment of the Pentagon Papers appeared in the *Times*: "Vietnam Archive: A Consensus to Bomb Developed Before '64 Election, Study Says."

While candidate Goldwater was calling for the immediate bombing of North Vietnam, the story said, the Johnson administration had privately concluded two months before the election that he was right. The sustained bombing – known as Rolling Thunder – began three months after the election.

At the *Post* we had gone to General Quarters, and were trying desperately to get our own copy of the Pentagon Papers, or any reasonable substitute, and getting on with the job of rewriting the *Times*'s Monday story for our Tuesday paper. At breakfast Monday morning, my friend Marcus Raskin, a former member of Kennedy's National Security Council, and then a part of the leftist Institute of Policy Studies (IPS), offered me the manuscript of a book by IPS scholars, "Washington Plans an Aggressive War," which he said was "based on" the Pentagon Papers, and which had been written after "access" to the Pentagon Papers, whatever that meant. We were so far behind the *Times*, I expressed an interest, but the manuscript was a polemic against the war, and it carried only the quotes from the papers that served the cause. We read it with interest, but felt it was a poor substitute for the real thing.

Phil Geyelin had a friend in Boston who offered him what was described as two hundred pages of excerpts from the Pentagon Papers. That is apparently exactly what they were, but we had no idea of their context, and before we could get any idea, the substance of those two hundred pages showed up in the *New York Times*'s third installment, on Tuesday, June 15: "Vietnam Archive: Study Tells How Johnson Secretly Opened Way to Ground Combat." We were going out of our minds, especially when we read that US Attorney General John Mitchell had sent a telegram to the *Times* asking them to cease publishing anything from the Pentagon Papers, and to return all documents to the Defense Department.

That same Tuesday, the Justice Department went to court and got an injunction against the *Times*, restraining a newspaper in advance from publishing specific articles, for the first time in the history of the republic. At least the *New York Times* had been silenced, never mind how.

Wednesday night, the *Post*'s thorny National editor, Ben Bagdikian, was contacted by someone and given a telephone number, to be called only from a pay telephone, where he could reach his friend, Daniel Ellsberg.

Dan Ellsberg was a zealous Harvard intellectual, who had served voluntarily for two years in the Marine Corps before becoming a defense research expert for the Rand Corporation. He had volunteered in Vietnam, where he served as an "apprentice" to General Edward Lansdale. He had seen plenty of action in the Mekong Delta in 1965 and 1966, and actively supported the American pursuit of the war, until he returned in early 1969 to Rand, where he had been a colleague of Bagdikian.

Ellsberg was also the source of the New York Times's 7,000-page copy of the Pentagon Papers, because of his friendship with and respect for the Times's legendary Vietnam reporter, Neil Sheehan.

Late Wednesday, the 16th, Bagdikian flew to Boston, and first thing Thursday morning, he flew back with two first-class seats, one for himself and one for a large cardboard carton full of Pentagon Papers. The Post's package consisted of something over 4,000 pages of Pentagon documents, compared to the 7,000 received by the New York Times. At 10:30 a.m., Thursday, June 17, Bagdikian rushed past Marina Bradlee, age ten, tending her lemonade stand outside our house in Georgetown, and we were back in business.

For the next twelve hours, the Bradlee library on N Street served as a remote newsroom, where editors and reporters started sorting, reading, and annotating 4,400 pages, and the Bradlee living room served as a legal office, where lawyers and newspaper executives started the most basic discussions about the duty and right of a newspaper to publish, and the government's right to prevent that publication, on national security grounds, or on any grounds at all. For those twelve hours, I went from one room to the other, getting a sense of the story in one place, and a sense of the mood of the lawyers in the other.

With the Times silenced by the Federal Court in New York, we decided almost immediately that we would publish a story the next morning, Friday, the 18th, completing in twelve hours what it had taken the New York Times more than three months to do. For planning purposes, we had to take that decision so that we could re-thread the presses to include four extra, unplanned pages . . . an operation that cannot be done on the spur of the moment. At 4:00 p.m., we stopped reading and arguing to hold a story conference, to talk out what we had, and what we could get written and laid out in the five hours left before the first edition deadline. Our first choice was a piece to be written by diplomatic correspondent Murrey Marder about how the Johnson administration had stopped and restarted bombing North Vietnam to influence American public opinion, not to further U.S. military goals. But Murrey, one of the world's most thorough reporters, was also one of the slower writers. As a precaution, Chal Roberts started on a story about U.S. diplomatic strategy in Vietnam under the Eisenhower administration. Chal had the fastest typewriter in the business, and we knew he'd get it done. Don Oberdorfer was outlining his story for Day Three.

But things were getting a little stickier in the living room.

There the lawyers were marshaling strong arguments against publishing, or at least urging that we wait for the injunction against the New York Times to be litigated. The lawyers were Roger Clark and Tony Essaye, two young partners in the firm of William P. Rogers, who had been the Post's lawyer until he quit to become Nixon's Secretary of State. In midafternoon, they were joined by our own Fritz Beebe, now chairman of the board of The Washington Post Company. My heart sank when Beebe announced that our deliberations were not to be influenced by the fact that The Post Company was about to "go public" with a $35 million stock offering. Under the terms of this offering, the *Post* was liable for a substantial claim by the underwriters if some disaster or catastrophe occurred. No one wanted to say whether an injunction, or possible subsequent criminal prosecution, qualified as a catastrophe. Just as no one wanted to mention the fact that any company convicted of a felony could not own television licenses, a fact which added another $100 million to the stakes.

The lawyers were throwing a lot of case law at me and my allies: Howard Simons, Phil Geyelin, and his editorial page deputy, Meg Greenfield (managing editor Gene Patterson was minding the store on 15th Street), citing legal arguments that seemed curiously irrelevant in a Georgetown living room, where Marina was selling lemonade, Tony was serving sandwiches, and telephones were ringing off the hooks. It was bedlam.

Two decades later it's hard to figure out why the hell the Pentagon Papers had become such a *casus belli* for the administration. I knew exactly how important it was to publish, if we were to have any chance of pulling the *Post* up – once and for all – into the front ranks. Not publishing the information when we had it would be like not saving a drowning man, or not telling the truth. Failure to publish without a fight would constitute an abdication that would brand the *Post* forever, an establishment tool of whatever administration was in power. And end the Bradlee era before it got off the ground, just incidentally.

But I wasn't winning with the lawyers. A federal judge had enjoined the *New York Times* from publishing the same material, they argued. Therefore we did in fact have "reason to believe publication would damage the United States."

"Bullshit," a reporter would comment, not particularly constructively.

"Maybe we should tell the Attorney General that we have the papers and are going to publish them on Sunday," a lawyer suggested, looking for a compromise.

"That's the shittiest idea I ever heard," said Don Oberdorfer, constructively. Chal Roberts announced he would quit, and make a big stink about it, if we did that.

I was getting painted into a corner. I had to massage the lawyers, especially Beebe, into at least a neutral position, while preventing the reporters from leaving him no maneuvering room during what we all knew was going to be the ultimate showdown with Kay Graham. She was getting ready to host a goodbye party for Harry Gladstein, the veteran circulation vice president, at her house about ten blocks away.

Suddenly, I knew what I had to do. I snuck out of the living room to an upstairs telephone and placed a call to Jim Hoge, then the managing editor of the *Chicago Sun-Times*. Would he please, urgently, send a copy boy down to whatever Chicago courthouse was trying the divorce case of president of McDonald's Harry Sonneborn, vs. June Sonneborn, starring Edward Bennett Williams for the defendant, and give Ed this message: "Please ask for a recess ASAP. Need to talk to you now. URGENT"?

I had known Williams for more than twenty years and trusted his common sense more than anyone else. He was the best in the business. Fifteen minutes later, he called back all business, with a curt, "What's up?" Without loading the dice – really – I took him through everything: what the *Times* had written, how we had tried to match them for three days, how we had finally gotten our own set of the Pentagon Papers, what we planned to do *tonight*, what the lawyers were advising us, how Beebe was getting caught in a bind, the public stock issue, the threat to the *Post*'s three TV stations, how we were headed for a Fail-Safe telephone call with Kay. Maybe ten uninterrupted minutes, and then I shut up.

Nothing from Williams for at least sixty seconds. I was dying. And then, finally: "Well, Benjy, you got to go with it. You got no choice. That's your business." I hugged him, long distance, and walked casually downstairs back into the legal debate. When I had the right opening, I told them what Williams had said, and I could see the starch go out of Clark and Essaye, and I could see the very beginning of a smile on Beebe's face. Such was the clout of this man. After another hour of argument, it was Show Time, and Fritz, Phil, Howie, and I went to the four different phones in our house and placed the call to Kay. I didn't want to think about what I would have to do if the answer was no.

Fritz outlined all of our positions, with complete fairness. We had told her what we felt we had to, we told her what Williams had said, we told her the staff would consider it a disaster if we didn't publish. She asked Beebe his advice. He paused a long time – we could hear music in the background – then said, "Well, I probably wouldn't." Thank God for the hesitant "Well," and the "probably." Now she paused. The music again. And then she said quickly, "Okay, I say let's go. Let's publish."

I dropped the phone like a hot potato and shouted the verdict, and the room erupted in cheers.

The cheers were instinctive. In those first moments, it was enough for all of us – including, let it be said quickly, the lawyers who had been arguing against publication – that Katharine had shown guts and commitment to the First Amendment, and support of her editors. But I think none of us truly understood the importance of her decision to publish the Pentagon Papers in the creation of a new *Washington Post*. I know I didn't. I wanted to publish because we had vital documents explaining the biggest story of the last ten years. That's what newspapers do: they learn, they report, they verify, they write, and they publish.

What I didn't understand, as Katharine's "Okay . . . let's go. Let's publish" rang in my ears, was how permanently the ethos of the paper changed, and how it crystallized for editors and reporters everywhere how independent and determined and confident of its purpose the *Washington Post* had become. In the days that followed, these feelings only increased. A paper that stands up to charges of treason, a paper that holds firm in the face of charges from the president, the Supreme Court, the Attorney General, never mind an assistant attorney general. A paper that holds its head high, committed unshakably to principle.

What was immediately obvious to us was the amount of work still to be done before we hit the street with a Pentagon Papers story. In fact, we missed the first edition, while Beebe and I argued – for the first time – about Ellsberg. Beebe had not realized Ellsberg was Ben Bagdikian's source, and when he learned it, he tried briefly to revisit Kay's decision, wondering if Ellsberg had stolen the Pentagon Papers, in fact or in law. But there was no steam in that last spasm, and finally we published . . . and waited for the Nixon administration's response and for a look at how the *New York Times* would handle our story – with an AP wire story, page one.

We didn't have long to wait. Just after 3:00 p.m., Friday, June 18, with Kay and some editors in my office, I got a call from Assistant Attorney General William H. Rehnquist. After a minimum of I-guess-you-know-why-I'm-calling and I-suspect-I-do, the future Chief Justice came to the point, and started reading what turned out to be the same message he had read to the *New York Times* four days earlier:

> I have been advised by the Secretary of Defense that the material published in *The Washington Post* on June 18, 1971, captioned "Documents Reveal U.S. Effort in '54 to Delay Viet Election" contains information relating to the national defense of the United States and bears a top-secret classification. As such, publication of this information is directly prohibited by the provisions of the Espionage Law, Title 18, U.S. Code, Section 793. Moreover, further publication of information of this character will cause irreparable injury to the defense interests of the United States. Accordingly, I respectfully request that you publish no further information of this character and advise me that you have made arrangements for the return of the documents to the Department of Defense.

My hands and legs were shaking. The charge of espionage did not fit my vision of myself, and all I knew about Title 18 spelled trouble. That's the Criminal Code. But with as much poise as I could muster I said, "I'm sure you will understand that we must respectfully decline." He said something like he figured as much, and we hung up.

Soon afterward, the Justice Department contacted Clark and Essaye and told them to be in District Court at 5:00 p.m. The *Times* editors and lawyers were in various courts, arguing appeals and appealing decisions against them. At no time did they – or we – consider violating court orders, damning the torpedoes and proceeding with publication.

For the next eight days – until just after 1:00 p.m. on Saturday, June 26, in the Supreme Court of the United States – we were almost full time in the U.S. District Court for the District of Columbia, the U.S. Court of Appeals for the District of Columbia, the District Court again, the Court of Appeals again (sitting *en banc* this time), or in various legal offices, researching and actually writing affidavits and legal briefs.

At 6:00 p.m. on the 18th, the government asked District Court Judge Gerhard A. "Gary" Gesell to enjoin the *Post* from any further publication of the Pentagon Papers. Two hours later, he ruled for the *Post*. It took the government only another two hours to round up three judges on the U.S. Court of Appeals to ask them to overrule Judge Gesell. That made it just before 10:00 p.m. – when we were desperately trying to get Murrey Marder's story into the paper and get the presses started. They were supposed to start at 10:15 p.m., but as luck would have it, this night they were late. Herman Cohen, the news dealer who used to take the very first copies of the paper off the press to the newsstands in the major hotels, was waiting, waiting, waiting, and the three-judge appellate panel was deciding whether to reverse Gesell's ruling. We figured if we could get a thousand copies on the newsstands we could argue that we had effectively published, therefore any injunction could not affect that day's installment. In addition, we had put the story on the *L.A. Times–Washington Post* News Service wire, with a special warning to editors that the Appellate Court was deliberating even as they were reading.

Finally, after 1:00 a.m. on the 19th, the court enjoined us, but agreed with Roger Clark that we could complete the publication of that day's paper.

Scenes from the next chaotic days remain frozen in my mind like frames from a Cocteau movie:

- We defendants had to be given emergency security clearances before we could even attend our own trial on charges of publishing documents we had already published.
- Courtroom windows were specially draped with blackout cloth, presumably to prevent unauthorized lip-readers (Soviet spies? Comsymps from Hanoi?) from watching testimony.
- Reporters had to spend hours explaining the Pentagon Papers to lawyers who had never had to cope with the arcane Pentagon world of classified material, before the lawyers could decide what affidavits they wanted from editors and reporters, or what questions to ask.
- Many times, stories that had already appeared in either the *Times* or the *Post* were included in the Pentagon Papers, but now classified top secret by the government.
- Often *Post* reporters plainly knew so much more than government prosecutors and government witnesses about U.S. involvement in Vietnam it was almost embarrassing . . . until one remembered how high were the stakes. My favorite ludicrous moment came when Gesell asked some poor Deputy Assistant Secretary of Defense, Dennis J. Doolin, to identify the one thing in the Pentagon Papers that would most damage the interest of the United States, if published by the *Post*. The poor guy blanched. The government lawyers caucused furtively, and quickly asked for a recess. We were almost as worried, trying to figure out what they would come up with. (We had collectively read most of the Pentagon Papers, surely more than the government had read, but none of us had read them all.) Finally, the trial resumed. The last question was reread, and the witness responded (you could almost hear the roll of drums): "Operation Marigold."

The more studious defendants among us – Chal Roberts, Murrey Marder, and Pentagon correspondent George Wilson – had brought a dozen reference books with them to court, just in case, and damned if they weren't able to find quickly three already published, detailed explanations of Operation Marigold, a June 1966 effort by President Johnson to get representatives of Poland and Italy to explore possible peace settlements with Ho Chi Minh. The following week's edition of *Life* magazine – not yet public – featured a signed article by Britain's prime minister, Harold Wilson. It was headlined "Operation Marigold."

Later, in a secret session – closed even to us defendants – before the US Court of Appeals for the District of Columbia, the government tried to supplement an affidavit by Vice Admiral Noel Gayler, director of the National Security Agency. Gayler wanted to describe as particularly dangerous to U.S. security a specific radio intercept reported in the Pentagon Papers, allegedly proving that North Vietnamese ships fired on U.S. destroyers in the Gulf of Tonkin in the summer of 1964. The remarkable George Wilson stunned everyone by pulling out of his back pocket a verbatim record of the intercept, in an unclassified transcript of Senate Foreign Relations Committee hearings.

As the Pentagon Papers bounced their way from court to court – in New York and Washington – on their way to The Supremes, I made a decision which now makes me blush.

In an effort to be prepared for any eventuality, we had assigned two reporters to go out to Chief Justice Warren Burger's house in nearby Arlington, after trying unsuccessfully to reach him by phone. If the U.S. Court of Appeals ruled for the *Post en banc,* we knew the government would apply to the Chief Justice for an immediate stay – to stop us from publishing – while they appealed to the Supreme Court. We didn't want the government to sneak out unnoticed from Burger's house, so we sent our own emissaries: Spencer Rich, who normally covered the Senate, and Martin Weil, a former CIA type, who worked nights on rewrite as a city reporter.

Together, they walked up the driveway to the Chief Justice's home and rang the doorbell. It was almost midnight. Marty Weil's memo describes the next few minutes better than I can:

> After about a minute or two, the Chief Justice opened the door. He was wearing a bath robe. He was carrying a gun. The gun was in his right hand, muzzle pointed down. It was a long-barreled steel weapon. The Chief Justice did not seem glad to see us. Spencer explained why we were there. There was a considerable amount of misdirected conversation. It seemed for a bit that people were talking past each other. Spencer, who held up his credentials, was explaining why we were there, but the judge seemed to be saying that we shouldn't have come. Finally, after a little more talk, everybody seemed to understand everybody. The Chief Justice said it would be all right for us to wait for any possible Justice Department emissaries, but we could wait down the street. He held his gun in his hand through-out the two or three minute talk. Sometimes it was not visible, held behind the door post. He never pointed it at us. He closed the door. We went down the street and waited for three hours. Then we went home.

I was at home when the desk called to report this brief encounter and ask where we should play the story – page one, or inside?

"What story?" I shouted. "Just because the Chief Justice of the United States comes to the door of his house in the dead of night in his jammies, waving a gun at two *Washington Post* reporters in the middle of a vital legal case involving the *Washington Post*, you guys think that's a story?"

Over the years, I have prided myself in recognizing a good story when I see one, even when no one else sees it. This is what I do best. But of course I had momentarily taken leave of my senses. All I could think of was how much Chief Justice Burger disliked the press in general, and the *Post* in particular, how ridiculous the alleged story would make him look (I could visualize the Herblock cartoon with clarity), and how much I wanted to avoid pissing him off a few days before he took our fate into his hands.

No story, I ruled, and there was no story, until after the Supreme Court had decided our fate, when Nick Von Hoffman slipped it into a column.

No story? I hereby apologize.

On Monday, June 21, 1971, Judge Gesell again ruled in favor of the *Post*, after the three-judge Appellate Court asked him to hold an evidentiary hearing on whether the publication of the Pentagon Papers would "so prejudice" U.S. interests, or cause "such irreparable injury," that prior restraint could be justified. On Thursday, June 24, the nine judges of the U.S. Court of Appeals ruled 7–2 in the *Post*'s favor. On Friday, June 25, the Supreme Court granted certiorari and agreed to hear the case. On Saturday, June 26, the case was argued in the Supreme Court. And on Wednesday, June 30, 1971 – seventeen days after the *New York Times* broke the story, and ten days after the *Post*'s first publication – the Supreme Court ruled for the two newspapers. The next day, both of us resumed our stories about the Pentagon Papers.

For the first time in the history of the American republic, newspapers had been restrained by the government from publishing a story – a black mark in the history of democracy.

We had won – sort of.

What the hell was going on in this country that this could happen?

How could a judge of the highest Court of Appeals in the land, Judge Malcolm R. Wilkey, a Nixon appointee who had been general counsel of the Kennecott Copper Corporation, and an Eisenhower appointee to the Appellate Court, seriously argue that the Papers "could clearly result in great harm to the nation," bringing about "the death of soldiers, the destruction of alliances, the greatly increased difficulty of negotiation with our enemies, the inability of our diplomats to negotiate"?

How could a president (who was three years from resigning in disgrace) and an Attorney General (who was three years later sent to jail himself) and an assistant attorney general (who was fifteen years from becoming Chief Justice of the United States) rush headlong and joyous down this reckless path?

Why this persecution/prosecution when the Pentagon Papers dealt entirely with decisions taken exclusively by Presidents Eisenhower, Kennedy, and Johnson, and ended some months before the Nixon administration took office?

And how come there was never a peep out of any of the principals when the Solicitor General of the United States, who argued the government's case before the Court of Appeals and the Supreme Court, the distinguished former dean of the Harvard Law School, Erwin N. Griswold, confessed *eighteen years later* that the government's case against the newspapers was a mirage? "I have never seen any trace of a threat to the national security from the Pentagon Papers' publication. Indeed, I have never seen it even suggested that there was an actual threat," Griswold wrote in a brave – and almost unheard of – correction of the record.[2]

We had no answers to those questions beyond recognition that the Cold War dominated our society, and realization that the Nixon-Agnew administration was playing hardball.

We did know that the Pentagon Papers experience had forged forever between the Grahams and the newsroom a sense of confidence within the *Post*, a sense of mission and agreement on new goals, and how to attain them. And that may have been the greatest result of publication of the Pentagon Papers.

After the Pentagon Papers, there would be no decision too difficult for us to overcome together.

NOTES

1   Reprinted with permission of Simon & Schuster Adult Publishing Group from *A Good Life: Newspapering and Other Adventures* by Ben Bradlee. Chapter 13, copyright © 1995 by Benjamin C. Bradlee.
2   It appeared in an Op-Ed piece in *The Washington Post* dated February 15, 1989.

Bibliography on Moral Leadership

The list below is by no means exhaustive, but it contains a number of books, mostly works of fiction, that offer a variety of insights into issues of leadership and responsibility.

Jonathan Alter, *The Defining Moment: FDR's Hundred Days and the Triumph of Hope*.
> This biography analyzes the background and early actions of US President Franklin Delano Roosevelt, who came to office in 1933 in the heart of the American Depression.

Louis Auchincloss, *The Rector of Justin*.
> A fascinating portrait of the life and work of the founder of a New England prep school – a story of entrepreneurship, idealism, shrewdness, and pragmatism.

Louis Auchincloss, *Collected Short Stories of Louis Auchincloss*.
> For the most part, these are stories of men and women in the social and economic elite of New York City, written by a man who spent his life within this milieu and made a dual career as an attorney and prolific author.

Howard Bahr, *The Year of Jubilo: A Novel of the Civil War*.
> A novel about the challenges of a returning Confederate soldier as he navigates the transition to civil life, a transformed town, and new and old loyalties and conflicts.

Russell Banks, *Cloudsplitter*.
> Author of *The Sweet Hereafter*, this is Banks' historical novel about John Brown, American abolitionist and leader of the failed attempt to capture a federal arsenal in Harper's Ferry, Virginia.

Tom Barbash, *On Top of the World: Cantor Fitzgerald, Howard Lutnick & 9/11*.
> 658 of 1,000 Cantor Fitzgerald employees died at the World Trade Center on September 11, the single largest loss of any WTC business. A chronicle of CEO Howard Lutnick's actions in response to this organizational and personal crisis.

Albert Camus, *The Plague*.
> A story about the resilience of the human spirit in the face of almost overwhelming horror, as the bubonic plague sweeps through a quarantined city in Algeria.

Raymond Chandler, *The Big Sleep.*
> A classic American detective story, first published in 1939, which can be read as a story about the pursuit of professional excellence and the moral dilemmas arising from dedicated service to a client.

Terrence Cheng, *Sons of Heaven.*
> Many remember the Tiananmen Square Massacre by the photograph of a single student who stands alone, facing a line of incoming government tanks. The identity of this student has never been determined. This novel is a fictional 'back story' that creates a description of the student's life and motivations for the actions he took.

Joseph Conrad, *Typhoon.*
> A story of moral courage at sea, involving an unlikely hero – a quiet, unassuming ship's captain.

Theodore Dreiser, *The Financier.*
> The rise and fall, and subsequent rise, of a nineteenth-century financier – a counterpart in many respects to 1980s corporate raider Michael Milken.

F. Scott Fitzgerald, *The Great Gatsby.*
> The famous story of Jay Gatsby, a successful Roaring Twenties financier, and his deluded quest for the good life.

Allegra Goodman, *Intuition.*
> Set in a prestigious medical research laboratory, this novel traces the accusations, and their consequences, that one of the laboratory's star young postdocs has been falsifying his research results.

Nadine Gordimer, *My Son's Story.*
> Gordimer is a Nobel Prize-winning South African writer who has chronicled that country's search to free itself from apartheid. This novel describes the evolution of a family led by an anti-apartheid activist, and the impact of his actions on his family and the cause.

Nadine Gordimer, *Six Feet of the Country.*
> A collection of Gordimer's short stories. The story "A Chip of Glass Ruby" has been used as a reading in prior versions of "The Moral Leader" course.

Jonathan Harr, *A Civil Action.*
> The non-fiction account upon which the recent movie was based. A fascinating story of moral leadership, in all its complexities, as seen through the efforts of a young lawyer bringing a class-action environmental suit against two large companies.

Nathaniel Hawthorne, *The Scarlet Letter.*
> One of the greatest American novels, this is the story of Hester Prynne, a Puritan woman convicted of committing adultery, her husband, and her lover, who is also an admired clergyman. Prynne, in many respects, some surprising, emerges as the moral leader in the story.

Joseph Heller, *Something Happened.*
> A black comedy, by the author of *Catch-22*, about success in corporate life and a fast-track executive adept at living on the surface of things.

Henrik Ibsen, *A Doll House.*
> The classic play about a wife's moral choices and her actions of self-liberation, set in Victorian times.

Edward P. Jones, *The Known World*.

This Pulitzer-Prize-winning novel and "book of tremendous moral intricacy" (*The New Yorker*) describes the little-known history of African-Americans who were themselves slave-owners.

Tracy Kidder, *Mountains Beyond Mountains: The Quest of Dr. Paul Farmer, A Man Who Would Cure the World*.

This book describes the work and life of Dr. Paul Farmer, celebrated infectious-disease specialist and Harvard professor who devotes himself to fighting tuberculosis in rural Haiti.

Barbara Kingsolver, *The Poisonwood Bible*.

The story of the quiet and heroic leadership of a mother who takes her children to the Congo, following her missionary husband, and then leaves him and Africa and reassembles a life from the wreckage of these decisions.

David Lodge, *Nice Work*.

A serious and funny book about what two people learn from the collision of their very different worlds. One is a factory manager; the other a deconstructionist professor of literature.

David Mamet, *Glengarry Glen Ross*.

A Pulitzer Prize-winning play about the brutal competition among a group of real-estate agents.

John Marquand, *Point of No Return*.

A successful investment banker returns to his hometown and reflects on the choices that shaped his life.

Arthur Miller, *All My Sons* and *Death of a Salesman*.

Two classic, powerful plays about identity and family.

William Shakespeare, *Macbeth*.

A study of ambition, the murkiness of values, and the powerful seduction of short cuts to success.

Michael Shaara, *The Killer Angels*.

A great historical novel that tells the story of the Battle of Gettysburg in brilliant detail. It presents a wide range of leaders, moral and otherwise, including the remarkable Colonel Joshua Lawrence Chamberlain.

George Bernard Shaw, *Major Barbara*.

A witty, complex, surprising play about an arms manufacturer and his idealistic daughter.

Anita Shreve, *The Pilot's Wife*.

The story of moral challenges faced by a wife of a secret member of the IRA.

Leo Tolstoy, *War and Peace*.

One of the great books, worth reading and rereading for a multitude of reasons, among which are Tolstoy's vivid and unforgettable portraits of men and women who change the world, on both the grand stage of life and in subtle, everyday ways.

Leo Tolstoy, *The Death of Ivan Ilyich*.

The somber tale of an ambitious, successful man and his discovery of the vacuum his life had become.

John Updike, *Rabbit at Rest*.

The final book in Updike's highly acclaimed trilogy recounting both the life of Harry Angstrom, a middle-class everyman, and the evolution of American society from the 1950s through the 1980s.

Gore Vidal, *Lincoln.*

A long, masterful work of historical fiction that portrays not only the story of Lincoln's presidency but his thoughts and feelings, as well as those of the people Lincoln lived and worked with.

Tom Wolfe, *The Bonfire of the Vanities* and *A Man in Full.*

Two long, entertaining, often satirical portraits of American business life and society. The first views the world through the experience of a New York investment banker during the 1980s; the second through an Atlanta real-estate developer during the 1990s.

Index

Note: *italic* page numbers denote references to Figures/Tables.

For Product Safety Concerns and Information please contact our EU
representative GPSR@taylorandfrancis.com
Taylor & Francis Verlag GmbH, Kaufingerstraße 24, 80331 München, Germany

www.ingramcontent.com/pod-product-compliance
Ingram Content Group UK Ltd.
Pitfield, Milton Keynes, MK11 3LW, UK
UKHW050954280425
457818UK00038B/353